GREEN EYE
OF THE STORM

Professor Arthur Rendle Short and John, his son

GREEN EYE
OF THE STORM

Controversy between Science and Christianity
in the Lives of

ARTHUR RENDLE SHORT
(1880–1953)

PHILIP HENRY GOSSE
(1810–1888)

GEORGE JOHN ROMANES
(1848–1894)

and the author,
JOHN RENDLE-SHORT

THE BANNER OF TRUTH TRUST

THE BANNER OF TRUTH TRUST

3 Murrayfield Road, Edinburgh EH 12 6EL
PO Box 621, Carlisle, Pennsylvania 17013, USA

*

© John Rendle-Short 1998
First published 1998
ISBN 0 85151 727 7

*

*

Typeset in 11 / 12 pt. Baskerville
at The Spartan Press Ltd,
Lymington, Hants
printed and bound in Great Britain by
The Bath Press, Bath

CONTENTS

PART FOUR   JOHN RENDLE-SHORT

APPENDICES

ACKNOWLEDGEMENTS

I would like to extend my sincere thanks to Mrs Fayette Gosse for making available to me a photocopy of the book *Omphalos* by Philip Gosse. Several people who knew my father have now died, but I would be remiss if I did not especially remember his great friends Mr Melville Capper and Dr Douglas Johnson, who together wrote his two biographies.

The preparation of this book has taken many years, and in the early stages I received assistance from a number of people. Latterly I must mention particularly Mr Iain Murray of The Banner of Truth Trust, without whose encouragement and guidance this work would never have come to fruition. Production of the final manuscript was greatly assisted by Dr Carl Wieland and Mrs Kym Holwerda.

Most importantly, my very sincere thanks go to my wife Angel for years of support and loving care.

INTRODUCTION

Four men whose lives span two centuries –
All four were professing Christians.
All four were deeply influenced by Darwinism, and reacted to it
in markedly different ways.
The four men are:

Philip Henry Gosse, FRS, (1810–1888). A notable zoologist
and marine biologist; inventor of the institutional aquarium for
long-term housing of marine animals. He compiled the first
descriptive catalogue of British marine invertebrates and
authored more than ten books, notably a *Manual of Marine
Zoology*.

George John Romanes, FRS, (1848–1894). Pioneer physiologist, poet, friend and disciple of Charles Darwin and one of his
literary executors, he published more than twenty-five books,
and many articles.

Arthur Rendle Short, BSc., MD, FRCS, (1880–1953). Physiologist, geologist, surgeon. He wrote many books on surgery and
physiology and also on biblical topics mainly in the field of
apologetics.

John Rendle-Short, AM, MD, FRCP, (1919–). The author.

*   *   *

Modern evolutionism is particularly British. It was popularized in the nineteenth century by such major proponents as Sir Charles Lyell, Charles Darwin, Alfred Russel Wallace and Thomas Huxley. By 1900, Britain and the Continent had capitulated to the theory and, to a major extent, have remained in that state. Not until well after the Second World War has there been an arguing of the case for scientific creationism.

The situation on the other side of the Atlantic has been very different. As it has been extensively reviewed from many different aspects, I will not refer to it here.

I have not attempted formal biographies, and make no apology for the fact that I am more concerned to follow the flow of ideas than strict chronology. My objective has been to select episodes from the lives of each of the four to demonstrate how they responded to a persuasive scientific theory, which as the decades passed, revealed itself as a philosophy which sapped their Christian faith like a bug in the bud of an orchid.

The examples I have chosen from the nineteenth century, Gosse and Romanes, personify the way in which many scientifically-minded professing Christians reacted when first confronted with Darwinism. Gosse fought back vigorously, but unavailingly; Romanes capitulated reluctantly to materialism, but later crawled his way back to a faith of some kind.

For these two, my information has been limited. In the case of Philip Gosse I have had to rely mainly, but not entirely, on *Father and Son*, a biography by his son Edmund[1] – not, you will discover, an unbiased observer.

I noticed frequent mention of 'poor George Romanes' in sermons preached by my father, Arthur Rendle Short, during his early years. This intrigued me. Who was this Romanes? I determined to discover more. I was fortunate to find a copy of *The Life and Letters of George Romanes* compiled by his wife.[2] I soon discovered why my father was so interested in him. Here was another searcher after truth.

Beside *The Life*, there are many references to Romanes in histories of science, *Darwin and the Emergence of Evolutionary*

[1]Edmund William Gosse, *Father and Son: Study of two temperaments* (London: William Heinemann, 1907).
[2]Ethel Romanes, *The Life and Letters of George Romanes* (London: Longmore, Green & Co., 1896).

[x]

Theories of Mind and Behaviour by Robert Richards[1] being of particular value. There are also Romanes' own writings, especially his poems.

The stories of Gosse and Romanes, briefly told, serve as a nineteenth-century back-drop to the life of my father in the first half of the twentieth century. Of the four men I describe, he is the principal figure and receives the greatest attention throughout.

For information on Rendle Short (or ARS as I shall often call him), I am greatly indebted to the two biographies edited by Mr W. Melville Capper and Dr Douglas Johnson. The first of these, *Arthur Rendle Short, Surgeon and Christian*, published in March 1954 (IVF), itself relied heavily on autobiographical material such as a series of little day-books, or diaries, from his early years, and an unpublished manuscript written for family consumption during the latter part of his life.

The second biography, *The Faith of a Surgeon: Belief and experience in the life of Arthur Rendle Short*,[2] supplements the first. In addition I have consulted numerous religious and medical books which ARS authored over fifty years of writing. A list of these is provided in Appendix III of *The Faith of a Surgeon*.

I have also made considerable use of my father's sermon notes dating from his early years to the year of his death. Virtually unexamined, these had been in storage in the garages of various homes I have occupied since we came to Australia over thirty years ago. After I retired from the University, I began to study them. It was then I discovered, for the first time, something of the struggle for truth which had occupied my father from his teens until the year of his death.

Lastly, of course, I have my own memories. I have to confess that only as I have written about him have I appreciated the incalculable debt I owe to my father's life and teaching. Part Four is autobiographical, and I have included a few personal details about myself. These, as with the stories from the life of my father, have been included for interest, and to help the flow

---

[1]Robert J. Richards, *Darwin and the Emergence of Evolutionary Theories of Mind and Behaviour* (University of Chicago Press, 1987), p. 127.

[2]W. M. Capper and D. Johnson, *The Faith of a Surgeon: Belief and experience in the life of Arthur Rendle Short* (Exeter: Paternoster Press, 1976).

of the narrative. But the main purpose of the section is to show the way in which God, by his providence, has been at work in my own life, guiding, prodding, restraining or halting me in my tracks, to lead me, by his grace, from wrong paths into more correct ones. I say *more* correct, as I certainly do not consider the task is yet completed.

*   *   *

That classical Darwinism with its numerous subsequent variations comprises a comprehensive philosophical belief system is now abundantly obvious. It is not a fact, it is a theory – indeed, perhaps it could better be called an hypothesis. It cannot be proved scientifically, any more than creation can be proved scientifically. Ultimately, each has to be accepted by faith.

New scientific evidence is constantly appearing which may at first appear to bolster evolution. But as this affirmative data is absorbed, ideas which had previously been accepted are shown to have been incorrect and have had to be abandoned. The situation in science is never static. Indeed, as things are at present, the net loss for evolutionary theory is outstripping the net gain. In this book I have touched only lightly on scientific evidence. The subject is too vast (see Appendix 1).

Darwinism can be considered historically as occupying five eras of roughly fifty years each.

1 1750–1800: The era of Charles Darwin's grandfather, Erasmus Darwin (1731–1802).

2 1800–1850: Pre-Darwinism [Gosse].

3 1850–1900: Darwin triumphant: era of scientific and theological consolidation [Romanes].

4 1900–1950: Era of universal acceptance: no substantial scientific voices raised against [ARS].

5 1950–2000: Era of rapidly increasing scientific challenge to evolution and its associated time scale.

Evidence for the truth of Christianity is provided not only by

Scripture, but also by science, and by secular history down the centuries. God does not expect men and women to accept the gospel without any supportive testimony, and he has graciously provided evidence in two principal forms:

1 *General Revelation:* The world around us, by its beauty and design, shouts aloud that there must be a Sovereign Creator God, and our senses and Scripture confirm this (*Rom.* 1:19, 20; 2:14–15 ; *Psa.* 19:1–6).

2 *Special Revelation:* The Bible, God's infallible, written communication to mankind, is a chronological and panoramic review of the history[1] of the world. I find it helpful to consider it under four headings:

(i) The first two chapters (Genesis 1 and 2) tell us about the world as it was when first created, perfect in every sense of the word. Chapter 1 gives a panoramic account of creation, while chapter 2 concentrates on the origin of man and woman.

(ii) Genesis chapter 3. In the earlier part we read how Adam and Eve sinned and allowed Satan to hijack God's beautiful creation, so introducing death into the world.

(iii) The second half of chapter 3 gives a brief picture of the awful effects of sin on both men and women. However, in chapter 3 verses 14 and 15 we are given a glimpse of God's plan to send a deliverer (Jesus Christ), who would 'bruise the head of the serpent'.

(iv) Lastly, Genesis 4 and all the rest of Scripture, through to the end of Revelation, relates how all mankind has followed Adam by disobeying God, and God's response.

If we consider the Bible in this way, it is obvious that we must accept it *in toto,* as a package deal. If any part is discarded, all biblical Christianity is compromised. Especially does this apply to the foundational early chapters of Genesis. But theological, historical and scientific evidence alone is not enough. Christianity can be studied as an academic exercise in a theological college and yet remain a dry and worthless exercise. Living, spiritual knowledge requires the exercise of

---

[1]Trevor McIlwain and Nancy Everson, *Firm Foundations: Creation to Christ. A chronological and panoramic course of Bible study* (Sanford, Florida: New Tribes Mission, 1993).

faith. But even before this, there must be a willingness to accept the evidence (*John* 7:17). God will help the willing seeker and confirm the evidence to the one who believes.

*   *   *

Readers of a book like this can be divided into three main categories:

1 There may be a few non-christian, atheistic, evolutionists. I hope they will enjoy the book if only as a record of history.

2 At the other end of the scale are people who accept the first chapters of Genesis as literal historical truth. Some may even wonder what all the fuss is about. 'Yes', they say, 'Of course I believe in Genesis. How can you be a Christian unless you do?'

3 But primarily, I have written for Christians who believe in evolution, those sometimes called theistic evolutionists, old-earth creationists, or progressive creationists.[1] Many such people believe God used some evolutionary mechanism in the creation and maintenance of the world over billions of years. Their motto could be summed up as: 'God wrote two books, the Book of Nature and the Book of the Bible, and so it stands to reason that they should agree. But unfortunately they don't seem to do so. As evolution (long ages) is a scientific fact – everyone accepts it – the problem must lie in how one interprets the first chapters of Genesis.'

This was my own position for many years. But I have changed, and the fourth section of *Green Eye of the Storm* explains why.

[1]See Hugh Ross, *Creation and Time: A Biblical and Scientific Perspective on the Creation–Date Controversy* (Colorado Springs: Nav. Press, 1994) and M. van Bebber and Paul S. Taylor, *Creation and Time: A Report on the Progressive Creationist Book by Hugh Ross* (Eden Productions, 1995).

PROLOGUE

Green Eye of the Storm

It was new and ominous. I had never seen anything like it before. There were no obvious clouds, but the sky on the western horizon was darkening, while overhead it remained a brilliant blue.

My family and I had been in Australia only a short time. We were taking our summer holiday on the Pacific coast of northern New South Wales and had pitched the large tent and small caravan on a narrow spit between an estuary and the sea. For the first few days all was calm, then gradually the wind rose to gale force from the east. We congratulated ourselves that we were protected from the pounding surf by substantial sand dunes. Yet over the estuary, to the west, the sky was becoming somehow too dark a blue. As the wind grew stronger, and the sky blacker, the eye of the approaching storm slowly changed to emerald green – beautiful, ethereal, seductive, yet strangely menacing.

At that time I had no idea that the green eye presaged a storm of exceptional ferocity which had the ability to change direction with startling speed. We huddled in the tent as protection from the stinging sand whipped from the dunes. A bizarre touch was the sound, above that of the wind, of a small, low-flying aircraft following the line of the surf up the coast.

About mid-day, I wandered down to the protected water of the estuary, harboured by the spit from the east wind. Off-shore lay a number of small boats, each anchored by a line from their bows, all facing east, up into the wind. Suddenly, as I watched, one by one they swung around 180 degrees. The wind had strengthened and dramatically changed direction and was now coming from the *west*, from the green eye of the storm. I dashed up the beach and across the road to the tent. Too late. It had blown away. Caravans were rocking to and fro. Through the roar of the storm, we could hear the crash of falling trees.

Such a sudden change of direction in the wind in a tropical storm is not rare. Daniel Defoe, writing around 1700, recorded that his hero, Robinson Crusoe, was sailing down the coast of South America, just north of the equator, 'in good weather, when a violent tornado, or hurricane took us quite out of our knowledge; it began from the South-East, came about to the North-West and then settled to the North-East, from whence it blew in a terrible manner for twelve days . . . During that twelve days, I need not say that I expected every moment to be swallowed up; nor did any of the ship expect to save their lives.'

My family and I spent a restless night in the home of some kindly strangers. The next day we traced the million-dollar path of destruction left by the tornado – a boat up a tree, a Methodist chapel flattened, the highest remaining point being the small harmonium protruding above the rubble.

And the fleeing aircraft? We searched the local newspaper for any mention of it, but nothing was reported. It must have reached safety.

PART ONE

PHILIP HENRY GOSSE

PHILIP AND EMILY

Philip had watched the progression of similar storms during his years in Jamaica: the calm beauty, the darkening sky, the freshening wind, the tell-tale green fluorescence – then suddenly like the strike of a cobra, the full force of the tornado, often unleashed from the opposite direction.

Philip Henry Gosse, FRS, (1810–1888) was born in Worcester, England. His father had studied painting briefly at the Royal Academy and was known as Thomas the Painter. He was a strange man who followed in whole or part a diet devised by a Dr Cheyne. This consisted of 'Vomits, gentle bleeding, easy purges. Exercise and a low diet'. He made a precarious living by painting beautiful miniatures on ivory. He was constantly on the move, sometimes living in more than ten different towns in the same year; a schedule he continued into his seventies. Despite this, he had married Hannah Best and they had four children, the second of whom was Philip Henry.

According to Fayette Gosse in her book, *The Gosses, An Anglo-Australian Family*[1], the family made a home in Poole, Dorset, and here Philip had his limited schooling, although his father continued his peregrinations. At the age of seventeen he was sent as a clerk to Carbonear, Newfoundland, where his brother, then aged nineteen, had recently preceded him.

Carbonear is the third largest town in Newfoundland. At

---

[1]Fayette Gosse, *The Gosses, An Anglo-Australian Family* (Canberra: Brian Coulston, 1981). This book is valuable in placing Philip Henry and his son Edmund in the context of their extensive and distinguished family. Much of the information on Philip's life is quoted from this book.

that time it was a scene of bustle when the fishing fleet was in port, and dreariness when the boats were absent. It was noted for its Irish brand of Roman Catholicism, but in the late eighteenth century had experienced a Methodist religious revival.

Philip was fortunate to find a well-stocked library, and he devoured biography, poetry, travel and science. But more importantly, it was here that he discovered his two life interests – evangelical Christianity and a love of nature; although the latter, at that time, consisted mainly in collecting insects. Later he continued his collection in Canada. Then in Alabama he became fascinated by the butterflies, 'to the extent of making 233 exquisite paintings of them'. Unfortunately while in the United States, he succumbed to headaches, fever and depression, and was compelled to return to England in poverty.

After some abortive efforts, Philip discovered his skill in writing. His first successful book was *The Canadian Naturalist* for which the publisher offered him a hundred guineas, a princely sum in those days. Mrs Gosse tells us the poor man was so overwhelmed that he burst into hysterical sobs. The publisher tried to soothe him with a glass of wine, saying, 'My dear young man! My dear young man!'

His biographer continues:

Philip Henry Gosse had at last found his vocation. The book was well received. Being self-taught and isolated from other naturalists, there was a kind of fresh and personal wonderment in his descriptions. Though he became more learned this happy enthusiasm for the world of nature remained in his writing which never dried into the academic. It was a style of precise description that charmed the lay reader without bewildering him.

Philip's literary works show extreme originality; a strange mixture of erudition with a whimsical love of all natural things. They point with gentleness from the beauty of the creation to the surpassing glory of the Creator who fashioned them. Many of them are illustrated with skilful woodcuts and like his father, he also painted beautiful miniatures. *The Dictionary of National Biography* lists nineteen books which he wrote: some, like *The Ocean*, ran to several editions. He also contributed over sixty papers to the *Proceedings of the Royal Society* (London).

Philip was one of the first to succeed in keeping marine

animals and plants alive artificially. An appendix to *A Naturalist's Rambles on the Devonshire Coast* (1852) describes how he successfully preserved some sea creatures in captivity for up to eleven months, a feat previously regarded as impossible. As a result, he was engaged to establish the world's first aquarium in the recently opened Regent's Park Zoo in London.

His popularity with lay folk can be gauged by an occasion in later life when Philip and his son Edmund were exploring the sea shore of the Devon coast. Edmund tells us they came across a party of ladies 'cackling joyously over a rarity they had discovered'. On enquiry they told Philip that it was a very scarce species 'and held it up for us to examine. My father at once civilly set them right; it was a so-and-so, something much more commonplace. The ladies drew themselves up with dignity and sarcastically remarked that they could only repeat that it was the rarity, and that "Gosse is our authority".'

But all that was in the future. Meanwhile in 1844, Gosse was recommended by the authorities of the British Museum to undertake the collection of previously undescribed birds and insects in the tropics. Accordingly, he sailed for Jamaica where he remained for two years. It was here that his role as a professional naturalist was established. He published *Birds of Jamaica*, accompanied by a folio of splendid plates. He was regarded as a coming man of science, a friend of the renowned scientists and authors of the day (Charles Kingsley, for example, expressed admiration for his books), yet with the remarkable gift of being able to speak and write in a way that lay-people could appreciate.

On his return to London, Philip, again poor and lonely, left the Wesleyan church of his father, and joined one of the newly formed Assemblies of Christians, known simply as 'The Brethren'. Beside satisfying spiritual doctrine, he found among them warm fellowship and it was there that in due time, he met Emily Bowes. They were married a year or so later; he was now thirty-eight and she past forty-two.

The Family

Emily was born in North Wales in 1806. She, like Philip, was accustomed to a life of intellectualism. She had been brought up as an Anglican, and was converted in her teens through reading William Law's *Serious Call to a Devout and Holy Life*. She was always deeply interested in the things of God which she considered 'the greatest pleasure in her life'. By the time Emily met Philip, she had already written two books of hymns and verse, and was on her way to renown as a writer of tracts. Her most successful, *The Young Guardsman of the Alma*, tells the story of a young man whom Emily had led to Christ shortly before he left England for the Crimean War, in which he was killed. This tract alone had a circulation of well over half a million.[1]

Philip and Emily had only one child. The event was recorded cryptically in Philip's diary as, 'E. delivered of a son. Received green swallow from Jamaica.' The boy was named Edmund. In later life he too found fame as a writer, and became Librarian to the House of Lords. He was knighted in 1925. Edmund wrote the definitive biography of his father,[2] and in 1907 a more detailed and popular account of his own early life with the title *Father and Son*.[3] Almost all that is known about Philip can be traced back to these writings of his son.

During the five years following his return from Jamaica, Philip had produced eighteen books, and the strain and tension took its toll. His headaches returned, and he collapsed while working in the British Museum. The doctor ordered a rest, and the little family returned to their beloved Devon, to a little cottage in St Marychurch. Here he entered what was probably the happiest and most tranquil period of his life with rewarding work, aided by his gentle wife.

Edmund recalls that in his early childhood,

The family were always cheerful and often gay. My parents were playful with one another.... [They] lived so completely in the atmosphere of faith, and were so utterly convinced of their intercourse with God, that, so long as that intercourse was not clouded by sin, to which they were delicately sensitive, they could afford to take the passing hour very lightly.

---

[1] L. R. Croft, 'Emily Gosse and the Tract Movement' (*Evangelical Times*, Darlington, July 1991).

[2] Edmund William Gosse, *The Life of Philip Henry Gosse* (London: Paul Trench, Trubner & Co., 1890).

[3] Gosse, *Father and Son*.

The year 1856 commenced well. More books were due to be published. But in April, Emily noticed a hard lump in her breast. Next morning, she went early to London to see Dr Edward Laseron. It was late afternoon by the time she returned home to her husband. 'Philip', she said with her usual quiet smile and unbroken calm, 'The doctor says I have got cancer'.

As soon as possible they consulted the famous London surgeon, Sir James Paget, a kindly man remembered even today for his pioneer work on breast cancer. After examining her, he confirmed the diagnosis and turning to Philip, gently pronounced the fateful words, 'I regret to inform you that the only possible treatment for your wife's condition is immediate removal of the breast.'

They were appalled. In dismay they consulted a third doctor, who recommended they get a fourth opinion from an American physician, Dr. Fell,[1] newly arrived in England. He had devised a non-operative treatment for breast cancer. This consisted of local applications of a powerful ointment for a period of six weeks. After much discussion and prayer they decided to return to London and try the therapy. But the ointment caused ulceration of the skin and extreme pain, and the excursion three times a week from their home in Islington to Pimlico to see Doctor Fell caused Emily great fatigue and distress.

Edmund, now eleven years old, usually accompanied his mother on these nightmare journeys by horse-drawn omnibus. He writes:

She was such a woman of faith that she carried on her evangelistic work as long as she possibly could, continuing to converse with her fellow passengers on spiritual matters . . . In those last months she scarcely ever got into a railway carriage or on an omnibus without presently offering tracts to the persons sitting within reach of her.

Everything seemed to combine, in the course of this fateful year 1856, to harass and alarm them. Just at the moment when illness created a special drain upon their resources, their slender income,

---

[1] It was probably this Dr Fell who gave rise to the satirical poem:
I do not love thee, Dr Fell,
The reason why I cannot tell,
But this I know, and know full well,
I DO NOT LOVE THEE, Dr Fell.

instead of being increased, was seriously diminished . . . Even their food . . . became Spartan indeed.

The state to which Emily was reduced defies description. I am reminded of the only occasion on which I saw my own father angry and deeply distressed. It was by the case of a young woman who crept into his hospital out-patient department in a condition similar to that of Emily. Her family, 'Christian Scientists',[1] had refused to allow her to receive treatment for her breast cancer. At last she could bear the pain and stench no longer, and escaped.

By October it was clear that the treatment Emily was receiving was not working and Dr Fell decided the tumour must be removed. The operation, according to Edmund, was performed in an extremely brutal manner.

But how could it have been otherwise? Dr James Young Simpson (1811–1870) had discovered chloroform anaesthesia in November 1847, only about ten years previously. It was some time before the discovery was universally accepted, theologians particularly objecting to the use of anaesthesia in childbirth. They quoted Genesis 3:16, God's curse on Eve: 'To the woman He said, "I will greatly multiply your sorrow and your conception; in pain shall you bring forth children".' As late as 1871, twenty-four years after his great discovery, Sir James Simpson (as he was to become), in exasperation, wrote a fifty-page defence against critics of anaesthesia in midwifery and surgery.[2]

Simpson himself nearly gave up the study of medicine when at the age of sixteen, he watched the suffering of a woman

---

[1] The cult of Christian Science was founded in Boston, Massachusetts, in 1877 by Mrs Mary Baker Eddy (1821–1910). It bears little resemblance to either Christianity or science. It is not related to the 'creation science' movement. The cardinal point of their doctrine is that 'matter and evil, including all sin, disease and death are *unreal.*' From Mary Baker Eddy, *Miscellaneous Writings*, p. 21. Quoted by Anthony Hoekema, *The Four Major Cults* (Exeter: Paternoster Press, 1963), p. 186.

[2] Simpson's article was entitled 'Answer to the religious objections advanced against the employment of anaesthetic agents in midwifery and surgery.' It included twenty pages of trenchant refutation of religious objections. A modern obstetrician, Dr Rex Gardner, writes, 'His only apology for this devastating broadside, with its evidence of profound biblical knowledge, is that it was hastily written in a single day while convalescing from influenza!' Simpson was an active member of the Free Church of Scotland. Rex Gardner, *A Great Physician's Greatest Discovery* (Journal of the Christian Medical Fellowship, January 1992), p. 6.

undergoing mastectomy without anaesthesia. Did Emily have an anaesthetic? I do not know. But one thing is certain, she suffered severe secondary infection. It could scarcely have been otherwise. It would be another ten years before Joseph Lister, inspired by Pasteur, used a carbolic acid spray to control infection. Lord Lister (as he later became) is described as 'a gentle, shy, unassuming man, yet firm in purpose because he humbly believed himself to be directed by God.'[1]

Edmund writes that his mother 'was so agonized by the treatment that she could neither stand up nor sit down, she was forced to take a room adjacent to Dr Fell's surgery. Here she dragged herself around in utter agony.' Yet despite all, her faith did not fail. She even continued to publish tracts. Her son continues,

What must be recorded was the extraordinary tranquillity, the serene and sensible resignation, with which my parents faced the awful hour. Language cannot utter what she suffered, but there was no rebellion, no repining; in their case even an atheist [and the mature Edmund acknowledges that he writes as one] might admit that the over-powering miracle of grace was mightily efficient.

The merciful release came in February 1857: Emily died in her husband's arms. Philip was stricken. It was now patently obvious that the treatment they had chosen, so far from retarding the disease, or even alleviating suffering, had the reverse effect, yet they had believed so sincerely that they had acted according to the Lord's will. At a later date Philip was to write, 'But it was not the Lord's will that we should decide differently. He surely guided us with infinite wisdom, to fulfil his purpose, which was infinitely good.'

How can we a century and a half later, in an era of antiseptic surgery, skilled anaesthesia, hormone therapy and control of pain by palliative care in a modern hospice, dare to pronounce any other verdict?

[1] *World Book Encyclopaedia* (Chicago, 1968), vol. 12, p. 307.

2

THE EVOLUTION OF EVOLUTION

In order to understand something of the cataclysm which was about to overtake Philip Gosse, and his reaction to it, I must turn the clock back; but only briefly, as there are many excellent books on the history and philosophy of evolutionary theory, written from both the secular and religious viewpoint.[1]

The Greek Era

The Greek philosopher, Aristotle (384–322 B.C.), has had an immense influence on Western thought down the centuries. In contrast to the prophets of the Old Testament he reduced God to the status of an absentee landlord, and so can be given credit as the first notable evolutionist. From the time of Aristotle, two schools of thought developed: the Graeco-Roman, leading to modern humanism, and the Judaeo-Christian. Down the running centuries, these two rival philosophies have warred against each other, with sometimes one, then the other in the ascendancy. The conflict has been superbly illustrated in the film series, *How Shall We Then Live?* by Francis Schaeffer.

Ancient Chronology

From earliest times, man has felt a compulsion to keep records of times and dates. Stonehenge for example, probably dating from the Druids or Neolithic times, seems to have been built as

[1]M. Bowden, *The Rise of the Evolution Fraud* (San Diego, California: Creation Life Publishers, 1982); Ian T. Taylor, *In the Minds of Men* (Toronto: TFE Publishing, 1984).

a massive astronomical calendar or clock. But all dates have to be hung on some notable historical event, and for the last two millennia in Western countries, this has been the birth of Christ; so we talk of B.C. and A.D.. True, because of humanistic pressure there have recently been attempts to discard this method of dating. In his *Analytical Concordance of the Bible*, under the heading 'Creation', Robert Young (quoting a Dr Hale) lists thirty computations for the date of creation based on the Scriptures. These range from 3616 to 6984 B.C.. But the only one commonly remembered today is 4004 B.C., computed by Archbishop Ussher (1581–1656). Details such as '9 a.m. on 17 October' (or similar) are not by Ussher although sometimes ascribed to him by sceptics in order to ridicule him.

The Seventeenth and Eighteenth Centuries

A notable follower of Aristotle was Descartes (1596–1650). A mathematician and philosopher, he published his *Discourse on Method* in 1637. In this he proposed that the universe is a mechanism governed by strict mathematical laws, an idea confirmed by Isaac Newton in 1687 with the discovery of the law of gravity.

By the eighteenth century the fashionable creed for intellectuals was deism.[1] It was accepted that a God was necessary at the beginning of the world, to wind it up like a clockwork toy. Pascal in his *Pensées*,[2] complained that Descartes, although a noted agnostic, could not resist invoking God to give 'the flick of His little finger to set the world in motion, but after that has no further use for Him.'

An influential figure in the late eighteenth century was Erasmus Darwin[3] (1731–1802), a popular physician, poet and free-thinker. His views on evolution anticipated Lamarck, and also those of his own more famous grandson, Charles Darwin. But today his philosophy of nature is regarded as untenable and incomprehensible.

[1]For a comparative definition of deism, theism etc. see page 71.
[2]Blaise Pascal, *Pensées* (Penguin Classics, repr. 1984).
[3]Darwinian properly pertains to the doctrine of Erasmus Darwin (1731–1802), but is more normally applied to the work of his grandson, Charles Darwin (1809–1882). Hence correctly Darwinianism, but usually shortened to Darwinism (*OED*).

The Early Nineteenth Century

Charles Lyell was born in 1797 in the family estate Kinnordy, Forfarshire, Scotland. In 1819 he entered Exeter College, Oxford to study law, and in due course was called to the Bar. However, he developed an intense interest in geology, and this became his life's interest. Lyell's major work, *Principles of Geology*,[1] was first published in 1830, and became the standard reference work for the next fifty years. Charles Darwin took the first volume to while away the hours during his celebrated voyage on the *Beagle*, and eagerly awaited the second instalment. Today the *Principles* is only remembered for popularizing 'Uniformitarianism', the theory which states that the present is the key to the past. 'Processes that have been actually observed to modify the face of the earth in historic times may be taken as a safe and sufficient guide in interpreting the record of events during the long ages of the geological past' (Sir Edward Bailey, FRS, 1962). The theory is essential to Darwinism, although most students of earth history in Lyell's early days opposed the doctrine.

Uniformitarianism assumes that all natural processes have continued almost unchanged from the beginning of time. Certainly it is agreed that there have been many relatively small catastrophes such as the eruption of Mount St Helens in 1980,[2] but no world-wide cataclysm has ever occurred. Obviously, if correct, the theory at one stroke rules out a six day creation and the world-wide flood of Noah. Thus Lyell's uniformitarianism has been every bit as destructive to the biblical story of creation as Darwin's *Origin of Species*. Of course, Lyell was not the first or only geologist to suggest such a theory, but his active propagation of the idea laid the foundation on which Darwin's work rests.

Lyell's Hidden Agenda

What was it that so strongly motivated Lyell? In the *Principles*,

---

[1]Sir Charles Lyell, *Principles of Geology* (London: John Murray, 10th ed., 1867), vol. 1, pp. 30–31.

[2]Mount St Helens. The significance of this eruption is the light it has thrown geologically on how long it may have taken for the world-wide development of rock strata (see Appendix 1).

he devotes the first four chapters of volume one to a history of geology. In these he gently derides as 'prejudiced', scientists, such as the medieval geologist Steno who 'displayed great anxiety to reconcile his theory with the Scriptures'. Then under the page heading 'Diluvial Theory', Lyell cites a seventeenth-century Sicilian painter called Scilla (1670), who produced an elegant work on fossils, written in Latin, and illustrated by fine engravings. Lyell writes: 'Like many eminent naturalists of his day, Scilla seems to give way to the popular persuasion, that all fossil shells were the effects and proof of the Mosaic deluge. It may be doubted whether he was perfectly sincere.'

'Certainly', Lyell concludes, 'some of his contemporaries who took the same course, were not. [Theologians] who refused to subscribe to the position that all marine organism remains were proof of the Mosaic deluge, were exposed to the imputation of disbelieving the whole of the sacred writings.'

Later, Lyell makes the dogmatic assertion:

Never did a theoretical fallacy, in any branch of science, interfere more seriously with accurate observation and the systematic classification of facts . . . [The diluvialists] saw the phenomena only as they desired to see them, sometimes misrepresenting facts, and at other times deducing false conclusions from correct data.

Lyell continues: 'A sketch of the progress of geology, is the history of a constant and violent struggle of new opinions against doctrines sanctioned by the implicit faith of many generations, and supposed to rest on scriptural authority.'

In 1830, in a letter to a geologist friend who had been asked to review the first volume of the *Principles* for the *Quarterly Review (QR)*, Lyell wrote:

I am sure you may be able to get into the *QR what will free the science from Moses*,[1] for if treated seriously, the party [i.e., theologians] are quite prepared for it . . . [Some bishops] see at last the mischief and scandal brought on them by Mosaic systems. If we don't irritate, which I fear that we may, we shall carry all before us . . . (my italics)

---

[1]Freud, similarly, considered it his mission to destroy Moses, who represented the Law and the guilt of the Law. In *Moses and Monotheism* he set out to portray Moses as an Egyptian, for if he could accomplish this, he would have thrust Moses out of Jewry. (Freud, *Moses and Monotheism*, quoted by R. J. Rushdoony, *Freud* (Phillipsburg, NJ: Modern Thinkers Library, Presbyterian and Reformed Pub. Co., 1979), pp. 37–38.

P.S. I conceived the idea five or six years ago, that if ever the Mosaic geology could be set down without giving offence, it would be by an historical sketch.

Lyell's basic plan, therefore, was to discredit Genesis and thus the whole of Scripture. This he hoped to do by undermining the Genesis accounts of creation and the flood. The slow steady demise of Christianity, he believed, would inevitably follow. Darwin was prepared to follow his example. Bowden quotes a letter Darwin wrote in 1873 to his son George:

Lyell is most firmly convinced that he has shaken the faith in the Deluge far more effectively by never saying a word against the Bible, than if he had acted otherwise . . . Voltaire insists strongly that direct attacks on Christianity (even when written with the wonderful force and vigour of Voltaire) produce little permanent effect: *real good* seems only to follow the slow and silent attack. (my italics)

Not Less Than; Not Greater Than

Lyell was probably the first to make use of the concept that 'the world *can not be less than* . . . X years old', where X is a figure considerably in excess of Ussher's computed date for creation of 4004 B.C.. Lyell's purpose was to undermine faith in this date by showing from scientific evidence that the world could not possibly have been created as recently as 4004 B.C., that is about 6,000 years ago from the present time. He believed he had found evidence for which he was searching during a visit to Niagara in 1841 to study the rate of recession of the Falls.[1] Water pouring over the escarpment for hundreds of years had gradually eroded the cliff. He talked to local residents and was told the Falls retreated about three feet per year. 'He assumed that this was an exaggerated claim, and concluded that one foot per year would be a more likely figure.' On the basis of this guess he calculated that it must have taken *at least* 35,000 years 'to cut the gorge from the escarpment to the place it occupied in the year of his visit'. Such was the persuasiveness of his pleading, that for the next few generations this calculation was accepted and helped to demolish any credence for Ussher's date, and with it orthodox belief in the Mosaic Flood.

[1]Taylor, *In the Minds of Men*, pp. 81–83.

According to Taylor, the figure has recently been revised to about 7,000–9,000 years. The importance of Lyell's theory of uniformitarianism is that it stretches the supposed biblical time frame, thus permitting the aeons desired by Darwin for the death and extinction of millions of animals, and the laying down of the great fossil graveyards.

Not Greater Than

How the plausible theory of uniformitarianism could be countered, and geology returned to the biblical belief in a relatively young earth, was a question occupying the minds of many Christians in the nineteenth century. It was the great Christian and mathematician, William Thomson, later to become Lord Kelvin (1824–1907),[1] who first conceived the idea of turning the tables on Lyell by showing scientifically that the age of the world could '*not be greater than* . . .'. In this case he selected the figure of 20 million years, based on the assumption that the earth had cooled at a certain rate. This figure, of course, is much greater than Ussher's 4,004 years, but Darwin recognized angrily that even so it was far too short to accommodate his theory, which he believed required at least 100 million years. Although Lord Kelvin's calculations were correct, we now know that the basic data on which it was based was faulty. Nevertheless, the episode points to a profitable line of research into the age of the earth which can be used in the present day. Many modern calculations based on standard scientific assumptions demonstrate that the age of the earth *can not be* anything approaching the billions of years now required by evolutionary theory.

* * *

Lyell rose to the summit of his profession. He was made a Professor of Geology at King's College, London, and repeatedly President of the Geological Society. Knighted in 1848, he was created a baronet in 1864. By a strange 'quirk of fate' – call it what you will – Darwin and Lyell are buried near each other in Westminster Abbey. As founders of the theory of evolution,

[1] *Ibid.*, pp. 292–94.

and destroyers of Christianity, they surely rank equal. Yet everyone has heard of Darwin and his work, but comparatively few know about Lyell. Sir Charles lies under a headstone of fossil marble from Derbyshire bearing the lengthy inscription –

CHARLES LYELL
BARONET F.R.S.

Author of
'The Principles of Geology'
Born at Kinnordy in Forfarshire
November 14 1797
Died in London February 22 1875

Throughout a long and laborious life
he sought the means of deciphering
the fragmentary records
of the earth's history
in the patient investigation
of the present order of nature
enlarging the boundaries of knowledge
and leaving on scientific thought
an enduring influence
'O Lord how great are thy works
and thy thoughts are very deep'.
Psalm xcii. 5.

As I ponder this epitaph, I have to agree that every word is factually true. But whether such endeavours qualify a man to be interred in a building dedicated to the glory of God – I wonder! Was the Bible text appended as an afterthought by the Dean of Westminster?

Meanwhile, in his coming fight against Lyell and Darwin, Philip Gosse had only the Bible and his collections of butterflies to guide him. Credible scientific evidence demonstrating that the earth may be young after all did not come to light until more than a hundred years later.

3

THE STORM STRIKES

Without Emily, Philip threw himself into his scientific work and his involvement in the Brethren movement as never before. But there was a basic incompatibility between the two. As a non-conformist he was not acceptable as a student at the universities of Oxford or Cambridge. Nevertheless his biology, though almost entirely self-taught by experimental observation, was of such a high standard that he was elected a Fellow of the Royal Society (FRS), which was then, as now, the highest academic accolade England can bestow. I doubt, however, whether this achievement was appreciated in the Gospel Halls he frequented; any more than his particular brand of religion in the corridors of science. It was an odd mix, though not unique.

Some months after Emily's funeral, Philip decided to take his grief and his only son away from the rigours of London and return to his beloved Devon. He invited his widowed mother to join them in St Marychurch. This location had the dual advantage of a small Brethren Assembly and a wealth of marine life on the sea shore for study.

In the summer of 1857, just before the move, he attended a last meeting of the Royal Society. Here it was that the full force of the storm struck, and from a new, but not totally unexpected direction. At the close of the meeting Gosse was approached in secretive fashion by Joseph Hooker (1817–1911), and later by Charles Darwin. Their purpose was to apprise him of the imminent publication of *The Origin of Species*.[1]

[1]Charles Darwin, *The Origin of Species by Natural Selection: Or The Preservation of Favoured Races in the Struggle for Life* (John Murray, 1859).

Hooker was eight years younger than Darwin, but Darwin had befriended him, originally perhaps because the younger man, like Darwin himself, had been on a long sea voyage during which he had collected scientific specimens. Darwin apparently felt that Hooker was someone who could be useful to him for various tasks. Making initial contact with Gosse was one of these.[1]

According to Edmund Gosse, it was Sir Charles Lyell who had suggested to Charles Darwin that 'before the doctrine of natural selection was given to a world which would be sure to lift up at it a howl of execration a certain body-guard of sound and experienced naturalists, expert in the description of species, should be privately made aware of its tenor.'

So it is probable that Philip Gosse was the first active Christian to hear of the Darwinian theory. If Lyell wanted to learn the views of a notable but probably antagonistic scientist, he could not have chosen better.

When informed of Darwin's theory Philip reacted, so his son tells us, as a scientist should:

every instinct in his intelligence went out at first to greet the new light. It had hardly done so, when a recollection of the opening chapter of Genesis checked it at the outset . . . Through my father's brain, in that year of scientific crisis, 1857, there rushed two kinds of thoughts, each absorbing, each convincing, yet totally irreconcilable. Here were two theories of physical life, each of which was true, but the truth of each was incompatible with the truth of the other.

The storm he had dreaded at last enveloped him, and just at the time when he was most vulnerable. 'Where was his place, as a sincere and accurate observer?' asks Edmund:

Manifestly it was with the pioneers of the new truth, it was with Darwin, Wallace and Hooker. But did not the second chapter of Genesis say that 'in six days the heavens and earth were finished, and the host of them, and that on the seventh day God ended his work which He had made?' Here was the dilemma! Geology certainly *seemed* to be true, but the Bible, which was God's word, *was* true. If the Bible said all things in Heaven and Earth were created in six days,

---

[1]Gosse, *Father and Son*, p. 75. I have followed this book by Edmund Gosse even though according to Ross it may not be acurate (see chapter 6 postscript). See also Adrian Desmond & James Moore, *Darwin* (London: Penguin Books, 1992), p. 313.

created in six days they were, – in six literal days of twenty-four hours each . . . A mind so acute, and yet so narrow as my Father . . . has not the relief of a smaller nature, which escapes the dilemma by some foggy formula . . . My Father, although half suffocated by the emotion of being lifted, as it were, on a great biological wave, never dreamed of letting go his clutch of *the ancient tradition.* (my italics)

So writes Sir Edmund. But I would question him on two counts. Firstly, why does he include Wallace? At that time Wallace was still in the Far East. He did not send Lyell and Darwin his so-called 'Ternate' paper proposing the 'survival of the fittest' mechanism until 1858. This was the paper which incited Darwin to publish the *Origin*.

Secondly, it was not mere 'ancient tradition' on which poor embattled Philip relied in his extremity, but on the infallibility of the Holy Scriptures. Edmund points accusingly at his father for lacking 'that highest modesty which replies, "I do not know", even to the question which Faith, with menacing finger, insists on having most positively answered.'

Reaction

Philip Gosse's reaction was, I think, totally predictable. He was thunderstruck by the enormity of the threat to Christianity and to his beloved science. For some time he, like many other Christians with a scientific bent, had become increasingly alarmed by the obvious inroads geology was making into religion, particularly concerning Lyell's theory of the age of the earth. But here was an attack from a different direction – biology. How then could he, an accomplished writer on scientific matters, appreciated by both scientists and lay people alike, best utilize his considerable skills to defend the Faith he loved so much? Of course, he would write a book! But on what? Obviously a book on creation, but which aspect? It was such a vast subject . . .

*   *   *

In the early nineteenth century, fossil hunting was the great sport of gentlemen – and ladies too, if they could manage to clamber up and down the cliff-face in their impractical garments. Charles Lyell and Gosse were both examples of diligent gentlemen geologists.

Gosse had read Lyell's *Principles*, and as he did so he realised that, sooner or later, an open attack on biblical creation, and so on the integrity of the whole Bible, was inevitable. But the terrible events of the past year had left little time for meditative thought.

According to Edmund, his father enjoyed the company of Darwin but was overawed by Sir Charles Lyell with his Scottish accent, worldly wisdom and lawyer's sagacity. Darwin relied on him much for advice and prompting, and used to refer to him as 'My Chancellor of the Exchequer'. Darwin was happy to be the 'front man' with Lyell the careful background manipulator.

His son tells us the elder Gosse did not wish to attack Darwin outright, although he could have done so more safely as biology was a topic in which he himself was an expert. Instead he moved against Lyell, with a book to be entitled *Omphalos*,[1] thus entering the field of geology in which he had less expertise. 'His son tells us . . .'! And here is the difficulty. I have found few references to Philip Gosse and *Omphalos* in the literature, and of these almost all,[2] as far as I can tell, judge the book by what Edmund says about it. Only Mrs Fayette Gosse[3] quotes the book directly, and that in one short sentence.

What amazes me is the speed with which (assuming Edmund's dates are correct) his father moved. Emily had died in February 1857, and not long thereafter he had that fateful meeting with Hooker and Darwin in the Royal Society. Then, in the summer he vacated London for good; transporting his widowed mother, his young son, his priceless collections of specimens, his books, and his scanty household belongings to live in a hamlet near Torquay on the Devon coast – yet the

---

[1]Philip Henry Gosse, *Omphalos: An attempt to untie the Geological Knot* (London: John Van Voors, 1857).

[2]For a notable exception see chapter 6, Postscript: Philip Gosse and Sir Edmund Gosse.

[3]Fayette Gosse, *The Gosses* (Canberra: Brian Clouston, 1981). I searched for the book, *Omphalos*, for a number of years, but in vain. I am grateful to Mrs Gosse for allowing me to make a photostat from her copy. In the next two chapters I have purposely quoted freely from *Omphalos*, both because of the book's intrinsic interest, and because I believe few readers will be able to obtain a copy for themselves.

preface to this new book of over 370 pages, with 56 intricate, scientifically accurate woodcuts is dated October 1857, only eight months after the horrific death of his wife. His industry astonishes me. For in the same year he also published[1] a *Memoir of Emily Gosse*, and *Wanderings through Kew*! True, as we shall see, *Omphalos* contained much material with which he was completely familiar, and the thesis on which it was based was not original. He explains in the preface that, 'It was suggested to me by a Tract, which I met with some dozen years ago, or more; the title of which I have forgotten: I am pretty sure it was anonymous, but it was published by Campbell, of 1 Warwick Square.'

It appears possible, therefore, that Philip had been considering the topic for some time. Perhaps he had been almost ready to publish before the Royal Society meeting.

But this still begs the question: Why the great haste? Could it be that Philip Gosse wanted to produce *Omphalos* before his friend Darwin published the *Origin*, and so perhaps limit the damage he knew it would cause?

He certainly hoped to counter Lyell's uniformitarian theory. The age-of-the-earth controversy had been going on for years, but the threat he now foresaw was that it would be linked with a viable new theory to account for the mutability of species.

Perhaps also he hoped that, after all, Darwin might be persuaded not to publish his manuscript. He probably knew that Darwin's wife was a Unitarian and vehemently opposed.

But all the while Darwin was being secretly urged on to publish by Lyell. Then occurred that strange coincidence of a little-known man with malaria in a jungle hut in the Dutch East Indies, who independently reached the same conclusion of a survival-of-the-fittest mechanism, and so threatened Darwin with that greatest dread for a researcher – to be forestalled in publication.

So the time seemed propitious and Philip hoped and prayed. He chose the title, *Omphalos*, with care. The name means navel. By this Gosse revived the medieval question, 'Did Adam have a navel?' For obviously, if the Genesis story is true, he did not

---

[1]See *Dictionary of National Biography* (1885–1900), vol. 22, p. 260. The annotation is signed E.G. (almost certainly Edmund Gosse), as is an entry on Gosse, Emily (1806–1857), p. 268.

require one, as he had no mother. Yet all complete humans have a navel . . . so? It takes the writer many pages to reach his surprising conclusion, and then the navel turns out not to be the most significant part of the story after all.

4

OMPHALOS

I suspect Philip Gosse regarded *Omphalos* as the most important book he had ever written. He sent it out with high expectations. His earnestness is indicated by the way that, in order to make a point, he piles illustration upon illustration, and in the end was driven to finish the book as fast as possible. I'm sure he would have agreed with the man who wrote: 'Sorry this letter is so long. I didn't have time to make it shorter.'

I make no apology for providing lengthy quotations. Indeed, I feel a certain responsibility in recording Philip's exact words as I suspect few people sympathetic with Gosse's general position have studied the book.

Omphalos is interesting, not least because of the light it shines on a godly man confronted by a dire situation. In this chapter, italics are original, unless otherwise specified.

*   *   *

The preface to *Omphalos* begins with the words: '"You have not allowed for the wind, Hubert," said Locksley, in *Ivanhoe*; "or that would have been a better shot."'

Gosse then recounts the story of the foundering of the *Elizabeth* off Newfoundland in 1830; a brig belonging to the firm in which he was at that time a clerk. This ill-fated ship 'plunged against the cliffs of Ferryland . . . and presently went down . . . The captain *had not allowed for the polar current.*'

Philip Gosse (PG) next refers to the planet Uranus, the orbit of which 'had been calculated by astronomers with scrupulous care.' Its expected path had been laid down 'according to the recognized law of gravitation. But it would not take this path.' Every reason for the disturbance had been considered without success; but, 'The secret is now known; *they had not allowed for the disturbance produced by Neptune'*. PG at last reveals the motif of the book:

I venture to suggest in the following pages, there is an element hitherto overlooked, which disturbs the conclusions of geologists respecting the antiquity of the earth. Their calculations are sound on the recognised premises; *but they have not allowed for the Law of Prochronism*[1] *in Creation.*

And what is this Law? 'The reader', replies Gosse, 'will find it at p. 124; or p. 347. All the rest of the book is illustration.'

I imagine he hoped to keep his readers in suspense, as in a modern detective novel. Personally, I turned immediately to those pages, and I guess most other readers did likewise. Gosse ends the preface:

I would not be considered an opponent of geologists: but rather a co-searcher with them after that which they value as highly as I do, *truth.* The path which I have pursued . . . [is] at variance with theirs. I have a right to expect that it be weighed; let it not be imputed to vanity if I hope it may be accepted.

But what I more ardently desire is that the thousands of thinking persons, who are scarcely satisfied with the extant reconciliations of Scriptural statements and Geological deductions, – who are silenced but not convinced, – may find, in the principles set forth in this volume, a stable resting-place. I have written it in the constant prayer that the God of Truth will deign to use it; and if He does, to Him be all the glory.

On p. 3, PG continues his apologetic:

I hope I shall not be deemed censorious in stating my fear that those who cultivate the physical sciences are not always sufficiently mindful of the *'Humanum est errare.'* . . . Even if our observations be so simple, so patent, so numerous as *almost* to preclude the possibility of mistake in them, and our process of reasoning from them be without a flaw, still we may have overlooked a principle, which, though perhaps not very obvious, ought to enter into our investigations and which, if recognised, would greatly modify our conclusions . . . In this volume

[1]Prochronism: The referring of an event, etc., to an earlier date than the true one (*OED*).

I venture to suggest such a principle to the consideration of geologists . . . I am not assuming here that the Inspired Word has been rightly read; I merely say that the plain straightforward meaning, the meaning that lies manifestly on the face of the passages in question, is in opposition to the conclusions which geologists have formed, as to the antiquity and genesis of the globe on which we live.

p. 5: Now while there are unhappily a few infidels, professed or concealed, who easily seize on the apparent discrepancy between the works and the Word of God, in order that they may invalidate the truth of the latter, there are, especially in this country, [in the geological and other branches of science] those to whom the veracity of God is as dear as life. They can not bear to see it impugned; they know that it cannot be overthrown; they are assured that He who gave the Word, and He who made the worlds, is the one Jehovah, who cannot be inconsistent with Himself. But they cannot shut their eyes to the startling fact, that the records that *seem* legibly written on His created works do flatly contradict those which *seem* to be plainly expressed in His word. Here is a dilemma. A most painful one; and many reverent minds have laboured hard and long to escape from it. They did not rejoice in the dilemma; they saw it at first dimly and hoped to avoid it. At first they . . . thought that the deluge of Noah would explain the stratification, and the antediluvian era account for the organic fossils. As the 'stone book' was further read, this mode of explanation appeared to many to be untenable.

PG appends a footnote:

The Rev. Samuel Charles Wilks long ago observed [that], 'Buckland, Sedgwick, Faber, Chalmers, and many other Christian geologists, strove long with themselves to believe that they could [avoid the dilemma]; and they did not give up hope or seek for a new interpretation of the sacred text, till they considered themselves driven from their position by the facts as we have stated. If *even now a reasonable, or we might say a possible solution were offered, they would we feel persuaded, gladly revert to their original position' (Christian Observer*, August 1834).

PG prefers not to name 'those good men who merely *denounce* Geology and geologists. . . . There are the facts, "written and graven in stones," and that by the finger of God.' 'How', he asks, 'can they be accounted for?' Gosse presents a number of theories which have been suggested whereby science and the Bible can be reconciled. He tells us that the opinion that 'the six

[25]

days in the Inspired Record signify six successive periods of immense, though indefinable, duration . . . is as old as the Fathers at least, e.g., Origen, Augustine.' He also quotes other propositions 'whereby science and the Bible can be reconciled.' He does not mention the Gap theory. Magnanimously, PG concludes chapter I, 'I am not blaming, far less despising, the efforts that have been made for harmonizing the teachings of Scripture and science. I heartily sympathize with them. What else could good men do?'

The High Court

To set the stage, in chapters II and III Philip imagines the scene in a courtroom. He cites what he calls, 'A High Court of Inquiry [which] has been sitting now for a number of years, whose object is to determine a chronological question of much interest. It is no less than the age of the globe in which we live.'

First there is 'The Witness of Macro-Chronology'. He states that there is general agreement that the fossils proclaim a very long age for the earth. And chapter III ends with the words, [all the above] ' . . . shows the lapse of time to have been *very long*. Such then is the evidence for the macro-chronology. And a mighty array of evidence it certainly is.'

'But is there no alternative? . . . I verily believe there is another.'

The Cross-Examination

PG says his first task is to examine, and disprove this testimony. His main contention is that:

there is nothing here but *circumstantial* evidence; there is no *direct* evidence. There is no actual observation of the processes above enumerated.

You will say, 'It is the same thing; we have seen the [fossil] skeleton of [this animal], the crushed bones of that'. No, it is not the same; it is not *quite* the same thing; *not quite*. Strong as is the evidence, it is not *quite* so strong as if you had actually seen the living things, and been conscious of the passing of time while you saw them live. It is only by a process of reasoning that you infer they lived at all. The process is something like this. Here is an object in a mass of stone which has a definite form – the form of a beast. The more minutely you examine it the more points of resemblance you find . . .

Allowing for the difference in species, the skeleton . . . is precisely like that of the little beast at whose death you were actually present, whose bones you cleaned with your own hands and mounted in your own museum.

Thus far is a matter of fact – observed, witnessed fact; you have found in a stone a real skeleton. You immediately infer that this skeleton belonged to a living animal that breathed, and fed, and walked about, exactly as animals do now. This conclusion seems so obvious and unavoidable, that we naturally conclude it rests on the same foundation of fact . . . But really it rests on a totally different foundation; it is a conclusion deduced by a process of reasoning from certain assumed premises.

PG ends the chapter with the bold pronouncement, 'I think I can show enough, greatly to diminish, if not altogether to destroy, the confidence with which you inferred the existence of vast periods of past time from geological phenomena. I can deduce a principle, having the universality . . . of *law*.'

Gosse tells us he takes for granted the following two premises:

1 *The Creation of Matter:*
   If any geologist takes the position of the necessary eternity of matter . . . I do not argue with him. I assume that at some period or other in past eternity there existed nothing but the Eternal God, and that He called the universe into being out of nothing.

2 *The Persistence of Species:*
   I demand also, in opposition to the development hypothesis, the perpetuity of specific characters, from the moment when the respective beings were called into being, till they cease to be. I assume that each organism which the Creator educed was stamped with an indelible specific character, which made it what it was, and distinguished it from everything else, however near or like. I assume that such character has been, and is, indelible and immutable; that the characters which distinguish species from species *now* were as definite in the first instant of their creation as now, and are as distinct now as they were then. If any choose to maintain, as many

[27]

do, that species were gradually brought to maturity from humbler forms . . . he is welcome to that hypothesis, but I have nothing to do with it. These pages will not touch him.

By the 'development hypothesis', I assume Gosse refers to what we would call evolution. If so, this statement is in direct contradiction to Darwin's manuscript which he had recently viewed in the Royal Society. Here is the rift between Gosse and Darwinian evolution. Furthermore he indicates in the last sentence that he will not contend on this topic: 'These pages will not touch him.'

He continues,

I believe however, that there is a large preponderance of men of science, at least in this country, who will be one with me here. They acknowledge the mighty *fiat* of God, as the energy that produced the being; and they maintain that the specific character which He then stamped on His creation remains unchangeable.

In the next chapter, Gosse came to the crux of his argument, which he dignifies as, 'A Law: The course of nature is a circle . . . I am not alluding to any *plan* of nature, but to its *course, cursus,* – the way in which it *runs on.* This is a circle.'

*   *   *

The bulk of the rest of the book is a succession of botanical and zoological examples by way of illustration of this Law. Here is the first:

In my garden is a scarlet runner. It is a slender twining stem, some three feet long, beset with leaves, with a growing bud at one end, and the other inserted in the earth. What was it a month ago? A tiny shoot protruding from between two thick fleshy leaves, scarcely raised above the ground. A month before that? The two fleshy leaves were two oval cotyledons, closely pressed, face to face, with the minute plumule between them, the whole enclosed in an unbroken, tightly-fitted, spotted, leathery coat. It was a bean, a seed. Was this the commencement of its existence? O no! Six months earlier still, it was snugly lying, with several others like itself, in a green fleshy pod, to the interior of which it was organically attached. A month before that, this same pod, with its contents was the centre of a scarlet butterfly-like flower . . . within which, if you had split it open, you would have discerned the tiny beans, whose history we have been tracing backwards . . .

But where was this flower? It was one of many that glowed on my garden wall all through last summer; each cluster springing as a bud from a slender twining stem, which was an exact counterpart of that with which we commenced this little history. And this earlier stem – what of it? It too had a shoot, a pair of cotyledons . . . and so backward, *ad infinitum*, for aught I can perceive.

The course, then of a scarlet runner is a circle, without beginning or end: that is, a natural, a normal beginning or end. For at what point in its history can you put your finger and say, 'Here is the commencement of this organism, before which there is a blank; here it began to exist?' There is no such point, no stage which does not look back to a previous stage.

PG repeats the illustration with a Liverwort, and with a Hawkmoth. He even goes on to include,

That cow that peacefully ruminates under the grateful shadow of yonder spreading beech, was, a year or two ago, a gamesome heifer with budding horns. The year before . . . [we can trace its lineage] back to the ovum . . . part of an ovary – of another cow – and so on, through a vista of receding cows, as long as you choose to follow.

PG sums up his proposition like this: looking through the light of experience and reason, there can be but one of two possible theories: 'The development of all organic existence out of gaseous elements, or the eternity of matter in its present state.'

He considers neither satisfactory. But, he tells us:

Creation solves the dilemma. I have, in my postulates, begged the fact of creation, and I shall not, therefore, attempt to prove it . . . But what is creation? It is *the sudden bursting into a circle* . . .

At whatever stage is selected by the arbitrary will of God, the commencing point must be unnatural, or rather preternatural. The life-history of every organism commenced at some point or other of its circular course. It was created, called into being, in some definite stage . . . Before that course began there was nothing . . . its previous history presents an absolute blank; *it was not.*

But the whole organisation thus newly called into existence, looks back to the course of an endless circle in the past. Its whole structure displays a series of developments, which as distinctly witness to former conditions as do those which are presented in the cow, the butterfly, the fern, of the present day. But what former conditions? The conditions thus witnessed unto, as being necessarily implied in the present organisation, were non-existent; the history was a perfect blank until the moment of creation. The past conditions or stages of existence in question can indeed be as triumphantly inferred by legitimate deduction from the present, as can those of our cow or the butterfly; they rest on the very same evidences; they are identically the same in every respect, except in this one, that they are *unreal*. They exist only in their results; they are effects which never had causes.

Those unreal developments whose apparent results are seen in the organism at the moment of creation, I will call *prochronic*, because time was not an element in them . . .

Now again I repeat . . . Every argument by which the physiologist can prove to demonstration that yonder cow was once a foetus in the uterus of its dam, will apply with exactly the same power to show that the newly created cow was an embryo, some years before its creation.

Permit me to repeat, as having been proved, these two propositions:

All organic nature moves in a circle.

Creation is a violent irruption into the circle of nature.

*　　*　　*

The next section Gosse calls 'Parallels and Precedents'. Since every organism was created at a moment of time, but we do not know exactly when, Gosse is prepared, for now, to leave out of his argument consideration of the exact chronological date: 'It may have been 600 yrs ago, or 6,000, or sixty times six million; let it for the present remain an indeterminate quantity. Only please to remember that the date *was* a reality, whether we can fix it or not.'

Plants

PG's first illustration in this new series is the Tree Fern (*Alsophila aculeata*). I will recount this in fair detail, because it illustrates his method of writing, repeated many times. PG supposes that he asks a botanist to date a Tree Fern. The botanist replies that he can do so only approximately:

Let us take it in order. The most recent development is the growing point in the centre of the arching crown of leaves. Around this you can see . . . close ring-like bodies, or perhaps more like snail-shells, protruding from the growing bud; then young leaves, partially opened in various degrees, but coiled up scroll-wise at their tips, and around them, these elegant fretted fronds, which expand broadly outward in a radiating manner, and arch downward.

Now every one of these broad fronds was at first a compactly coiled ring; but it has, in the course of development, uncoiled itself, growing at the same time from its extremity.

But let us look further. The outermost fronds that compose this exquisite cupola, you see are nearly naked; indeed, the extreme outermost are quite naked, being stripped of their verdant honours . . . and left mere dry and sapless sticks . . . Some of them, you see, are hanging down, almost detached from the stem, and ready to drop at the first breath of wind. Now remember, each of these brown unsightly sticks was once a frond, that had passed through all the steps of uncoiling from its circinate condition. This process has certainly occupied several months.

Look now . . . the stem is marked with great oval scars, and see, this old frond-rib has come off in my hand, leaving just such a scar, and adding more to the number of them than there were before . . .

These scars are ocular demonstration of former fronds . . . They are the record of the past history of this organism, and they evidently reach back into history. The periodic ratio of development of new fronds may be, perhaps, roughly estimated at eight in the course of a year. Now there are about a hundred and fifty leaf-scars that we can count with ease . . . I have no hesitation, then, in pronouncing this plant to be thirty years old; it is probably much older.

Such is the report of our botanical adviser; such his argument; and we can not but admit it is invulnerable; his conclusion inevitable, but for one fact, which he is not aware of. There is one objection – a fatal one; You and I know that the Tree-fern is not five minutes old, *for it was created but this moment.*

PG repeats this line of argument for the next forty-nine pages. He describes twenty-seven plants, mainly tropical. Many of them grow well in my vicinity: Bamboo; Couch grass; Travellers Tree; the giant Australian Fig; Mangrove; Tulip Tree and so on.

Philip further illustrates his Law by describing invertebrate animals: twenty-eight of them in fifty-nine pages, including such surprises as white ants and the human intestinal parasite, Taenia. Lastly he gives examples of vertebrates, considering eighteen specimens in thirty-seven pages.

On each occasion he explains that the signs, which to the

expert confirm the age of the organism, 'are illusory, or rather that they are prochronic'. So that, 'as in the case of this crab, the evidences of age are fallacious, because the Crab has been created this morning'. Whatever the organism he is quoting, be it plant or animal, PG assumes that in every case we are privileged to view it at the moment of its creation, 'but a short time ago'.

*　　*　　*

Man

'We have knocked at the door of the vegetable world, asking our questions; then at those of the lower tribes of the brute creation.' Now Philip turns his attention to the primal head of the human race. He asks the same questions as before: 'Does the body of the Man, just created, present us with any evidence of past existence?' After some anatomical discussion, he asks the question which, one might say, has been the trigger for his whole book:

What means this curious depression in the centre of the abdomen, and the corrugated knob that occupies the cavity? This is the *navel*. The corrugation is the cicatrix left where once was attached the umbilical cord, and whence its remains, having died, sloughed away. This organ introduces us to the foetal life of Man, for it was the link of connection between the unborn infant and the parent.[1]

If it was legitimate to suppose that the first individual of the species Man were created in the condition answering to that of a new-born infant, there would still be the need of maternal milk for its sustenance, and maternal care for its protection for a considerable period; while if we carry on the suggested stage to

[1]In a footnote on p. 279, PG observes that 'Sir Thomas Browne, indeed denies Adam a navel . . . The following is his verdict: "Another Mistake ther may be in the Picture of our first Parents, who after the manner of theyre Posteritie are both delineated with a Navill: and this is observable not only in the ordinarie and stayned peeces, but in the Authenticke Droughts of Vrbin, Angelo, and others. Which, notwythstandynge cannot be allowed, except wee impute that vnto the first Cause which we impose not on the second . . . *Pseudodoxia Epidemica* 1643"'. This footnote is the only place in *Omphalos* where Adam is called by name. Eve is nowhere mentioned. Two years before Sir Edmund Gosse published *Father and Son*, he wrote a major work on Sir Thomas Browne. Perhaps he had been thumbing through his father's old library.

the period when this provision is no longer indispensable, the development of hair, nails, bones &c, will have proceeded through many stages.

And thus the life of the individual Man before us, passes by necessary regression, back to the life of another individual, from whose substance his own substance was formed by generation.

Triumphantly, Philip Gosse, FRS, the scientist, throws down the gauntlet: 'How is it possible to avoid this conclusion?' [We will leave out of consideration a lengthy chapter on Germs, a term by which PG refers to nuts; eggs of the butterfly, the Gipsy moth, the Cockroach; the egg-purse of the Shark; the egg of the fowl; the foetus of the Kangaroo – to name just a few. (The word 'germs' in the modern sense of microbes, had scarcely been invented.)]

Lastly, Gosse comes to a chapter entitled:

The Conclusions
We have passed in review before us the whole organic world; and the result is uniform; that no example can be selected from the vast vegetable [or animal] kingdom, which did not at the instant of its creation present indubitable evidence of a previous history. This is not put forth as a hypothesis but as a *necessity*; I do not say that it was *probably* so, but that it was *certainly* so; not that it *may have been thus*, but *it could not have been otherwise.*

Creation can be nothing else than a series of interruptions into circles; that supposing the interruption to have been made at what part of the circle we please – we can not avoid the conclusion that each organism was from the first, marked with the records of a previous being . . . but such records are *false* so far as they testify to time. The question of the actual age of any species whether plant or animal, is one which can not be answered except on historic testimony.

To illustrate the above, PG pictures a toy coach running round and round on a table and asks the question : 'How long has the coach been running?'

Answer, 'We cannot tell unless we saw the tramp [now hidden under the table] winding up the clockwork.' 'The only evidence worth a rush is that of the lad who saw him set the whirligig a-going . . . ' 'So', Gosse continues, 'I am not attempting to show that the globe existed for no more than six thousand years . . . *because I was not there to see it happen!*'

[33]

Here Philip Gosse is making a profound statement. When today someone talks confidently about an event as having occurred millions of years ago, it is surely legitimate to ask, 'How do you know? Were you there?' This is the Lord's question addressed to Job, in chapter thirty-eight, verse four.

Fossils

As with all skilled writers, Gosse leaves the most interesting and contentious issue of his whole thesis to the end – what about fossils?

He suggests a geologist finds a fossil skeleton. His knowledge of anatomy enables him to recognize that the bones had been hollow. Presumably they contained cavities for bone marrow, and foramina (holes) for blood vessels. So he understands that once there must have been flesh and blood. Blood implies life, and life implies the passage of time. He therefore concludes unhesitatingly that the skeleton was once alive, and that time passed over it in the living condition.'[1] On p. 345, Gosse provides us with probably the clearest explanation of his Law. He writes:

It is certain that when the Omnipotent God proposed to create a given organism, the course of that organism was present to his idea, as an ever revolving circle, without beginning or end. He created it at some point in the circle and thus gave it an arbitrary beginning; but one which involved all previous rotations in the circle, though only as an ideal, or in other words, prochronic.

Here we come to perhaps the most contentious statement in the book:

Who will say that the suggestion, *that the strata of the surface of the earth, with their fossil flora and fauna, may possibly belong to a prochronic development of the mighty plan of the life-history of the world,* – who will dare to say that such a suggestion is a self-evident absurdity?

---

[1] There is also a curious footnote on Coprolites. 'The existence of Coprolites [the fossilized excrement of animals] has been considered as more than ordinarily triumphant proof of pre-existence.' [I think he must be referring to the long age of the earth.] 'But,' he suggests, 'just as blood-vessels presume that there must have been blood, and therefore life, so coprolites indicate excrement located in the intestine of the first Man.'

PG seems to have anticipated the cries of vituperation which would probably arise. And indeed this is the statement which was seized upon by his scientific colleagues, journalists, and others, friends or foes, whether agnostic or Christian; virtually everyone, in fact, who has ever heard of *Omphalos*, from the date of its publication to the present time. For he continues:

It may be suggested that, to assume the world to have been created with fossil skeletons in its crust – skeletons of animals that never really existed – is to charge the Creator with forming objects whose sole purpose was to deceive us. The reply is obvious. Were the concentric timber-rings of a created tree formed merely to deceive? Were the growth lines on the created shell intended to deceive? Was the navel of Man intended to deceive him into the persuasion that he had a parent? . . . Some unscientific reader may say, 'Could not God have created plants and animals without these retrospective marks?' I distinctly reply, 'No! Not so as to preserve their specific identity with those with which we are familiar.' [PG provides several further illustrations.]

*   *   *

Let me interpose a personal suggestion: As I ponder on Philip's two propositions, it seems to me that there is the world of difference between the first Man being 'deceived' by observing his own navel (at most only Adam and Eve would have been concerned), and fossils being created, preformed, in the earth. If the latter were so, the deception would indeed have been great and would have been maintained in perpetuity.

I notice also that PG does not mention the possible involvement of Noah's flood in the formation of fossils. He must have known of this idea but seems to have abandoned it, perhaps after reading Lyell's *Principles*.

Gosse speculates further:

Let us suppose that this present year, 1857, [was the year which] the Creator selected [for] the actual beginning [of the world]. At his fiat it appears; but in what condition? . . . There would be cities filled with swarming men; houses half-built; castles falling into ruins; wardrobes filled with half-worn clothes. &c &c.

'Many persons,' he continues, 'have been inclined to take refuge from the conclusions of geology in the absolute

[35]

sovereignty of God, asking, "Could not the Omnipotent Creator make the fossils in the strata, just as they appear now?"' PG replies with vigour, 'No reason could be adduced for such an exercise of mere power, which would be unworthy of an Almighty God. This suggestion is totally different from what I am contending. I am endeavouring to show that a grand *Law* exists.' Despite Philip's protestations, in point of fact, this suggestion is precisely what his enemies, and even his friends, assumed to be his central message.

The Age of the Earth

Finally,[1] Gosse refers again to the crucial question of the chronology of events. He concedes that, 'We might still speak of the inconceivably long durations of time, provided we understand *ideal* instead of *actual* time – that is, the duration was projected in the mind of God, and did not actually exist.' PG has this comfort for 'the geologist with his Stone Book', maintaining that his thesis in no way denigrates the work of God in the fossils. 'The geologist would still find in the fossil forms, evidence of that complacency in beauty, which has prompted the Adorable Workman to paint the rose in blushing hues, and to weave the fine lace of the dragonfly's wing.' In the end Gosse returns to the analogy of the Court Room: 'The field is left clear and undisputed for the Witness on the opposite side, whose testimony is as follows:

In six days Jehovah made heaven and earth, the sea,
and all that in them is
Finis.'

*   *   *

Summary

Gosse's critics maintained that in *Omphalos*, God is represented as a divine deceiver. The 'howl of execration' envisaged by

---

[1]Toward the end of the book, evidences of hustle appear. For example, 'Man' and 'man' are capitalized inconsistently, as are 'He' and 'he' for God. There are repetitions, and over-statements. Later arguments on the origin of the mountains, and the velocity of light, lack Gosse's usual meticulous presentation.

Lyell for the *Origin* certainly broke, but on the head of the unsuspecting Philip, not of Darwin. Some journalists mockingly questioned whether God had hidden the fossils in the rocks to tempt latter-day geologists into infidelity. Charles Kingsley wrote to his friend reprovingly that: 'For twenty-five years I have read no book which has so staggered and puzzled me'. He refused to review it. He could not believe that 'God had written in the rocks one enormous and superfluous lie'.

Poor Gosse was devastated by the universally adverse reaction to his book, although, according to Mrs Fayette Gosse, 'he was too stubborn to alter his mind.' And in *Father and Son*, Edmund derides him as 'a narrow-minded Calvinist'.

For myself, I accept that when God created the world he must have placed upon it mature creatures – Eve was not given into Adam's arms as a squawking baby. By the will and power of God, the *fiat* Creator, she was presented as a fully grown, beautiful woman.[1] But as for preformed fossils hidden in the rocks – that is quite another story.

[1]According to Dr Werner Gitt, 'The basic principle of creation is that an understanding of the original creation can only be obtained through a biblical "temper of mind" [from a biblical viewpoint]. Biblical revelation is the key to understanding the world. The Bible is the basic, irreplaceable source of information. It is a fact of creation that we may not extrapolate the currently valid natural laws into the six days of creation. Our present experiences do not allow us to really evaluate something that has just been created. Example: All adults were children. But Adam could not have been created as a baby, he was a grown man. He never was a child, and it does not make sense to extrapolate a number of years into his life, just because our present experiences require that every adult should have been a child. Similarly all the stars were immediately visible in spite of immense distances. Trees were not made as seedlings; they were fully grown and complete. Neither did birds hatch from their eggs and eventually grow up. The old question of "which was first – the hen or the egg?" has a clear and unambiguous biblical answer' (Werner Gitt, *Did God use Evolution?* [Bielefeld, Germany: Christliche Literatur-Verbreitung e. V., 1993], p. 17).

5

AFTER THE STORM

I am glad we are not left with only the errors of *Omphalos* and the vituperation of *Father and Son*. I have had the pleasure of reading a literary gem from the hand of the older Gosse: *The Romance of Natural History*, a book he wrote in Torquay in 1860, only two years after the death of Emily.

In the preface he explains that there is more than one way of studying natural history:

There is the way which consists of mere accuracy of description and differentiation; statistics as harsh and dry as the skins and bones of the museum where it is studied. There is the field-observer's way; the careful and conscientious accumulation and record of facts bearing on the life-history of the creatures; statistics as fresh and bright as the meadow where they were gathered in the dewy morning. And there is the poet's way; who looks at nature through a glass peculiarly his own; the aesthetic aspect, which deals, not with statistics, but with the emotions of the human mind, – surprise, wonder, terror, revulsion, admiration, love, desire and so forth, – which are made energetic by the contemplation of the creatures around him . . . Now this book is an attempt to present nature in this aesthetic fashion. Not that I presume to indicate – like the stage directions in a play, or the 'hear, hear' in a speech – the actual emotion to be elicited; this would have been intrusive and impertinent; but I have sought to paint a series of pictures, the reflection of scenes and actions in nature, which in my own mind awaken poetic interest, leaving them to do their proper work.[1]

[1]Philip Henry Gosse, *The Romance of Natural History* (London: James Nisbet, 1860).

Gosse obtained much of his material from his own observations in Jamaica, Newfoundland, Canada and as far south as Alabama. He also quotes extensively from the observations and travels of others. Throughout the book he points to 'the mighty works of God', but in such a natural and unobtrusive way as to give little opportunity for offence. Several times he refers critically to passages from Darwin's *Naturalist's Voyage* (1852). Concerning blind animals in caves, and blind fish in deep water – a subject on which Darwin expresses distinctly Lamarckian views – Philip comments, 'I am very far, indeed, from accepting Mr. Darwin's theory to the extent to which he pushes it, completely trampling on Revelation as it does; but I think there is a *measure* of truth in it.'[1]

The French scientist, Jean-Baptiste de Lamarck (1744–1829), had proposed that the organs of an animal could be modified by the environment in which the creature found itself. These slight changes could then be passed on to the offspring. The idea is known as 'the inheritance of acquired characteristics', or Lamarckism. The theory has now been abandoned, yet as recently as the beginning of this century was still alive and well.

Rudyard Kipling certainly subscribed to the idea. His beautifully written *Just So Stories* reveal classic Lamarckism, as even the titles of some of the chapters illustrate – 'How the Whale got its Throat'; 'How the Camel got its Hump'; 'The Beginning of the Armadillos'; 'The Elephant's Child'.

Peter Leys, who edited the Penguin reprint of *Just So Stories*,[2] acknowledges the fact. He writes: 'These stories are a kind of bad-taste of Darwin's theory of the evolution of species, and the truth about that subject is so overwhelmingly interesting as to make fantasies about it insipid. Yet Kipling could not have written without Darwin.'

I was brought up on the *Just So Stories*. They were my favourite bed-time stories, particularly when I could persuade my father to read them to me. Take the story of 'The Elephant's Child' for example. Kipling explains that all elephants in 'the high and far-off days' had 'a little blackish, bulgy nose, as big as

---

[1] *Ibid.*, p. 81.
[2] Rudyard Kipling, *Just So Stories For Little Children* (1902, Penguin edition 1987), p. 13.

a boot'.

Now, because of his "satiable curtiosities *(sic)*', the Elephant's Child went to see the crocodile who lived on the 'banks of the great grey-green greasy Limpopo river, all set about with fever trees', to ask him what he had for dinner. The crocodile was most co-operative, and told him to come closer so that he could whisper the answer, but when he did so the crocodile suddenly lunged out of the water, and grasped him by his 'little blackish bulgy nose as big as a boot', and pulled as hard as he could. The Elephant's Child planted his feet out in front of him and pulled too, shouting the while through his slowly elongating nose, 'Led go! You are hurtig be!' This for me, was the highlight of the tale, particularly when I could persuade my father to allow me to hold his nose as he said these words. The Lamarckian moral of the story comes in the last lines:

And ever since that day, O Best Beloved, all the elephants you will ever see, besides all those that you won't, have trunks precisely like the trunk of the 'satiable Elephant's Child.

I enjoyed Philip Gosse most in his book entitled *The Minute*. Was he thinking of his fourteen-year-old son Edmund when he wrote, 'Highly attractive to the young observer is the variety of life which meets the eye as he examines with a good microscope a drop of water from some pool rich in organisms'? Philip was particularly fascinated by the organism, *Melicerta*:

The smallest point you could make with the finest steel pen would be too coarse and large to represent its natural dimensions; yet it inhabits a snug little house of its own construction, which it has built up, stone by stone, cementing each with perfect symmetry, and with all the skill of an accomplished mason, as it proceeded. It collects the material for its mortar, and mingles it; it collects the material for its bricks and moulds them; and this with a precision only equalled by the skill with which it lays them when they are made . . . The whole apparatus is exquisitely beautiful . . . It is impossible to witness the constructive operation of the melicerta without being convinced that it possesses mental capacities, at least, if we allow these to any animals below man.

Gosse concludes the chapter:

Truly, the world which we are holding between our finger and thumb – this world in a globule of water – this world of rollicking, joyous, boisterous fellows, that a pin's head would take up, is even more wonderful than the shoals of whales in Baffin's Bay, or the herds of elephants that shake the earth in the forests of Ceylon. Truly the great God who made them is *maximus in minimis*.

In this delightful book there is no hint of sorrow.

*   *   *

But another disaster befell the embattled Philip Gosse. Edmund recalls that on her deathbed, as her mind was becoming clouded, his mother had gathered all her strength together to say to his father:

'I shall walk with Him in white. Won't you take your lamb and walk with me?' Confused with sorrow and alarm, my Father failed to understand her meaning. She became agitated and repeated two or three times: 'Take our lamb and walk with me!' Then my father comprehended, and pressed me forward. Thus was my dedication, that had begun in my cradle, sealed with the most solemn, the most poignant and irresistible insistence, at the death-bed of the holiest and purest of women.

But alas, poor Philip was not able for the task. He was not the man to undertake the successful rearing of a highly intelligent, motherless child.

My father then, like an old divine, concentrated his thoughts on the intellectual part of faith. In his obsession about me he believed that if my brain could be kept unaffected by any of the seductive errors of the age, and my heart centred on the adoring love of God, all would be well with me in perpetuity. He was still convinced that by intensely directing my thoughts, he could compel them to flow in a certain channel . . . The great panacea was now, as always, the study of the Bible.

Philip and Edmund

The memory of Philip Henry Gosse has suffered from the terrible fate of having as his exclusive biographer – who has been copied again and again – a son who was a literary genius, an acute and close observer, yet whose total world-view was completely alien and opposed to that of his father. So far from seeing his father through rose-coloured spectacles, or even with the impartiality of a neutral observer who endeavours to present his subject objectively, Edmund allows his love/hate relationship to intrude, and, I believe, warp his judgement. He was torn between irritation at the subjection in which his father kept him, and guilt at the distress he was causing one for whom, despite all, he seems to have retained some filial affection.

The basic trouble was that he could not understand his father. But this is only to be expected. St Paul writes, 'The natural man does not receive the things of the Spirit of God, for they are foolishness to him; nor can he know them because they are spiritually discerned' (*I Cor.* 2:14). There was surely fault on both sides.

Edmund was the product of a most dangerous combination: a highly intelligent only child, who had been brought up by an anxious, fastidious, sensitive, grieving yet outwardly unemotional, lonely Christian father. Furthermore, although Philip frequently acknowledged the sovereignty of God, and Edmund even refers to him as a Calvinist, yet in his anxiety to follow the dying wish of his wife, coupled with his own strong natural desire, he felt he must aid God in the salvation of Edmund's soul. He was not prepared to leave this task in the hands of the Holy Spirit, and rest content to play the supporting role of demonstrating the love of God by deeds rather than by narking words.

Satan hates to see men and women walking by faith. He will stand in their way and obstruct them all he can. But if that fails, he has a nasty habit of going round to the back and pushing from behind so that they run faster and faster and at last trip and fall.

The result was inevitable. Edmund became a spiritual prig. For example: Philip would not allow Christmas to be celebrated in his home, pointing out, quite correctly, that it is a religious festival grafted onto an old pagan custom. When Edmund was twelve years old, feeling sorry for the boy, the two maids in the house smuggled a small plum pudding into the kitchen. When pressed to eat, Edmund developed a sudden pain. He ran from the room, crying wildly, 'Oh, Papa, Papa, I have eaten of the flesh offered to idols.' Philip collected the remains of the pudding, and holding his son firmly by the hand, rushed to the rubbish tip at the bottom of the garden to dispose of the unfortunate remains.

A few years later, because of his son's mental brilliance, Philip persuaded the elders of the church to allow the boy to be baptised, by immersion, at an unusually early age. Following this, so Edmund tells us, his behaviour deteriorated. He became familiar with his father, condescending to the governess, haughty with the maid and insufferably patronizing with anyone of his own age. He admits, 'I was puffed up with a sense of my own holiness.' Edmund had developed the worst type of spiritual precocity – he became a pharisaical hypocrite.

The Break

Events moved relentlessly to a conclusion. For his twentieth birthday, Philip Gosse gave his son Dean Alford's edition of the Greek New Testament in four great volumes, magnificently bound in full morocco. 'The work shone on my poor book-shelf of sixpenny poets like a duchess among dairy-maids', wrote Edmund. He had learned to hate the Bible.

At last, when he was twenty-one, the abscess came to a head and burst. 'There was a meeting, in the hot-house at home, among the fragrance of the gorgeous waxen orchids, . . . when my forbearance or my timidity gave way.' After a tumultuous altercation, Edmund escaped the 'odoriferous furnace of the conservatory', and fled to London. The following day he received a long and pleading letter from his father. But in it, all he was offered was, 'Everything or nothing'.

Certainly, as seen through the eyes of his son, the elder Gosse acted unwisely on many occasions.

*   *   *

So we leave Philip, alone among the beauty and fragrance of his orchids, dejected, bemused, overwhelmed, pondering the strange workings of God.

For the thousandth time his mind returned to his beloved Emily, so happy in her home and blessed in her work for her Lord. What a future of service had seemed to be opening before them both. Until that terrible day when their earthly dreams were shattered. There was the fateful decision to forsake the sound advice of a renowned and kindly surgeon, and follow instead a plausible charlatan. Fear of mutilation had, of course, driven them; yet still they firmly believed it was God who was guiding them. Now he saw it was all a terrible mistake. Yet who was to blame? Was Emily? Was he? Was God? But they had prayed so earnestly, and they sincerely believed what they were doing was right.

Scarcely had Emily died in his arms than the new horror had arisen. A few days had sufficed to show him the dire effects of Darwin's theory. If evolution were true, then the Bible was not. It was as simple as that. And if the authority of the holy Word of God were shattered, then the greatest love in his life – yes, greater even than his love for Emily – his love for Jesus Christ, the living water, was revealed as a mirage.

With nothing to fall back on except the Scriptures, he had written that unfortunate book. Perhaps, after all, both the science and the theology were suspect. Perhaps the journalists were right to pour scorn on it, and on him too. Unwittingly, he now realized, he had given occasion for the enemies of the Lord to blaspheme (*2 Sam.* 12:14).

If the Bible were true, then Lyell and Darwin must be wrong; and despite all scientific appearances, it *was* true – he would stake his life on it. So God *was* still in control. God *did* still love him, despite everything, despite even his failure with Edmund.

If asked, Philip could have quoted the words of Naomi on her return from the land of Moab, 'Do not call me Naomi; call me Mara, for the Almighty has dealt very bitterly with me' (*Ruth* 1:20)

Would not the Master have answered, 'Blessed are those who have not seen, and yet have believed' (*John* 20:29)? 'Well done, good and faithful servant . . . Enter into the joy of your Lord' (*Matt.* 25:21).

6

POSTSCRIPT: PHILIP GOSSE AND SIR EDMUND GOSSE

These are some of the epithets which have been hurled at Philip Gosse over the last hundred years or so: 'A scientific crackpot'; 'A bible-soaked romantic'; 'A stern, pulpit-thumping Puritan throwback to the seventeenth century, who mingled plodding scientific investigation with suffocating doses of scriptural literalism'; 'A religious maniac, bordering on the insane'; 'An insensitive automaton, gathering data with the same lack of imagination that set him labouring at a literal interpretation of the Bible'; 'A stern and repressive father'.

And what is the source of this mud? According to Frederic R. Ross[1] writing in the prestigious journal *Isis* (1977), an international review devoted to the history of science and its cultural influences:

For these, as for virtually all modern assessments, Gosse is indebted to his son Edmund, literary critic, minor poet, biographer, salon-keeper, sycophantic gadabout *par excellence*, and author of two ostensibly biographical works on his father, the temperate and objective *Life of Philip Gosse, FRS* (1890), and the legend-mongering *Father and Son* (1907).

Of the two, modern scholars invariably use *Father and Son* as their reference. I have certainly done so, as I found the *Life* unobtainable.

Ross devotes much space to the alleged incident when Hooker and Darwin met Gosse in the Royal Society in 1857. He

[1] Frederic R. Ross, *Philip Gosse's* Omphalos, *Edmund Gosse's* Father and Son and Darwin's theory of Natural Selection (*Isis*, 1977, vol. 68), pp. 85–96.

concedes that 'there is obviously an element of truth in Edmund's story', but concludes that it is doubtful whether the event was nearly as dramatic as Edmund makes out in *Father and Son*. For example, it is not corroborated in the *Life*, except for the statement that 'some time prior to *Omphalos* the two naturalists were exchanging memoranda which more and more directly tended to strengthen evolutionary ideas'.

Nor is there corroborative evidence in Darwin's *Autobiography and Letters*, although Darwin does write, 'I tried once or twice to explain to able men what I meant by Natural Selection but signally failed.' Ross finds no evidence that Gosse was included among these 'able men'. On the other hand, Ross makes much of the fact that Darwin became increasingly anxious to protect the priority of his theory. He was afraid someone might publish on Natural Selection before him. It was for this reason he was so fearful of Wallace. But if he knew his man at all well, I scarcely think Darwin would have worried that Philip Gosse would rush into print on this subject before him! In fact it may be because of this that Darwin had no fear of talking freely to a safe man like Philip.

As I have already hinted, to my mind the greatest problem with the story of the Royal Society meeting is that chronologically it seems virtually impossible. If Philip Gosse was spoken to by Darwin in the summer of 1857 and, according to Edmund, moved to Devon in September the same year, how could a book of the size and complexity of *Omphalos* have been published by October 1857 (the date given on my copy)? And in any case the argument in the book is primarily directed against Lyell, not against Darwin, so what was the hurry?

Turning to *Omphalos*, Ross comments:

It is easy to reprobate Gosse's theorizing, for the whole business is sadly lacking in rigor and consistency. But to object to *Omphalos* on this basis certainly does not legitimize Edmund's characterization of [his father] as a grimly bedevilled, emotion-wracked paranoid.

On the contrary, Ross continues, Philip is revealed as 'stable, temperate and surprisingly objective':

Although the response of reviewers to *Omphalos* must have given Philip much sorrow, Edmund's characterization of Gosse after

[46]

Omphalos as a wretched misanthrope skulking disconsolately about the bleak Devonshire coast is most likely more *Father and Son* fiction.

Finally Ross discusses why Edmund should have set out to 'fictionalize the historical record' which he had faithfully chronicled only seventeen years before in the *Life*. Edmund, he says, 'creatively reshaped history by suppressing facts he considered redundant to his drama and accentuating those he felt would add to it.'

Ross suggests that the 'principal motif in the story of *Father and Son* is *rejection*. Puritanism, barren scripture, Devonshire isolation, methodical science – indeed all that Philip Gosse stands for are ultimately rejected by Edmund.' The *Omphalos* incident was a variation on this motif. According to Edmund, not only Philip's fanciful theory but, symbolically, his entire approach to religion was rejected by the contemporary social order. Refusing to accommodate himself to society, Philip reacted by 'isolating himself physically, mentally and spiritually'. And, most importantly for Edmund, he sought to impose this triple isolation on his son, who eventually rebelled. Ross continues: 'By rejecting his father's isolation – that is by rejecting his father's rejection of the world – Edmund formally aligned himself with the world. He accepts the current social order by rejecting his father.'

In fact, as Edmund confesses elsewhere, he became a militant evolutionary atheist.

There is no doubt that Edmund's written record of this rejection has proved singularly effective. Ross maintains that, 'The modern world now rejects Philip Gosse, not because he wrote *Omphalos*, but because Edmund wrote *Father and Son*.'

In conclusion, Ross records the opinion of an anonymous contemporary literary reviewer, who in the *Times Literary Supplement* of 1907, 'captured the essence of the vexing problem which faces any literary artist who attempts what Edmund Gosse attempted'. The reviewer wrote that an author 'must settle with his conscience how far in the interests of popular edification and amusement it is legitimate to expose the weakness and inconsistencies of a good man who is also one's father.' Judged by these criteria, I have no hesitation in pronouncing *Father and Son* an intensely cruel book.

One thing is certain: Philip Gosse must have been regarded as a powerful voice in his age, otherwise why were so many people so bitterly against him? Yet he died a forgotten man.

*　　*　　*

I shall refer to Philip Gosse more than once in later chapters. To me he personifies such men – several of whom appear in this book – as find themselves crushed between their two major loves: the seemingly irresistible force of science, and the immovable inerrancy of Scripture. Many, especially those with an academic background, can only salve their conscience by concocting what Edmund rudely characterized as some 'fuzzy formula'. Such a compromise position was unsatisfactory in Gosse's day, and, as I hope to show, is equally unsatisfactory today.

PART TWO

GEORGE JOHN ROMANES

7

EARLY YEARS

Squalor, with grimy, boney fingers greeted many nineteenth-century children from the moment of their unwelcome birth.

At a fund-raising speech for the Hospital for Sick Children, Great Ormond Street, in 1857, Charles Dickens eloquently proclaimed, 'The two grim nurses, Poverty and Sickness, who bring these children before you preside over their births, rock their wretched cradles, nail down their little coffins, pile up the earth on their graves.' If they survived, by the age of five they might find themselves unprotected among the flying shuttles of a Lancashire textile mill, or at six, deep in the cavern of a coal mine pulling a heavily-laden skip.

In complete contrast, George John Romanes was born in May 1848, with a background as different as it is possible to imagine: cuddled into a smiling world of happiness and love. Everything he desired was freely available. Yet George had something in common with those unfortunates of the Industrial Revolution: in later life he too suffered overwhelming physical pain, mental and spiritual disillusionment and an early death at age forty-six. George John was born in Kingston, Ontario, the first child of George and Isabella Romanes. For the family it was a time of particular celebration, as on the same day that George John was born, his father came into a considerable fortune which George junior inherited in due course. The money enabled Professor the Reverend George Romanes, DD, to resign the chair of Greek at Kingston University and return with his Canadian-born wife and infant son to England to live the life of a perpetual student.

Isabella was a Canadian Scot of Highland descent; handsome, vivacious, unconventional and clever. The family settled in a big house in Regents Park, London, not far from the recently opened Zoological Gardens. Here two more sons and two daughters were born. For a short time young George attended a preparatory school near his home, but an attack of measles brought a premature end to his schooling. He never went to school again. According to his wife, 'He was educated in a desultory and aimless fashion at home and was regarded by his family as a shocking dunce.'¹ He grew up idle but marvellously happy, much of his time being spent in Heidelberg, making collections of various items and keeping pets with his sister Ethel, to whom he was deeply attached. He married another Ethel, and sometimes referred to the two as his 'brace of Ethels'. They both helped to nurse him through his last long illness. To add to the confusion, his eldest child was also called Ethel, which caused endless trouble until at the age of twenty-eight she joined an Anglican religious order and became Sister Ethelred. She studied theology at Oxford, obtaining a First. Tragically, six years later she died of sarcoma.

George's father, the Rev. George Romanes is described as a 'moderate' Anglican; whereas Isabella was a Presbyterian. The family attended an Anglican or Presbyterian church with 'entire impartiality'. Their religious convictions were 'genteel and respectable but hardly enthusiastic'.

When the younger George expressed the desire to enter Cambridge University and follow his father into the Church of England, he was not encouraged, yet religion and a love of music played a big part in his early life.

Fortunately Romanes had a stubborn streak in him. Being almost totally illiterate, he had to spend a year receiving intensive tutoring and in 1867 managed to secure a place in Cambridge at Gonville and Caius College² to read mathematics and to prepare for Holy Orders. Then 'some slight chance' caused him to abandon this course and to take a BA in the Natural Science Tripos instead. To his chagrin, but

---

¹ *The Life and Letters of George John Romanes: A biography edited by his wife* (London: Longman Green and Co., 1896). For most of the personal details of George Romanes' life I am indebted to this work.

² Universally known as Caius, pronounced 'keys'.

fulfilling his family's low expectation of his intellectual potential, he only achieved a second class degree. In view of his later brilliance, I think we can classify Romanes as a 'late developer' – a noble army of young men and women, led by Winston Churchill.

During his undergraduate days, Romanes developed an interest in physiology and commenced an in-depth study of invertebrate zoology in the newly opened laboratories in Cambridge. Later he moved to University College, London, and, with others, pioneered the subject of physiology in England.

Regretfully I have been able to uncover few details about George's wife, Ethel. She is described as 'deeply religious' and in later life went on at least one lecture tour in the United States, but in what capacity I do not know. In the biography of her husband she comes across as a highly intelligent woman with a more than passing understanding of George's scientific work and a useful knowledge of Latin, Greek and Italian if we can judge by the not infrequent quotations in these languages which she does not linger to translate. She demonstrates a Victorian reluctance to reveal herself, never using the personal pronoun (except in the preface), and mostly calling her husband 'Mr Romanes' – although once or twice toward the end of the book she allows 'George Romanes'. She always refers to herself anonymously as 'his wife'.

Ethel shows an intense and loving interest in George's spiritual pilgrimage. As a rare insight into her own religious beliefs I quote from the end of the Preface:

It is needless for me here to speak of what, to some extent, he has laid bare – of mental perplexity and of steadfast endurance and loyalty to Truth. It may be that others wandering in the twilight of this dimly lighted world, may be stimulated and encouraged and helped to go on in patience until on them also dawns that Light. If this be so it will not be altogether in vain that he bore long years of very real and very heavy sorrow.

Cambridge

Ethel tells us that when George went up to Cambridge,

he was half-educated, utterly untrained, with no knowledge of man or books. He left a trained worker, an earnest thinker with his life-work begun – an unwearied search after truth – an ever-increasing reverence for goodness, and, as the years went by, a disregard for the applause of reward.

She continues,

At first he fell completely under evangelical influences . . . at that time practically the most potent force in Cambridge . . . He was a regular communicant, and it is touching to look at the little Bible he used while in Cambridge: worn and marked, and pencilled with references to sermons which had evidently caught his boyish attention. He used to attend Greek New Testament study classes and enjoyed the distinguished preachers who visited the university.

He spent much time in theology and writing sermons, which, 'though crude and confused in style', according to his biographer, 'still show deep thought and a remarkable knowledge of the Bible'. At the end of his life the family was attached to what was called the 'evangelical Catholic' wing of the Anglican church (a term I had not met before).

Christianity in the Early Nineteenth Century

The eighteenth century evangelical revival under Whitefield and the Wesleys had proved mightily effective among the likes of factory workers and miners. John Wesley, in his autobiography, recalls visiting a colliery outside Bristol and seeing white streaks, furrowed by the tears which coursed down the coal-encrusted cheeks of Somerset miners. It is generally recognized that it was true biblical Christianity which saved England from a revolution such as overwhelmed France.

But there was only a sporadic response to the 'Methodies' from the wealthier classes, or from the latitudinarian theologians of the established Church of England. However, when high society looking across the English Channel saw the bloody outcome of the Revolution in France, and learned of the enthronement in Paris of the 'Goddess of Reason' (a notorious prostitute) on the high altar of Notre Dame Cathedral, they started to appreciate – perhaps for the first time – the dangers which lurked in the depth of poverty and social evil which plagued the industrialized cities of London and northern England.

England was a paradox of wealth and poverty, of elegance and despair. It took a Frenchman, Alexis de Tocqueville, to describe Manchester in 1835 in these terms:

From this foul drain the greatest stream of human industry flows out to fertilize the whole world.

From this filthy sewer pure gold flows. Here humanity attains its most complete development and its most brutish; here civilization works its miracles, and civilized man is turned into a savage.

An important result of Anglican evangelicalism in the first part of the nineteenth century was the involvement of the upper classes with their wealth in social change. This was spearheaded by such men as Wilberforce, Shaftesbury and the men of the Clapham Sect. The labours of these and others like them, and the respect they enjoyed, were to a large extent responsible for the resurgence of biblical Christianity, now not only among the Methodists in the factories, but also among the wealthy Anglicans in the universities. Particularly was this so in Cambridge where the legacy of the Anglican evangelical revival led by the godly Rev. Charles Simeon (1759–1836) still survived.[1] Not until the third decade of the nineteenth century, were Roman Catholics or 'Dissenters' allowed to study at Cambridge University. But for Anglicans like Simeon and Henry Martyn, narrow denominationalism had no appeal. The latter left Cambridge in 1806 to become a Military Chaplain to India and immediately formed affectionate links with the pioneer Baptist missionary William Carey.

Commencing Ill-Health

To return to George Romanes. In 1870, at the age of twenty-two, Romanes noticed the first ominous signs of ill-health: fainting attacks, incessant headaches and increasing lassitude. These disabilities, later including hemiplegia and partial blindness, were to dog him until his premature death twenty

[1]D. S. Allister, 'Anglican Evangelicalism in the Nineteenth Century', in *The Evangelical Succession in the Church of England*, ed. D. N. Samuel (Cambridge: James Clarke, 1979).

years later. Nevertheless, in 1873, despite chronic ill-health and a severe attack of typhoid fever, Romanes decided to enter the annual Christ College essay contest. The subject that year was: 'Christian Prayer considered in relation to Belief that the Almighty governs the World by Natural Laws'. Much to his surprise and that of his friends, his essay was successful, 'and the writer was more than once acclaimed as a defender of the faith on account of it.' The following year he published the essay under the title *Christian Prayer and General Laws*. In this tract he claimed that no logical or scientific barriers stood against the proposition that prayer is effective in a world governed by general laws. But although Romanes still evidenced his belief in the power of prayer, it is apparent that for the first time, he was starting to have doubts.

8

THE MATURE SCIENTIST

Signs of a slowly progressive neurological disorder, and a considerable fortune acquired from his father, determined George Romanes to give up a set profession and devote himself to free-lance scientific research.

His first major research interest was into the nervous system of the jelly-fish, *Medusae*. The painstaking anatomical dissection and physiological experimentation required was mainly carried out in his family's summer residence in Dunskaith, Scotland, interspersed with occasional weeks of deer-stalking. In 1875, at the age of twenty-seven, he presented a paper on *Medusae* to the Royal Society of London. This was selected for the Croonian Lecture, a high honour, awarded to the best biological paper each year. Over the next ten years, Romanes continued to contribute papers showing detailed research into invertebrate physiology which he believed to be important in establishing an evolutionary link between primitive and higher organisms. He became a Fellow of the Royal Society in 1879 at the young age of thirty-one, the same year in which he married Ethel.

Romanes had started to read books by Charles Darwin in 1870, and, Ethel records, 'It is impossible to overstate the extraordinary effect they had on the young man's mind.'

Vestigial Organs

Romanes first met Darwin in 1874 when, at the age of twenty-six, he wrote a series of short essays for the journal *Nature* on the subject of so-called rudimentary (vestigial) organs.[1] At that time, and indeed almost up to the present day, it was believed that certain parts of the body were useless, unnecessary.

It was a subject which greatly interested Darwin. In *The Descent of Man*,[2] he had devoted much of the first chapter entitled, 'The Evidences of Descent of Man from some Lower Forms' (subtitled 'Rudiments'), to this topic. He regarded these 'rudimentary organs' as very strong evidence that man and the higher apes are descended from some primitive mammalian stock.

Over the years, vestigial organs have continued to interest evolutionists as they seem to provide striking evidence of man's evolutionary past. Take the appendix as an example. While quite big in some animals, it is relatively small in man, and moreover has no obvious clinical function, so evolutionists believed it to be an organ which had outgrown its usefulness. Besides the appendix, Darwin named as vestigial, the thyroid, pituitary and thymus glands, the tonsils, and the coccyx. This list was later expanded by others to include over a hundred parts of the human anatomy. We now know that, so far from being useless, 'vestigial organs', including the appendix, play a significant role in the economy of the human body; some indeed, like the pituitary, fulfil an essential function.

This ill-fated evolutionary theory has had disastrous effects in my own medical lifetime, as follows.

It is not unknown for a young baby to die unexpectedly in its cot. This is now called the Sudden Infant Death Syndrome, or SIDS, but when I commenced paediatrics in the 1940s it was thought to be due to a condition called Status Thymolymphaticus ('Status'). This was because at autopsy on babies who had died suddenly of 'Status', the thymus was always found to be much larger than in the body of an infant of

---

[1]George Romanes, 'Natural Selection and Dysteleology; Rudimentary Organs; Disuse as a Reducing Cause in Species' (*Nature*, vol. 10, 1874). Quoted by Robert J. Richards, *Darwin and the Emergence of Evolutionary Theories of Mind and Behaviour* (University of Chicago Press, 1987), p. 332. This book is a valuable source of information on Romanes' scientific career. However, Richards appears to have little sympathy with his spiritual odyssey.

[2]Charles Darwin, *The Descent of Man and Selection in relation to sex* (London: John Murray, 1871; 2nd ed., September 1874).

comparable age who has died following a prolonged illness. It was therefore postulated that the sudden death was due to pressure by the enlarged thymus on the soft trachea (or wind-pipe) of the young baby, thus suffocating it. However, we now know that the thymus is always big in small infants who die suddenly - for example in a motor car accident.

In the past, since the thymus was regarded as useless, an unnecessary organ, to prevent 'Status' (or SIDS) some doctors advocated a prophylactic dose of deep X-ray therapy to the upper chest in a small infant. This was known to make the thymus shrink, so hopefully, the child would not die from 'Status'. And in fact, they seldom did - not because of the treatment, but because 'Status' (SIDS) is such a rare condition anyway.

Unfortunately it so happens that the thymus is situated only millimetres from the thyroid gland, which was inevitably irradiated too. Thus, ten to twenty years later, many of the children who had been so irradiated died from cancer of the thyroid, induced by radiation given on wrong premises:

First, that a big thymus is the cause of 'Status' (SIDS); and second, (following evolutionary hypothesis), that the thymus is an unnecessary appendage which can safely be discarded. However, we now know the gland has an essential role to play in the immunological system in infants.

Another evolutionary myth[1] which has taken a long time to die is the so-called 'Biogenetic Law' - the idea that the developing embryo passes through, or recapitulates, stages in the evolution of its entire phylum. This theory was advanced by Haeckel in his 1876 book *General Morphology of Organisms*. In it he coined the phrase 'Ontogeny recapitulates Phylogeny'. For

[1]See M. Milton, *The Facts of Life*, 'Shattering the Myth of Darwinism' (Fourth Estate Publishers, Cambridge University Press, 1992) for an instructive chapter on this topic. Incidentally, Milton tells us he commenced research for his book when he discovered that his nine-year-old daughter was 'beginning to absorb the general theory of evolution' at school. He writes that this fact had 'been giving me sleepless nights. Is Julia being taught the truth? Or is she – are we – being seriously misled?' Milton continues, 'Let me make it clear from the outset that my doubts do not arise from religious motives. I want my daughter to have access to the fruits of scientific enquiry . . . My doubt about the theory arises from a number of sources. It comes first and most importantly from the inability of Darwinism to pass this simple test . . . to show a thinking member of the public conclusive scientific evidence to substantiate the theory . . .'

example, Haeckel and others (including Darwin) believed that the early human embryo possessed gill slits, indicating the human's fishy past. These slits atrophy in later life.[1]

Romanes and Charles Darwin

To return to Romanes: His small contributions to *Nature* were observed by Charles Darwin, who very generously sent a friendly note of approval to the young writer. This kindness had an overwhelming effect on him. That the famous Mr Darwin should write to *him!* It was too wonderful to be true. He became an immediate and complete convert to Darwin and his theory. That summer Romanes journeyed to Down House, Darwin's home in Downe, south east of London, to meet his idol. The older man greeted him with outstretched arms, and exclaimed, 'How glad I am that you are so young!' And so commenced a long and very close friendship between the two men which ended only on Darwin's death. According to Ethel:

It was marked on one side by absolute worship, reverence and affection [and letters reproduced in the biography demonstrate that this statement is no exaggeration], and on the other side by an almost fatherly kindness and wonderful interest in the younger man's career. Perhaps no hero worship was more utterly loyal, or more richly rewarded.

Romanes became Darwin's disciple in the highest sense of the word. Indeed, according to Richards, 'Romanes was virtually anointed Darwin's successor by the old man himself; and he undertook the defence of Darwinism – and its further extensions into the evolution of mind and behaviour – with a zeal that made Huxley look the model of Victorian reserve.'[2]

On Darwin's death in 1882, Romanes wrote to Darwin's son Francis:

I have long dreaded this time, and now that it has come it is worse than I could anticipate . . . Half the interest of my life seems to have

---

[1]This suggestion has long been repudiated by respectable scientists, but is not dead. Only a few days ago I heard of a medical practitioner who told his patient that the swelling in his neck was because the gill slits had not atrophied.

[2]Richards, *Darwin and the Emergence of Evolutionary Theories of Mind and Behaviour*, p. 332.

gone when I cannot look forward any more to his dear voice of welcome, or to the letters that were my greatest happiness.

In memory of his great friend, Romanes composed a poem of over twenty-five pages. This was written only about two years before Romanes himself died. As a eulogy on a man of Charles Darwin's atheistic convictions, the *Memorial Poem* is strangely religious, and concludes on a highly personal note. Here are some excerpts: the first, strongly evolutionary; the second, strangely Christian:

> From hunger, terror, pain, and strife
> The beauty of a world arose:
> The life that grows to higher life,
> And ever lovelier as it grows.
> The more the travail and the toil
> The more magnificent the birth.
> And what gave man that god-like thought,
> Or put that meaning in his eyes?
> What splendid truth has he been taught,
> Or with what wisdom is he wise?
>
> Then Evil is perchance the soil
> From which alone the Good can grow.
> From Evil Good, and Joy from Pain,
> Derive their beauty and their light:
> And knowledge of the Wrong is gain
> If it can teach us more of Right.
> Or is there Right or is there Wrong
> Within the universal Whole?

*   *   *

> So let it be that, come what may,
> The very tomb that holds my dust
> Shall bear the message, 'Though He slay
> Me, yet in Him shall be my trust.'
>
> 'Who art Thou Lord?' We know Thee not;
> We only know Thy work is vast,
> And that amidst Thy worlds our lot
> Unknown to us, by Thee is cast.
> We know Thee not; yet trust that Thou
> Dost know the creature Thou hast made;
> And wrotest the truth upon his brow
> To tell Thy thoughts by worlds unsaid.

[61]

So help me, Lord, for I am weak,
And know not how my way to grope,
So help me as I seek, I seek
The source that sent that ray of hope.
Teach me I have not understood:
Thy ways are ways past finding out:
Our wisdom still shall find them good:
And in the darkness slay the doubt.

Through Darwin, Romanes became on friendly terms with many of the great scientific figures of the day: Lyell, Thomas Huxley, Hooker, Asa Gray and others. His research resulted in thirty or more articles and books on such topics as *Mental Evolution of Animals*, *Animal Intelligence* and *Scientific Evidences of Organic Evolution*. In addition he developed into a highly successful lecturer – popular, erudite and witty.

Today, much of Romanes' experimental work appears disarmingly simple, but at the time it was regarded as foundational to science and especially to evolutionary theory. Many of his experiments were first reported to the prestigious Royal Society of London.

Here, for example, is an account of one such painstaking experiment from 1892 (*Life*, p. 324). Hundreds of seeds of various types – beans, peas, etc. – were grown under a wide variety of conditions: sealed in a vacuum for three months, then transferred to tubes charged with such gases as hydrogen, oxygen, chloroform and so on. It was found that the germinating power of these seeds differed hardly at all from seeds grown under normal conditions. 'Further, in no single case, in the hundreds of seeds so treated, did the plants produced from them differ from the standard types grown from the control seeds even in the smallest degree.' That is, no mutation had been induced.[1]

In time Romanes became heir-apparent to Darwin's unpublished notes and MSS on psychological subjects. He pioneered the study of developmental psychology using material supplied by Darwin. His carefully argued belief was that not only do the bodies of man and animals have a common origin, but that the

[1]How different might have been the result if the seeds had been irradiated, thus damaging their DNA structure. But this technique had not at that time been discovered.

[62]

same is true of their minds also. After Darwin's death, Romanes wrote a three-volume work: *Darwin and After; An Exposition of the Darwinian Theory and a Discussion of Post-Darwinian Questions.*

*   *   *

A problem confronting evolutionists today is the origin of man's mind from that of an animal. This area of study particularly interested George Romanes.

I do not intend to give a résumé of Romanes' scientific work since this has already been extensively done by Richards,[1] and Moore[2]. In any case I am not appropriately qualified to do so.

In the light of modern knowledge, much of Romanes' work, and that of Darwin on similar topics – the instincts of neuter insects, and the evolution of morality, for example – strike one today as naive. But in mitigation, it must be remembered that Romanes and Darwin were both writing before the seminal work of Pavlov on conditioned reflexes; they had no knowledge of the discipline of molecular biology with its ramifications into modern neurophysiology and anatomy; Mendel was only just starting his experiments on genetics, and the discovery of DNA was far into the future.

Since Darwin and Romanes had both rejected any idea of a supernatural, and were relying solely on human reason, it is not surprising that they often fell into grave scientific error. Today, their work on the human mind is of little value except to researchers in pursuit of an historical PhD.

[1]Richards, *Darwin and the Emergence of Evolutionary Theories of Mind and Behaviour,* p. 127.
[2]James R. Moore, *The Post-Darwinian Controversies: A study of the Protestant struggle to come to terms with Darwin in Great Britain and America 1870–1900* (Cambridge University Press, 1979).

9

'A GOOD SQUIB'

The Reverend Professor Adam Sedgwick, DD, renowned Cambridge geologist, Canon of Norwich, vice-master of Trinity, friend and teacher of Darwin read the *Origin* as soon as it appeared in 1859, and viewed it with disgust. In his book *Darwin, Before and After*,[1] Dr. Robert Clarke tells us Sedgwick pronounced it 'a dish of rank materialism cleverly cooked and served up merely to make us independent of a Creator'. He prophesied that if Darwin's teaching were accepted, humanity 'would suffer a damage that might brutalize it, and sink the human race into a lower grade of degradation than any into which it has fallen since its written records tell us of its history' – a view shared by his friend Carlyle.

In the first flush of enthusiasm for Darwin and all his works, Romanes thoroughly disagreed with the old Professor, but he was to make similar comments himself in later years. Meanwhile Darwin laughed off the accusation from the 'old bird' as 'a good squib'.

[1]Robert E. D. Clarke, *Darwin, Before and After* (Exeter: Paternoster Press, 1948). I am indebted to this book for much of the material in this chapter. I had the pleasure of meeting 'Nobby' Clarke (as he was affectionately called) in 1939. He was regarded by my Cambridge Inter-Collegiate Christian Union (CICCU) friends, and I am afraid by myself, as an amiable eccentric. What a lot I could have learned from him if I had been prepared to listen! I was particularly impressed by his habit of noting even apparently trivial facts on a card index. I visited him at midday in his second floor room over a watch shop in the narrowest part of Sidney Street, Cambridge; only a few doors from where the young Charles Darwin had taken 'digs' a hundred years before. The shop had a large chiming clock protruding into the street. The mechanism for the clock was housed in Clarke's room. Conversation halted abruptly when the clock struck twelve.

'A Good Squib'

The *Origin* made an immediate impact on the Christian world. All the bottled-up anxiety over Lyell's conjectures about the age of the earth came to a head. The years 1860 to about 1880 became a time of deep perplexity for many devout people: Anglicans, Non-conformists, or Roman Catholics. Some lost their faith. Some even committed suicide.[1]

Ethel Romanes writes about those times of deep perplexity, 'It is impossible to exaggerate the influence Mr Darwin's great work has had on every department of science, of literature, and also of art.' She could have added – music: Wagner records the inspiration he received from Darwin; politics – Marx wished to dedicate *Das Kapital* to Darwin, and Hitler based his 'final solution', the genocide of Jews and the disabled, on Darwinism. Psychology too owes much to Darwin as acknowledged by Freud. Medicine too – see for example abortion and euthanasia; philosophy – as proclaimed by Nietzsche; education, by Dewey; aggressive capitalism, by Rockefeller and Carnegie – and much more.

I am particularly interested that Mrs Romanes mentioned art. It is not often realised how much artists down the decades have been affected by the work of Darwin. The Norwegian artist, Edvard Munch, for instance, celebrated painter of 'The Scream' (1895), has recorded his indebtedness to Darwin.

In a modern book, *American Art*, Sam Hunter[2] wrote concerning the years 1866 to 1890:

There was a moment of hesitation, Darwin, Huxley, Herbert Spencer and Matthew Arnold were novelties. They presented urgent prob-

---

[1]Gertrude Himmelfarb, *Darwin and the Darwinian Revolution* (London: Chatto and Windus, 1959). Surprisingly, according to Himmelfarb, despite having their faith in God destroyed by Darwinism (and Nietzsche's triumphant statement that 'God is dead') most English people in the nineteenth century retained their ethical and moral beliefs. But 'Their moral code did not originate in a supernatural disposition, and was not enforced by a supernatural judge with all eternity at his disposal, but by man himself in the here and now.' (She illustrates from Victorian novelists, such as Eliot and Hardy). [These] 'believed in retribution on earth all the more firmly for disbelieving in it in heaven . . .' [Himmelfarb continues], 'Frederic Harrison, arch-agnostic and high-priest of English Positivism when asked by his son what a man who falls in love but can not marry is to do, replied indignantly: "Do! Do what every man does under the circumstances. Do what your religion teaches you. Do what morality prescribes as right." When his son persisted in wanting to know why love was proper only in marriage, Harrison could barely contain himself: "A loose man is a foul man. He is antisocial. He is a beast". He finally put an end to the matter: "It is not a subject that decent men discuss."' (Quoted from pp. 337–38).
[2]Sam Hunter, *American Art* (1987), p. 15.

lems which thinking people had to cope with. Everything in belief and much more in practice had to be radically reconsidered, with the dire off-chance that only destruction was possible. There had been no time to think it through, nor less to adopt the defeatist policy of letting well alone . . .

One early victim was 'reality' in painting. Hence the rise of the Impressionists, the Cubists, Picasso and his followers, the Dada school and much more in so-called modern Art.

Why did Darwin, a self-taught biologist, have such a vast and long-lasting effect on such a wide variety of disciplines and professions in all countries and on all cultures from 1859 to the present day, and doubtless far into the future? Not, I am sure, because Darwin anticipated such effects. In his life story he comes across as a gentle, kindly man. Then again, not because of the scientific excellence of his theory. It has had to be revised more than once. The reason, I suggest, is because the theory destroyed the trustworthiness of the Scriptures, and especially the very foundation of the gospel in the first chapters of Genesis. And above all because Darwinism abolished the need for God and the Christian verities. Thus certainty was swept away. Nothing on the earth or in the sky could be guaranteed any more; everything was in the melting pot. Reality was nowhere to be found.

To any reader, brought up to believe in a 'real' world, this lack of reality may be difficult to appreciate, even shocking. When face to face with the concept it can be exasperating. I vividly remember speaking in a small, stuffy, crowded sitting-room of a little house in Manchester in 1957. A coal fire had been stoked up against the cold outside. I can't recall my topic, but I know I stood backed up against the wall. In the far corner stood a man maintaining nothing was real, not even the room. 'How can I *know*?' he cried. I regret to say I lost my temper. 'Come up here and I'll bang your head against this wall, then you'll know if it's real', I shouted back. At that time I had no understanding of the sincerity and awfulness of his plea. I thought he was making a game of me. But in truth he was voicing the dreadful logic of his evolutionary presuppositions. Do you know the story of the man who dreamed he was a butterfly? When he awoke he was not certain that he might not be a butterfly dreaming he was a man.

'A Good Squib'

We are told of the young Gilbert Chesterton,[1] that, 'In homes like his in 1880 (Gilbert's father was a successful estate agent in South Kensington, London – the firm is still operating today), fairy tales and myths and legends had taken the place of more orthodox Christianity, which had become one story among many.' It was Chesterton who maintained that when a man ceases to believe in God, he does not believe in nothing, but believes in anything. Not surprisingly, as a reaction to the dismissal of God, there was an increase in spiritism.

Loss of Faith

During these years, under the influence of his prestigious agnostic friends, Romanes found to his great distress, that his Christian faith was slipping away. In desperation he investigated psychic phenomena, probably encouraged by his friend Wallace.

Alfred Russel Wallace (1823–1913) flits like a phantom through the Darwinian saga. Although born of devout Anglican parents, Wallace became a wanderer travelling alone through the jungles of South America. He befriended some Indians who in turn introduced him to their black arts. He continued to dabble in spiritism, or the occult as we would now call it, for the rest of his life.

In 1848 he transferred to Malaya. There, by a strange coincidence, at much the same time as Darwin in England, he started to consider the possibility of a non-theistic origin of the world. One dark night in February 1858, in a jungle hut on the small island of Ternate between New Guinea and Borneo, Wallace became desperately ill with 'intermittent fever' (probably malignant malaria). Suddenly, so he tells us, in a moment of hallucinatory ecstasy all was revealed to him. Years later he wrote:

It occurred to me to ask the question, 'Why do some die and some live?' And the answer came clearly, that on the whole, the best fitted, lived . . . There suddenly flashed on me the *idea* of the survival of the fittest. The more I thought it over the more I became convinced that I

---

[1]Alzina Stone Dale, *G. K. Chesterton: The Outline of Sanity. A Life of G. K. Chesterton* (Grand Rapids: Eerdmans, 1982), p. 15.

had at last found the long-sought-for law of nature that solved the problem of the Origin of Species.[1]

Stated plainly like this, the 'survival of the fittest hypothesis' sounds so plausible. It merits Thomas Huxley's explosive response: 'It's so simple. Why didn't I think of it myself?'

I am reminded of a story told me in Burma during the war. A man under the influence of opium believed he had discovered the secret of the universe. But when he was lucid again, he found he had forgotten it. So before his next 'trip', he provided himself with pencil and paper so that he could record his thoughts. The morning after, written in scrawly letters on his pad he found the long-awaited secret. It read: 'The banana is great, but the skin is greater.'

Someone may ask, 'How can we determine who are the fittest?' Norman Macbeth replies in his excellent book *Darwin Retried: An appeal to Reason*:[2]

Very early . . . the answer came back that we determine this by the test of survival; there is no other criterion. But this means that a species survives because it is the fittest and is the fittest because it survives, which is circular reasoning and equivalent to saying that whatever *is*, is fit.

Macbeth proceeds to discuss how modern evolutionists cope with this problem. He believes they can only end with a tautology, 'struggling with a treacherous set of words'. He concludes:

Another strange aspect of the fitness problem is the vast gulf it reveals between the biologist and the ordinary layman. The biologists have discarded the survival of the fittest, together with the words *fit* and *fitness* in their normal usage, and they have been perfectly open about this. Yet if my acquaintances are typical, the layman has noticed nothing. They continue to talk of fitness in the old way and regard survival of the fittest as sound doctrine.

Wallace and Darwin

Wallace sent his proposition from Ternate to Sir Charles Lyell in London. In consternation, Lyell, knowing that Darwin had

---

[1]Brackman C. Arnold, *A Delicate Arrangement* (New York: Times Books, 1980), quoted by Ian Taylor, *In the Minds of Men*, pp. 77–78.

[2]Norman Macbeth, *Darwin Retried: An appeal to reason* (Ipswich, Mass.: Gambit, 1971), p. 62.

nearly completed a book on the same topic, showed him the paper. So it was arranged that a preliminary communication from Darwin and Wallace's observations should both be read at a meeting of the Linnaean Society on 1 July 1858. Neither Wallace nor Darwin was present at the meeting, and the topic passed almost unnoticed. However, Wallace's work, revealed to him during high fever under the spectre of death, was the goad which prodded Darwin into publishing the *Origin of Species*.

The Psychic

About that time, not only Wallace but many others started to take an interest in psychic phenomena.

As Darwinism spread among scientists, 'parson-bashing' by such charismatic speakers as Huxley and Hooker also spread. Perhaps as a reaction, this was followed by an increasing interest in the supernatural, mainly evidenced by séances and table-turning sessions in the parlours of the intelligentsia.

Huxley declined to become a party to the new fad. 'Having seized power from the priests, he was loath to see it devolved on dotty ladies.'[1] He and other sober scientists became fearful that the serious message they sought to proclaim might be diluted. They were therefore appalled when Wallace started to revamp evolution to take account of unseen spirits.

There is little doubt that in 1860–70 spiritism took under its sway many who had previously been loosely tied to the churches. Men and women who felt uncomfortable with godless evolution longed for some 'other world' to which they could give their allegiance – particularly in an emergency.

Now, in the second half of the twentieth century, an increasing threat to Christianity, and also paradoxically to orthodox scientific evolution, is coming from the New Age Movement and Eastern Religions,[2] linked sometimes with satanism. And recently, as though to give these movements

[1]Adrian Desmond and James Moore, *Darwin* (London: Penguin Books, 1992), p. 538.
[2]See, for example, Herbert J. Pollitt, *The Inter-Faith Movement* (Edinburgh: Banner of Truth Trust, 1996), pp. 109–146.

scientific respectability, there is developing the so-called 'new physics'.

Romanes tried to interest Darwin in spiritism. But he would have none of it. Romanes, however, continued to take a mild interest in the subject almost until the time of his death, although latterly this consisted only of telling ghost stories around the fire on winter evenings, with particular friends. Mrs Crawford, who shared this interest, beguiled many weary hours for him in this way, each endeavouring to 'cap' the other's tales.

To our modern evangelical ears this sounds darkly dangerous. Didn't he know the power of evil, that the devil is real? I agree. But before we become too censorious, we must remember that evenings were long and dark; lighting was confined to candles or an oil lamp, and there was certainly no television. At the end of his life George was almost blind and unable to read. Even in my Christian home, ghost stories were regarded as good innocent fun.

At the beginning of the twentieth century Sir Arthur Conan Doyle, creator of Sherlock Holmes, was heavily involved in psychic phenomena. My father tells the story that, as a medical student, he and a friend learned that Conan Doyle was to investigate a reported ghost in an old manor house in Somerset. The students felt it a pity the great man should journey down to the West Country for a long midnight vigil in vain. So they resolved to provide what was required. Borrowing a white operating gown from the hospital, my father's friend flitted in and out of the trees in the moonlight. Conan Doyle was thrilled and took several photographs. Years later he gave a lecture on spiritism in South Africa. He proudly projected his lantern slides of the Somerset 'ghost', telling his entranced audience they constituted the only genuine photographs of a ghost ever recorded. My father's friend happened to be present in the audience. He leaped to his feet and cried, 'I was that ghost'.

I think it probable that the more blatant evidences of satanism have only become evident recently. I once asked my father whether he believed in demon-possession. He replied he had to do so because it was in the Scriptures. Also, missionary friends had told him of such phenomena occurring in 'heathen parts'. But he added that he, personally, had never encountered an instance of demon-possession.

SPIRITUAL WARFARE

In 1876, plagued by headaches, and strongly attracted to the psychic, Romanes, now aged thirty, wrote a book, entitled *A Candid Examination of Theism*. This work, which relied heavily on Darwin and Spencer, is said to have effectively disposed of theism.

But what is theism? Darwin in his autobiography tells us that he was a theist in his early days, but confides that in later life even this belief grew dim.

English is a language of great exactitude, and sometimes there seems to be a gradation in philosophical (or theological) terms, like theism and deism. Whether the nineteenth century meaning of the words was the same as now, I do not know. But here are some modern definitions from Brewer's *Dictionary of Phrase and Fable:*

A *theist* 'believes there is a God who made and governs all creation; Christians, Jews and Moslems are included among *theists.*'

A *deist* 'believes there is a Supernatural Being who set the world in motion, and implanted in it certain immutable laws, called *The Laws of Nature*, which act *per se*, like winding up a clockwork toy, but afterward act with no supervision of the maker.' I suspect that in modern terminology, Darwin was a deist rather than a theist.

An *atheist* 'disbelieves even in the existence of God. He thinks matter is eternal, and what we call "creation" is the result of natural laws.'

An *agnostic* 'believes only in what is knowable. He rejects revelation. He is neither theist, deist nor atheist, as all of these subscribe to doctrines which are incapable of scientific proof.' In practice, if he rejects God's revelation in Scripture, he has already rejected God and should logically be called an atheist. In things theological, I doubt whether there really is such a person as an agnostic. Aldous Huxley, who called himself an agnostic, stated that he took it for granted that the universe had no value or meaning. He confessed, 'I had motives for not wanting the world to have meaning. Most ignorance is invincible ignorance – we don't know because we don't want to know.'

A *materialist* 'believes there is nothing in the universe but matter, and there is no ground for assuming a spiritual first cause . . . In the 19th century materialism was much influenced by the theory of evolution.'

Romanes had held the subject matter for *A Candid Examination* for a number of years. When he did at last publish, it was under the pseudonym 'Physicus'. In this book there emerges for the first time an inkling of the battle which was to dominate the rest of his life. He writes feelingly of 'the waning splendour' of the 'old faith' in which he once believed, and continues:

I am not ashamed to confess that with this virtual negation of God the universe to me has lost its soul of loveliness; and although from henceforth the precept to 'work while the day is', will doubtless gain in force from the terribly intensified meaning of the words 'for the night cometh when no man can work' (*John* 9:4). Yet when at times I think, as think I must, of the appalling contrast between the hallowed glory of the creed which once was mine and the lonely mystery of existence as now I find it – at such times I shall ever feel it impossible to avoid the sharpest pangs of which nature is susceptible.

What propelled Romanes into atheism? In a further manuscript left unfinished at the time of his death, he expressly declares that it was the theory of evolution which caused him to abandon religion. And this, according to Ethel, was compounded by the friendliness of Darwin, reciprocated by George's adoration for the older man.

Ethel, looking back at the end of the nineteenth century when Darwinism was triumphant, voices the opinion that,

We can now see that a man can fully accept the doctrine of evolution, and yet can also believe in a personal God and in the doctrines which logically follow from that belief. But it was not so at first. To many on both sides the new teaching seemed to threaten destruction to Theism . . . And German [Higher] criticism seemed to many to be rapidly destroying the credibility of the early documents of Christianity.

Many a noble soul made shipwreck of his faith, nor is this disaster wonderful . . . There were some who, amidst all the strife of tongues, kept their heads, remembered bygone storms, and did not lose their courage, their wholeheartedness, but they were few, and were not much heard or heeded.

From the time of the publication of *A Candid Examination*, Romanes was in constant spiritual turmoil, and it was then that he wrote the poem *Gloria Mundi* (see p. 114). According to his wife he was commencing a fight which became, as it were, a long rearguard action. Step by step he abandoned the position he had held at the time of the Burney Prize, 'with no great pauses, rather, as it seemed with startling rapidity, and with sad and reluctant backward glances he took up a position of agnosticism, for a time almost of materialism.'

Yet, as Ethel explains,

There are many who abandon belief for various reasons, who by various methods stifle regret and call in stoicism to their aid. There are those who really care very little about the 'ultimate purposes', and who find the world of sense quite enough to occupy them. And there are those souls who seem to be constantly crying out in their darkness for light . . . These last have the capacity for holiness, the capacity for a tremendous power to witness for the truth . . . To this class George Romanes belonged. By nature he was deeply and truly religious. Interested and absorbed as he was in science, it is no exaggeration to say he was just as keenly interested in theology, that is to say in the deepest and ultimate problems of theology.

So for the last years of his life George was constantly seeking. In 1883 he wrote to Professor Asa Gray, professor of botany and theologian at Harvard University – a man who said it was his aim to persuade people that it was possible to reconcile Darwinism with Christianity – 'How gladly I would enter your camp if only I could see that it is on the side of truth.'

Romanes was not unmindful of the peril of his position. With great sincerity he wrote:

Never in the history of man has so terrific a calamity befallen the race as that which all who look may now behold, advancing as a deluge, black with destruction, resistless in might, uprooting our most cherished hopes, engulfing our most precious creeds and burying our highest minds in desolation . . . The flood-gates of infidelity are open, and Atheism overwhelming is upon us.

Some modern secular writers have tried to dismiss these statements of Romanes as mere Victorian hyperbole. I do not agree. I see a man with a breaking heart, not only stating his profound beliefs, but echoing the sentiments of his old Professor Adam Sedgwick and many others.

Then, so his wife tells us, when at the height of his scientific success:

[Romanes] entered into a period of conflict between faith and scepticism which grew more and more strenuous, more painful as the years went by and which never really ceased until a few weeks before his death, and which was destined to end in a chastened, a purified and a victorious faith . . . As time went on he felt . . . the utter impossibility of a purely materialistic position, and as he pondered the final, ultimate mystery [death] . . . he arrived very slowly, very painfully, but very surely at the Christian position.

*　　*　　*

The Poet

Commencing about the time he first met Darwin in 1874, Romanes began to write poetry. He was then twenty-six, unmarried, and his health had already deteriorated to such a state that he was no longer able to engage in active work. He continued to express himself in verse, mostly in the form of sonnets, until the last days of his life.

Art in any form, be it painting, poetry, film making, novel writing – what you will – must reveal something of the interests, pleasures and griefs of the artist. True art wells up, unstopped, and unstoppable. To some extent, therefore, it is always autobiographical. So it was with George Romanes.

I have already introduced some of his poems elsewhere in this book. In 1896, two years after his death, a selection of his poems was published with an introduction by T. Herbert Warren, President of Magdalen College, Oxford.[1] According

[1] *A Selection of the Poems of George John Romanes*, with an introduction by T. Herbert Warren (London: Longmans, Green, and Co., 1896).

[74]

to Warren there is a certain literary deficiency in the poetry, probably stemming from Romanes' lack of regular education. He dismisses as irrelevant George's advantages, his study of nature at home and in the field, the influence of his foreign travel, his prolonged residence in Heidelberg, his preoccupation with sport in Scotland and his considerable knowledge of music and religion. Instead he points to the poet's lack of grammatical or stylistic training and considers that the Selection of Poems contained no work of great merit, there being a 'monotonous sameness about them.' But for all that he concedes 'they are part of the man, part of his voice, part of his soul; the index and the utterance of a beautiful, a loving and a loveable spirit.' Moreover, Warren continues, they have a 'pathetic interest', and reveal a spirit 'suffering, learning, struggling toward the light, seeking after God.' From this book I have selected only a small sample of George's work – almost all the poems are brief and I have presented them in full. The only exception is the '*Memorial Poem*' written on the death of his great friend and mentor – Charles Darwin (see p. 61). As far as I can ascertain, all the verses in this chapter are in chronological order.

A Hunt[1]

> I saw a monster hunting with two hounds,
> Which snuffled on the track of unseen game;
> For far away, beyond the utmost bounds
> Of vision, lay the pasture of the same.
> All day they tracked him, until he could see
> Them gliding through the valley like a spot;
> But basking in the noontide sun lay he:
> They were so distant that he heeded not.
> So when at evening they surprised his lair,
> And dog by dog were hanging flank by flank,
> He ran, and ran, and ran in his despair,
> Until, in midnight darkness, lo! he sank.
> I ask the hunter of their names: he saith,
> *We are Decrepitude, Disease, and Death.*

[1]'A Hunt': This was an early poem. In terms of poetry Warren singled it out as the best in the collection.

Day Dreaming[1]

Upon a day, in spring-time of the year,
I sat a-dreaming where a willow stood,
And watched my children playing in the wood.
Their joyous faces, and their laughter clear,
Aroused in me the once familiar cheer
When I, too, was a child; till in the mood
Thus caught, I murmured, 'Nature, thou art good!
'My little ones, my little ones, how dear!'

'Twas then I heard the voice of Nature say,
Behold, thy children shall lie down with thee
In homes of death and heritage of clay.
Yet, what was said but made them more to me;
And when they called that I should join their play,
I went with them, ah! more than willingly.

The Heart

The chambers of the heart were made to hold
Faith, Hope, and Love to God and Man; these four
Give life and warmth where else were cheerless cold:
If Doubt, Despair, or Hate break through the door,
To pillage, ravish, murder, and destroy,
They leave a ruin to record their crime,
And Desolation fills the house of Joy.
The tenement, enduring for a time,
Gives shelter now to evil birds of night,
And beasts of prey; while year by year it falls,
Decaying into dust. When these foes smite,
And Sin alone is left to fill those halls,
There stands, without a purpose, plan, or part,
The crumbling form of what was once a Heart.

Natural Theology[2]

Arrayed in beauty did the world arise;
Arrayed in beauty doth it ever stand.

[1]'Day Dreaming'; 'The Heart': Both of these poems could be described as an Ode to Nature. But what a desolate future they portray!

[2]'Natural Theology' was written at much the same time as 'The Heart'. It starts as a paraphrase of Psalm 104, particularly verse 24. But in the second stanza commencing, 'Arrayed in order did the world arise;/Arrayed in order doth it ever stand;' Romanes asks the perennial question, 'But who declares the order [of the earth] to be wise?/Or fondly finds in it a Father's hand?'

Spiritual Welfare

O children of mankind, lift up your eyes!
Behold Him in the clouds, the sea, the land!
The firmament His glory doth declare.
The hosts of Heaven, created by His breath,
As shining witnesses are standing there.
O all ye skies, and all that is beneath,
Bless ye and magnify with endless praise!
In us alone a stolid silence lurks:
The whole Creation else its voice doth raise.
O Lord, how wonderful are these Thy works!
Surely in wisdom hast Thou made them all!
On Thee, on Thee let now Thy servant call!

Arrayed in order did the world arise;
Arrayed in order doth it ever stand:
But who declares the order to be wise,
Or fondly finds in it a Father's hand?
Oh, blind to what ye see, and deaf to all
Ye hear! The beauty is in your own eyes:
The loving words, which on your hearing fall,
Are sounds which in your own poor hearts arise.
What man among you, had he made this earth,
But all his brothers would condemn to die?
The parentage of such a monstrous birth
Would brand him with inhuman devilry.
Believe in love for man alone designed,
Or else believe in God without a mind.

My soul was troubled by the sin and pain:
My heart was withered by the thought of God:
The order seemed an order to ordain
Infinite Evil, with bad tidings shod.
This was the only minister of things;
And if I saw a beauty of a joy,
It was the beauty of a dragon's wings
And folly of an infant with its toy.

For assuming, as he did, that the earth and all in it was made (by God?) over a vast period of time, what sort of a God would he be? A 'God without a mind'?; A God who ordains 'Infinite Evil'? Perhaps the wisdom and beauty we see is, after all, merely subjective. But in the last lines a reminder of George's children interrupts his gloomy thoughts and we see a glimmer of hope.

Then unawares, into mine idle hand
A touch of sweetest childhood gently crept;
A face was there that seemed my thoughts to brand;
A voice said, 'Father, Father,' and I wept.
The trust which to a little child is given,
Forbid it not a love that is of heaven.

Faith[1]

Can it be true, as all the Churches teach,
Nought is of Faith but what they hold as true?
Or is the Word set forth in human speech
More sure than when revealed to human view?
Nay, if the truth be all that they would show,
Let him who doubted be my witness here:
Faith's deepest joy were it at last to know
That, while I knew it not, the Lord was near.
So now, with groping hands, I feel for Thee,
Who hast such words as no man ever had:
Oh, count it sorrow that I cannot see,
And not a sin that I was born so sad.
Though dark the eyes that stream in sight-less grief,
Lord, I believe; help Thou mine unbelief.

The Riviera, 1894[2]

Calm Nature, in thy blue Italian guise,
How vainly dost thou smile upon a mind
Which, seeing beauty, is to beauty blind.
Yet smile thou on. Thou canst not sympathise
With any wearied thing that droops or dies.
And so, adieu. With strength and hope resigned,
'Tis well that I should soon and surely find
The peace of unawakenable eyes.

[1]'Faith': The title of this late sonnet is highly significant. In the latter part of this poem is an indication that, added to his other troubles, George was gradually going blind. Nevertheless, he is able to conclude with the words: 'Lord, I believe; help Thou mine unbelief' (*Mark* 9:24).

[2]'The Riviera, 1894': Written when he was away from home in the last year of his tortured life and as the mists of blindness closed in. Romanes addressed it to his long-suffering wife, who was about to give birth to their fifth child. It ends with the poignant lines: 'O my dearest, come at times with flowers/In darling memory of those short hours/We shared together as a holiday.'

Spiritual Welfare

That smile will then be no less warm and bright
For all thy children still untired of play
And strong in growing powers of young delight:
Yet, O my dearest, come at times with flowers
In darling memory of those short hours
We shared together as a holiday.

11

RETURN TO FAITH

George Romanes was a devoted family man. At the time of his death in 1894 he had five children, four boys and a girl. The eldest was not yet in his teens, and the youngest had been born only a few weeks earlier. Even at the height of his agnosticism, he believed that the children should be made familiar with the Bible, if only for their literary education.

Partly for the sake of the children, the family moved from London to Oxford. The beauty of this city gratified Romanes' poetic sense. There were libraries and abundant opportunities for scientific work. Added to this, both Ethel and George had a wealth of friends.

In 1889 he delivered a lecture in Toynbee Hall on the *Ethical Teaching of Christ*. In it he questioned whether Christ was divine, but ended, 'Whatever answers people may give to the questions, "What think ye of Christ? Whose son is He?" everyone must agree that, "His name shall be called Wonderful"' (*Matt.* 22:42; *Isa.* 9:6).

In the same year, Romanes took part in an important symposium before the Aristotelian Society in Oxford on *Design in Nature*. In his contribution he made the point that,

There is nothing in the constitution of nature inimical to the hypothesis of design . . . Innumerable, indeed, are the evidences of design in nature, *if once a designer is supposed;* but apart from any antecedent supposition, we are without any means of gauging the validity of the evidence presented. (my italics)

So in this lecture Romanes had taken another small step

toward the recovery of his faith. The 'antecedent supposition' (or, as Francis Schaeffer would term it, the 'presupposition') can only be a belief that 'God is, and he is the rewarder of those who diligently seek him' (*Heb.* 11:6).

This verse, I suggest, is the most basic in the whole of Scripture. For unless God *is* – not just *exists* as a theist or deist might affirm, and as some modern Bible versions translate – not only Christianity, but the whole hope for reason, truth and goodness in the universe, is null and void. Why do I emphasize the word 'is'? Because it encapsulates the holy name of God given by God himself to Moses: 'I am who I am'; Yahweh, the self-existent, eternal one (*Exod.* 3:14). ' "I am the Alpha and the Omega, the Beginning and the End," says the Lord, "who is, and who was and who is to come, the Almighty" ' (*Rev.* 1:8).

*   *   *

The Romanes Lectures

In 1891, Romanes presented the sum of £1,000 to the University of Oxford to endow an annual lecture, the subject of which was to be taken from Science, Arts or Literature. Neither politics nor religion were to be included. Rather oddly, despite these exclusions, the prime minister, Mr Gladstone, was asked to give the first lecture, and up to the present day, three other prime ministers have followed him. Down the years the subjects have varied and the speakers have included many notable scientists.

Thomas Huxley gave the second lecture. He told Romanes that he intended to speak on 'Evolution and Ethics'.[1] Perhaps he hinted something of its contents to his friend. Romanes was alarmed, so advance copies were sent to the two wives, Mrs Romanes and Mrs Huxley, for vetting. Both agreed that it was quite innocent.

The lecture was delivered before a packed audience in the Sheldonian Auditorium in Oxford. The topic, as might be expected, had given Huxley much heart-searching to prepare. It was a topic which had occupied not only him but many

[1]Thomas Huxley, *Ethics and Evolution.* Second Romanes lecture.

others for decades. In the eighteenth century, nature had for the most part been considered as the design of a benevolent Creator, with the acknowledged cruelty and wastefulness accepted with resignation as largely beyond human comprehension. But in the nineteenth century, the perception of nature oscillated to and fro. Early on, according to Irvine,[1] nature was thought of as 'an endless, divinely inspired picture-gallery or symphony concert, in which the lonely enthusiast, escaping the restraints of city life, might dreamily commune with God, and recover the primitive innocence of freedom and spontaneity.'

Later, according to Irvine, the 'city life' to be escaped from included vast hordes of slum dwellers. And by the middle of the century, 'Tennyson, deep in Lyell and personal bereavement, saw nature's pictures as hung in a charnel-house and her music played in a tomb'. Meanwhile, however, the evolutionary creed of 'survival of the fittest' was eagerly welcomed by capitalists such as Rockefeller and Carnegie as endorsing the business principles of *laissez-faire*. So it comes as no surprise that the impact of Darwinism on people with a humanitarian conscience, inevitably led to pessimism.

Romanes had himself painted a terrible picture. After millions of years of evolution:

More than half the species that have survived the ceaseless struggle are parasitic in their habits, lower and insentient forms of life feasting on higher and sentient forms; we find teeth and talons whetted for slaughter, hooks and suckers moulded for torment – everywhere a reign of terror, hunger and sickness, with oozing blood and quivering limbs, with gasping breath and eyes of innocence that dimly close in deaths of brutal torment.

How would Thomas Huxley in his lecture approach such a dismal subject? Faced with nature's indifference to human suffering, he was despondent: 'grief and evil fall, like the rain, upon both the just and the unjust . . . The biologically fit may survive but not necessarily the ethically fit.' Huxley maintained that while moral sentiments, no less than immoral sentiments, evolved as part of human character, nevertheless, this knowledge provides no moral rules; it establishes no moral ends.

[1]William Irvine, *Apes and Angels* (London: Weindenfeld and Nicholson, 1956), p. 268.

[82]

Since the lecturer rejected Christianity *a priori*, where could he point his audience for hope? In desperation, he considered Jewish culture, the Stoicism of the Greeks and the apparent peace of Indian culture with its doctrines of Karma – this he somewhat favoured. But eventually he resorted to what he termed 'the evolution of intelligence and will, guided by sound principles of scientific investigation'.

* * *

Meanwhile George's headaches grew worse. Focal blindness developed, and on 11 July 1893 a left-sided paralysis. From then on George's scientific activities were severely curtailed. I assume he was given laudanum, a tincture of opium, but the only treatment which I find recorded in his biography is that he should travel to Italy and Spain.

Here, as a physician, let me interpose a note. Reading the story of Romanes' illness, which lasted more than a decade, there is little doubt that he suffered from a benign, slow-growing, space-occupying tumour of the brain, probably a meningioma, or perhaps a vascular aneurysm. Had he been living now, the diagnosis would be made by a sophisticated scan, and early surgery might even have been curative. But there was no diagnosis, no effective therapy and no palliative care. Lacking certain knowledge of the underlying pathology, his days must have passed in alternate hope and despair, the future black and all unknown. With the development of hemiplegia, Romanes' worst fears were confirmed. From that time,

the Shadow of Death was ever on him, and he knew it . . . Sometimes the thought of leaving those whom he loved with such intense devotion, such wonderful tenderness, overwhelmed him; sometimes the longing to finish his work was too great to be borne, but generally he was calm, and always, even when most sad, he was gentle and patient, and willing to be amused.

He made a partial recovery from the paralysis. His intellect was as keen as ever, but primarily, 'he set himself to face the ultimate problems of Life and Being, to face the question of a possibility of a return to Faith.'

During these last months of his life, Romanes seems almost to have been two men in one. To the outer world he was the stalwart academic, with scientific face, as befitted one of Darwin's literary executors. 'He appeared', so his wife tells us, 'profoundly sincere, anxious, almost unduly anxious, to give no indulgence to his longings; to state to himself and to others unsparingly, unflinchingly what appeared to him as yet irrefutable arguments against the Faith.' Yet, when alone with his 'two Ethels' or close friends, he relaxed and poured out his inmost heart.

As we have seen, George had considerable gifts as a poet, and like all artists, in his chosen art form he allowed the inner man to appear as in this sonnet, written for his wife three years before his death.[1]

> I ask not for thy love, O Lord: the days
> Can never come when anguish shall atone.
> Enough for me were but thy pity shown,
> To me as to the stricken sheep that strays
> With ceaseless cry for unforgotten ways –
> O lead me back to pasture I have known.
> Or find me in the wilderness alone,
> And slay me, as the hand of mercy slays.
>
> I ask not for thy love, nor e'en so much
> As for a hope on thy dear breast to lie,
> But be thou still my Shepherd, still with such
> Compassion as may melt to such a cry
> That so I hear thy feet and feel thy touch
> And dimly see thy face before I die.

On Sunday, 28 January 1892, two years before his death, Romanes was on one of his 'health cures', staying in the Hotel

---

[1]In October 1890 George Romanes was in *Geanies*, his much loved country home in Scotland. He wrote to his wife, who was in London, 'I will not disappoint you about the sonnet . . . which is the first of a series which I wrote in the small hours, after reading your favourite Psalm [Psalm 27]. There was only one verse which remained appropriate to me, so I took it as a text'. (We are not told which verse this is. I suggest verse 8, which reads in the Psalter version 'Hearken unto my voice, O Lord, when I cry unto thee: have mercy upon me and hear me.') Ethel writes, 'The sonnet alluded to is so beautiful that I include it here. It shows better than any words could the attitude of George Romanes' mind. Profoundly sincere, anxious, almost unduly anxious, to give no indulgence to his own longings, to state to himself and to others unsparingly, unflinchingly, what appeared to him as yet irrefutable arguments against the Faith, when he was alone he poured out his inmost heart.'

l'Ermitage in Costeballa. Ethel had been out for a brief time. When she returned she was surprised to be greeted cheerfully:

His first proposition was, 'The church bell is tinkling, let's go to church.' The brightness and gladness of the two evening psalms was oddly appropriate, and chimed in with the feeling of greater gladness dawning on him, for he was leaving the strange land in which for years he had not been able to sing 'The Lord's Song'. Gradually, through the darkness, he became increasingly aware of the hand of the Lord stretched out to him.

The Psalms to which Mrs Romanes refers are the 137th and 138th. In the Anglican Book of Common Prayer (Miles Coverdale translation), Psalm 137 commences:

By the waters of Babylon we sat down and wept: when we remembered thee, O Zion.
As for our harps, we hanged them up : upon the trees that are therein.
For they that led us away captive required of us a song, and melody, in our heaviness: Sing us one of the songs of Zion.
How shall we sing the Lord's song: in a strange land?

Psalm 138 commences:

I will give thanks unto thee O Lord, with my whole heart: even before the gods will I sing praise unto thee.
I will worship toward thy holy temple, and praise thy name, because of thy loving-kindness and truth: for thou hast magnified thy Name and thy Word above all things.
When I called upon thee, thou heardest me: and enduedst my soul with much strength.

And the last two verses:

Though I walk in the midst of trouble, yet shalt thou refresh me: thou shalt stretch forth thy hand upon the furiousness of mine enemies, and thy right hand shall save me.
The Lord shall make good his loving-kindness toward me: yea, thy mercy, O Lord, endureth for ever; despise not the work of thine own hand.'

Romanes was blessed with many good friends, both in the scientific world and, as Ethel says, 'two or three of Mr Romanes' greatest and most intimate friends were Christian as well as intellectual men.'

[85]

The very last shopping he did before his death was to buy a Golden Wedding present for Sir James and Lady Paget. It was delivered after he had died.

'But,' as Ethel continues, 'of influence and argument and persuasion, as most people imagine them, there was nothing. Discussions many during the past years, but to these he owed little . . . Nothing can be more erroneous than to suppose that the change in point of view was sudden, or due to any fear of death . . . It is written, that those who seek find, and to no one do these words more fitly apply.'

However, books may have helped him; especially theological books. The one which 'bears marks of most careful study', was Pascal's *Pensées*. His copy, which used to lie by his bedside, was marked and annotated. It was the last book he read to himself 'in his own careful and student-like fashion'.

Now let Mrs Romanes give some personal recollections of her husband's last weeks:

And then began a time, often saddened by hours of intense physical exhaustion and physical depression, but also of what can only be called growth in holiness, in all that comes from nearness to God.

In the early autumn and winter there had been sad moments when still the clouds of darkness, of inability to grasp the Hand of God stretched out to meet him, hung over him, but in these months there had been some growth.

One to whom he often spoke of the deepest things in life and death, will never forget his saying [about three months before his death], 'I have come to see that cleverness, success, attainment, count for little, that goodness is the important factor in life'.

By way of explanation, his wife tells us that, 'In early days, Mr Romanes had attached, so it seemed to some of those who knew him best, an undue importance to intellect, to cleverness, to intelligence' .

During his student days in Cambridge, George had heard Earl Shaftesbury speak in Great St Mary's on the fate of slum children. But scientific success, ample finances, and above all estrangement from God had hardened his soft heart.

Now, however, so Ethel tell us, 'as the weeks passed on he would often plan a country house and a life in which "good works" were to have a share.'

What a pity the phrase 'good works' sounds so Victorian (in the derogatory sense) to our modern ear. But as a dying man he had little practical opportunity to show actively 'the fruit of the Spirit' (*Gal.* 5:22).

On his last Easter Sunday, only a few weeks before his death, Romanes composed a valedictory poem based on Luke 2:29 and Hebrews 11:10 (AV), which reads: 'He looked for a city which hath foundations, whose builder and maker is God.'

> Amen, now lettest thou thy servant Lord,
> Depart in peace, according to thy word:
> Although mine eyes may not have fully seen.
> Thy great salvation, surely there has been
> Enough of sorrow and enough of sight
> To show the way from darkness into light:
> And thou hast brought me through a wilderness of pain,
> To love the sorest paths if soonest they attain.
>
> As thou hast found me ready at thy call,
> Which stationed me to watch the outer wall,
> And, quitting joys and hopes that once were mine,
> Oh! may it be that, coming soon or late,
> Thou still wilt find thy soldier at the gate,
> Who then may follow thee till sight needs not to prove,
> And faith will be dissolved in knowledge of thy love.

During Whit-week, so Ethel Romanes tells us,

there was a curious feeling of preparation for some change. George made all his arrangements and was quite calm, quite gentle, quite merry at times; now and then the weary fits of physical lassitude or of headache would prostrate him, but when these were past he would placidly begin some bit of work.

On Thursday of Whit-week he went to the eight o'clock Celebration of Holy Communion in the Latin Chapel of Christ Church, and in the course of that day he said, 'I have come to see that faith is intellectually justifiable.'

Although he presently added, 'As yet I have not that real inward assurance; it is with me as the text says, "I am not able to look up."'

However, almost his last words to his wife were, 'It is Christianity or nothing.' The long pilgrimage from faith to materialism and back again was done.

*   *   *

Two decades[1] previously, George Romanes had written a book entitled, *A Candid Examination of Theism* (*Theism* for short). Then, shortly before he died, he commenced a further book to be called *A Candid Examination of Religion*, which he did not live to see completed (I shall refer to this as *Religion*). This was edited posthumously by his friend Canon Gore, and published in 1895 under the title, *Thoughts on Religion*.[2]

I found *Thoughts on Religion* a difficult book to assess since I was much more interested in Romanes' last statement of faith, than in Gore's comments, particularly as Gore was such a renowned High Churchman. I suspect he had little sympathy with the evangelicalism of Romanes' undergraduate days.

In *Religion*, Romanes records that, 'When I was a student at Cambridge, there was a galaxy of talent . . . all around me there were Christians'. In particular he cites Sir William Thomson (1824–1907), later Lord Kelvin, and four or five other notable scientists.

However, by the time he came to write *Theism*: 'the views which I entertained as a student were abandoned in the presence of the theory of evolution.' He considered that, 'Science has in several cases incontestably demonstrated that religious teaching has been wrong as a matter of fact . . . Sceptics were triumphantly confident that the light of dawning knowledge has finally dispelled the darkness of superstition . . . Religious persons were troubled to think of the future . . . I took it for granted that Christianity was "played out".'

So, with 'youthful enthusiasm', Romanes ascribed 'the attributes of Deity to Humanity, . . . which can therefore properly be called a Religion – the Religion of Humanity.'[3]

[1]This date is variously given as 1874, 1876 or 1878, without explanation.

[2]*Thoughts on Religion*, by the late George Romanes, MA, LLD, FRS, edited by Charles Gore, MA, Canon of Westminster (2nd ed., Chicago, 1895). Charles Gore (1853–1932), was a nephew of the Earl of Arran. At the time Romanes knew him, he was already a notable theologian; a Tractarian, and friend of Cardinal Newman. He was the first principal of Pusey House, Oxford; later Bishop of Birmingham, and subsequently Bishop of Oxford.

[3]According to the Oxford English Dictionary the term 'Religion of Humanity' was coined in 1860. However, it is notable that the entry explaining it is to be found under the entry Humanism, not under the word Humanity. Under the entry 'evolutionary humanism', the *Fontana Dictionary of Modern Thought* gives: 'A sort of secular *religion* or religion surrogate founded upon the deeply held conviction that *evolution* is the fundamental modality of all change in the universe, so that all agencies that provoke change and all that retard it can be described as "good" or "bad" respectively' (p. 219).

(Today we would probably prefer to call it the Religion of Humanism.) But, as Romanes later explains, 'I now see that I was wrong.'

Gore, in the preface to *Thoughts on Religion*, says of Romanes' *Theism*, that 'It contained a tone of certainty'; there was an almost exclusive reliance 'on the right of scientific reason, in the Court of Reason'. By contrast, the unfinished MS *(Religion)* 'represents the tendency of one "seeking after God . . . if haply he may find Him".'

What occasioned this change of direction? Romanes tells us it mainly came about as he studied 'the outcome of the great textual battle' (of German biblical criticism).[1] 'This', he continues, 'is importantly considered a signal victory for Christianity.' The epistles of Romans, Galatians and Corinthians, are 'agreed upon as genuine, and the same is true of the Synoptics' (Matthew, Mark and Luke). Turning to the 'main doctrine of Christ Himself', Romanes points to 'the important absence from the biography of Christ of any doctrine which subsequent growth of human knowledge has had to discount.'

He goes on to discuss the 'Body of Christianity', and in particular the story of the cross. The Bible, he concludes is 'adapted to all sorts of men and women . . . How good then is Christianity, as being the religion of love . . . the infinity of God's love for man.'

In these statements we can see firstly, how overwhelming had been the victory of evolutionary theory and the German biblical criticism movement if this was almost all the theological comfort which he could obtain!

What was this 'great textual battle' to which Romanes refers? It is so important to our story that I will devote further space to it in later chapters. For now, let me remind you that in the Prologue, I described a tornado which completely flattened a little Methodist church so that all that remained was the old harmonium sticking up out of the ruins. The wind which destroyed that church had come successively from two different directions: what the easterly gale left standing, the westerly blasts demolished. Similarly, the tempest which

[1]See footnote 1, page 121.

almost destroyed the historical accuracy and authenticity of the Bible in the late nineteenth and twentieth centuries came from two directions – evolutionary theory and biblical criticism.

But secondly, we can sense here (as elsewhere, for example in his poems) how Romanes' belief in Christianity as a religion of love, and particularly the love of God for man, was instrumental in undermining his trust in the stark cruelty of atheistic evolution, and drawing him back to God.

At the end of his apologia, Romanes asks, 'What then, is the answer to agnosticism?' And replies with the words of our Lord: 'Jesus answered them, and said, "My doctrine is not mine, but his that sent me. If any man will do his will, he shall know of the doctrine.'" (*John* 7:16–17 AV).[1]

As a life-long research scientist Romanes begs his readers,

To try the only experiment available – the experiment of faith. *Do the doctrine*,[2] and if Christianity be true, the verification will come, not indeed mediately, through any course of speculative reasoning, but immediately by spiritual intuition. Only if a man has faith enough to make this Venture honestly, will he be in a just position for deciding the issue. (my italics)

On the ground of reason alone, it should be allowed that [supposing Christianity to be] of God, it *ought* to appeal to the spiritual rather than to the rational side of our nature.

In this I differ from Romanes. I maintain that Christianity appeals fully to both the spiritual side of a man's nature, and to his reason. Or, as we might phrase it, to man's heart and his mind, or will.[3]

---

[1]This passage (*John* 7:17) has obviously caused difficulty to the translators. Here is a selection of some of the versions available: 'If anyone chooses to do God's will, he will find out whether my teaching comes from God' (NIV); 'If any man is willing to do His will, he will know of the teaching, whether it is of God' (NASB); 'Whoever has the will to do the will of God shall know whether my teaching comes from him' (NEB); 'If any man desires to do His will (God's pleasure), he will know – have the needed illumination to recognize, can tell for himself – whether the teaching is from God' (Amp.); 'If there be a man who desires to act in accordance with his (God's) will, he will know for himself whether the teaching I give comes of God' (*God's New Covenant*, Cassirer, Eerdmans, 1989).

[2]I think Romanes had already begun trying 'the only experiment available'. He had responded to his own call to *Do the doctrine*, by his desire to lead a life 'in which good work would have a share' (p. 86).

[3]See my book *Reasonable Christianity* (Darlington: Evangelical Press, 1991).

In summing up, Gore tells us that *Religion* is not written from 'a position of confirmed orthodoxy . . . It contains many things which would not come from a settled believer.'

Gore says that in *Religion* Romanes shows:

(1) Pure agnosticism in the realm of scientific reason. (This statement I believe is substantially true. At the time he lived Romanes had virtually no evidence with which to counter the overwhelming effect of Darwin's theory. Therefore in the realm of strict science perhaps he was right to say 'I don't know'. He was a true agnostic.)

(2) He had a vivid recognition of the spiritual necessity of faith.

(3) He had a perception of the positive strength of the historical and spiritual evidence of Christianity.

(4) He could state, 'It is reasonable to be a Christian believer'.

(5) In the end he surrendered to 'the infinity of God's love for man'.

Gore therefore concludes that there is no doubt George Romanes 'returned before his death to that full, deliberate communion with the church of Jesus Christ which he had for so many years been conscientiously compelled to forego . . . In his case the "pure in heart" was after a long period of darkness, in a measure before his death, "to see God" ' (*Matt.* 5:8).

Not surprisingly, Romanes' evolutionary friends viewed this change with dismay. One wrote that 'neither Gore nor Mrs Romanes was theologically disinterested in preserving the memory of a scientist returned to the "faith"'. Another even suggested that his final reconciliation to the church was itself 'an act of pure agnosticism.'

*   *   *

What sort of a man was George Romanes? Let the one who knew him best, his wife Ethel, give her final judgement:

Looking back over those two years of illness, it is impossible not to be struck by the calmness and fortitude with which the illness was met. There were, as has been said, moments of terrible depression and disappointment and of grief. It was not easy for him to give up ambition, to leave so many projects unfulfilled, so much work undone.

But to him the illness grew to be a mount of purification. More and more there grew on him a deepening sense of the goodness of God. No one has ever suffered more from the Eclipse of Faith, no one has ever been more honest in dealing with himself and his difficulties.

The change that came over his mental attitude may seem almost incredible to those who knew him only as a scientific man; it does not seem so to those few who knew anything of his inner life. To them the impression given is, not of an enemy changed into a friend, antagonism changed to submission; but rather it is of one who for long had been bearing a heavy burden on his shoulder bravely and patiently, who at last has had it lifted from him, and lifted so gradually that he could not tell the exact moment when it was gone, and himself standing, like the Pilgrim of the never-to-be-forgotten story, at the foot of the Cross, and three shining ones coming to meet him.

At his funeral, George's favourite hymn was sung, 'Lead, kindly Light'. It had been written by John Henry Newman in 1834 when at the age of thirty-two he had been becalmed for a whole week in the Strait of Bonifacio between Corsica and Sardinia. The hymn reflects Newman's unsettled state of mind as he grappled with deep religious questions. The words make a fitting epitaph for George Romanes:

> Lead, kindly Light, amid the encircling gloom,
>   Lead Thou me on;
> The night is dark, and I am far from home;
>   Lead Thou me on.
> Keep Thou my feet; I do not ask to see
> The distant scene; – one step enough for me.
>
> I was not ever thus, or prayed that Thou
>   Shouldst lead me on;
> I loved to choose and see my path, but now,
>   Lead Thou me on;
> I loved the garish day, and, spite of fears,
> Pride ruled my will: remember not past years.
>
> So long Thy power hath blest me, sure it still
>   Will lead me on,

Return to Faith

O'er moor and fen, o'er crag and torrent, till
   The night is gone.
And with the morn those Angel faces smile,
Which I have loved long since, and lost awhile.

PART THREE

ARTHUR RENDLE SHORT

12

THE BRETHREN CONNECTION

My father, Arthur Rendle Short (ARS)[1], was born on 6 January 1880 in Bristol, England, the elder son of Edward and Catherine Rendle Short. His father was a clerk in Fry's, the chocolate manufacturer. His parents had no great status in the material sense, but they were rich as Christians who put their beliefs into practice. For forty years they virtually ran a 'ragged school' known as 'Wagg's' with over a hundred children in the centre of Bristol. They regularly spent whole nights on the streets of Bristol bringing practical and spiritual help to drunks and prostitutes. In addition they were occupied with door-to-door visitation on behalf of the Chapel they attended.[2]

After the death of his wife, my paternal grandfather lived alone for many years in a big house near us in Clifton, Bristol. He obviously disliked change and his house was still furnished in Edwardian style, even to being fully lit by gas, until the time of the second World War.

My mother was Helen Henrietta Case, a first cousin of my father, and a year or so his senior. Her father, Henry Case, owned one of the two main milk suppliers in Bristol. I only remember seeing him on one occasion. His wife had pre-deceased him. From his photograph, Mr Case was an imposing, handsome, bearded gentleman with piercing eyes. Stories

---

[1] I shall use the title ARS for simplicity. Friends referred to him as 'The Doctor'; to relatives he was Rendle; my mother called him Ren. The name Arthur was never used.

[2] W. M. Capper and D. Johnson, *Arthur Rendle Short: Surgeon and Christian* (London: IVF, 1954); Peter Masters, 'More than a Surgeon' in *Men of Destiny* (London: Wakeman, 1968), p. 110.

were told of him. On one occasion a farm hand reported for work the worse for drink. My grandfather threw him by his breeches into the duck pond. Everywhere he went he was accompanied by a large, but normally friendly dog. The animal respected the Lord's Day and never followed him when he went to the local Anglican church on a Sunday. However, on one occasion his mental calculator must have failed and he followed his master into the church and slipped quietly under his feet. All went well until a late-comer crept up the aisle. The dog had been taught to attack anyone walking in a suspicious manner. He bounded from his hiding place and confronted the man with teeth bared. All might still have gone well, had my grandfather not leapt to his feet, and shouted in a stentorian voice, 'Lie down, you brute'.

My father's younger brother was named Latimer, after Bishop Latimer, the great Protestant reformer who was burnt at the stake in Oxford in 1555. The 'Rendle' part of the name came from family connections in the picturesque fishing village of Polperro in Cornwall. The old Talland church, on a cliff overlooking Polperro and the sea, contains many tombstones inscribed with the name 'Rendle' with that distinctive spelling.

Other places of origin on both my father's and mother's side of the family were Dartmouth in Devon, and Dulverton just over the border in Somerset, on the edge of Exmoor. We proudly considered ourselves a West Country family, and from the turn of the century my father and his parents had always taken holidays in the most inaccessible spots they could find on the barren north Cornish coast. A sister-in-law complained, 'The Shorts have no idea of a holiday except walking themselves silly.'

My father, his father and grandfather all came from Christian Brethren stock. In 1855 my great-grandfather had left Lincolnshire for Bristol to take up a position as teacher in the Ashley Down Orphan Homes recently opened by George Müller. It is scarcely surprising therefore that ARS and his parents were greatly influenced by that triumphant example of faith. As a family we regularly attended Bethesda Chapel, Great George Street, situated at the foot of Cabot Hill in Bristol. This historic building had been acquired by George Müller in 1832, and became renowned as the parent church of

[98]

the Brethren movement. During the Second World War, it was burned down in one of the early air raids on Bristol.

Although often called Plymouth Brethren (or PBs) the early history of the Brethren is more closely linked with Bristol than Plymouth. Unfortunately, despite their original high principles, the movement was early plagued by deep doctrinal divisions, which have left their scars to the present day. My father once told me, 'Don't trouble to read the early history of the Brethren. It's a sorry story and will only depress you.' The major cleavage was, and still is, between the Exclusive and Open Brethren, but even among the latter there is a range of 'tightness'. Some 'Assemblies', as the little churches are known, are more separatist than others. We belonged to the 'open' end of the spectrum. Even so there were some 'open' Assemblies which would not allow my father to minister in them, and certainly he was never admitted to an Exclusive chapel. Each Assembly was autonomous. In those days there was no central register listing the addresses of the many Gospel Halls in Great Britain. During World War II, this caused problems with the bureaucracy when they attempted to compile a register of all religious buildings.

On Sundays during our annual family holidays in Cornwall we would try first to find an 'Open' Assembly with which to worship. Failing that we would attend the local Methodist or Church of England.

In order to visit an Assembly in an unfamiliar place, we had first to find it. This often meant driving up and down deserted Sunday morning streets in a strange town. At last we would locate a likely building. But was it 'Exclu.' or 'Open'? To find out, I might be sent into the foyer to see which hymn book was offered. If it was 'Hymns for the Little Flock', we would beat a hasty retreat, but if 'The Believer's Hymn-book', we had arrived safely.

In my childhood days the huge Bethesda chapel was sparsely occupied on a Sunday morning – that is, except in fine weather when a couple of hundred orphans from the Müller's Homes would sit at the back. A well-known sight in Bristol was the long crocodile of boys or girls (never mixed), dressed in attractive blue and white serge uniforms, the girls with speckled straw bonnets, dating from the early nineteenth century, walking the five hilly miles each way from Ashley Down to Bethesda.

As I wriggled about in my seat, sitting secure between my father and mother, those orphans, so deathly still, seemed a world apart. I sometimes wondered what they made of the service. I don't remember anyone taking much notice of them. (Did they even have hymn books?) About once a month there would be one of those hoped-for occasions when, opening his Bible as he went, my father would climb slowly up into the pulpit after the breaking of bread to 'give a word'. This I could understand, and I'm sure the orphans could too. I feel he must have taken the unusual step of speaking from the pulpit on purpose to talk over the heads of the adults direct to the orphans, and to me. No one else ever spoke from the pulpit on a Sunday morning.

There were two pulpits. The lower one, capacious, plain and solid, was constructed from the same varnished wood as the pews. It was reached by three steps from either side. Above was the high pulpit, an elegant structure, beautifully proportioned, standing on a pedestal like a goblet. The woodwork was fluted, the only concession to decoration in the whole bare building. Above were big lofty windows of symmetrical Georgian design. The high pulpit was entered behind by stairs from the vestry. It was only used on those rare occasions when the tiered gallery on the three sides was occupied for some special meeting.

The historic building was destroyed by incendiary bombs during the first night blitz on Bristol on Sunday, 24 November 1940, when much of the city centre was destroyed by fire. The evening service was being held in the vestry when the first bomb fell in their midst. The little congregation escaped through the chapel, but further bombs soon set the galleries alight and nothing could be done to save it. By morning only the four walls and the safe in the vestry remained. So ended Bethesda Chapel after 132 years of service to the Brethren cause in Bristol.

During my school and university days the open Brethren were very active in interdenominational circles. At an Inter-Varsity Fellowship conference, for example, the members might well comprise 40% Brethren, 40% Anglican and 20% others. Surprisingly, evangelical Church of England and

Brethren worked well together. Perhaps this was because both held such a high view of the Lord's Supper. My father was loyal to the Brethren throughout his life. Although active in many evangelical organizations, he would always attend the Breaking of Bread service on Sunday mornings, refusing to speak for any other denomination if there was a Gospel Hall in the vicinity.

I ceased attending the Brethren soon after I went up to Cambridge, preferring to go to a Church of England service with my friends. I am afraid this change was not made for theological reasons, but because of what I presumed to be the lowly image of the Brethren. My move to Anglicanism was sealed in Burma during the War. There were no PBs there. In fact, the army did not recognise 'strange sects'. Although I have parted from them, I retain an admiration and affection for the 'peculiar people', as we used to call them.

ARS was much sought after as a preacher in local gospel halls in the Bristol area, and sometimes in the surrounding country. He bought a car later than most of his colleagues. Before we owned one, he would cycle to services in Bristol and even nearby villages. There were no buses at that time. Bristol had the reputation of being a very godly city, with no public transport on Sundays.

When I was small my father would carry me, perched precariously on the step of his bike. Men's bikes in those days were mounted from the back like a scooter with one foot on the step which protruded from the centre of the back wheel. I would stand with my left foot on the step, my right leg kneeling on the mudguard, and my arms grasping father's waist. It was pretty uncomfortable, and must have been heavy work for him. In this way, on fine Sunday evenings, we would occasionally travel to local chapels in the surrounding countryside, returning by train. I helped somewhat by pushing the bike up hills. Later, of course, we went by car, or sometimes by train.

I did not like trains so much. I was always nervous that we would miss it. Father considered it time wasted if we were at the station before the train came in. We would arrive at the last minute, sometimes having to buy a penny ticket from the slot machine to get onto the platform, and paying the correct fare at our destination. I cannot remember ever missing a train. I was impressed that my father so often seemed to pray on trains. I knew that because whenever he prayed he would lift his trilby hat an inch or so. So, Sunday night after Sunday night, I had the priceless privilege of listening to a gifted Bible expositor, expounding the gospel to ordinary folk in simple terms.

Preaching

In line with Brethren tradition, my father had commenced preaching at a young age. In this he was aided by great communicative ability and a phenomenal memory. It was reported that at the age of three years, when asked by an aunt whether he would like her to read a Bible story to him, 'Perhaps Daniel in the lions' den?', he replied, 'No thank you, I know all the Bible 'cept 'zekiel's vision.'

What was ARS like as a preacher? Perhaps I am not the best judge, as I mostly heard him speak in small village chapels and at the annual Missionary Study Class Conferences, an organisation which he had helped to found and at which he felt particularly at ease. He was not so much imposing, as friendly. Small, with a marked Bristol accent, he had the gift of making the obscure seem simple, although never distorting the truth, or speaking down to his audience.

He did not suffer from nerves, even when appearing before big gatherings. One such was a 'Bible Witness Rally' held in the great St. Andrew's Hall, Glasgow in May 1942. The meeting was reported a couple of days later by a veteran Glasgow reporter, Alexander Gammie in the *Evening Citizen:*

In all my experience of religious gatherings in Glasgow I have seen nothing more remarkable than the Bible Witness Rally held this week. On Tuesday evening . . . all around St. Andrew's Hall were queues of people eager to secure admission . . . After the hall had been packed in every corner, it was estimated that over 1,000 people had been turned away . . .

It was not only the largest gathering of its kind ever seen in Glasgow, but it was one of the most mixed. Never, perhaps had there assembled under one roof so many representatives of so many different creeds. The atmosphere was not ecclesiastical but evangelical. Almost every branch of the Church was represented, along with the Salvation Army, the Christian Brethren, and . . . [many others are named]. The speakers were worthy of so great an occasion. Professor D. M. Blair, as chairman, struck the right keynote. Professor Daniel Lamont, in speaking on the Authority of the Bible, was at once academic and evangelical, as is his wont . . . Professor A. Rendle Short of Bristol, eminent surgeon as he is, made ruthless and skilful use of the knife in dealing with some aspects of modern science. And with a rare intimacy of knowledge, revealed some aspects of the Bible.

The final speaker was Dr. Martyn Lloyd-Jones . . . who brought the meeting to a triumphant, and impressive climax. To him had been allotted the title of 'The Bible and Today' . . . His address was as gripping and as powerful as it was popular in its appeal. As an oratorical *tour de force* it would have roused a political audience to tumultuous enthusiasm.[1]

The Busy Speaker

One of the advantages – or disadvantages, depending on your point of view – of the Brethren system of church government is that there is no ordained ministry. Virtually all the preachers hold a 'secular' job. This means that the hierarchy is always looking for promising recruits. My father must have thought I had the makings of a preacher (or was it merely that I fell into the family tradition?). I can't remember his ever verbalizing the topic; however, he set about training me without my really knowing it was happening.

As the years went by, his programme of surgical consultations, operating, university lecturing and later administration of a professorial department, was so rigorous and exacting, that preaching and apologetics lecturing had to be fitted in wherever possible. Thus he developed the policy of being present at church functions for the minimum time possible. As I grew older I was able to help him. For example, if he was due to speak at some chapel at 6.30 p.m., he would send me on before to take the preliminary exercises – hymns, reading, and later the prayer. He promised to be there at 7.00 p.m. And he always was. However, he might arrive during the hymn before the sermon. From the pulpit I would watch some anxious elder scratching his head and thumbing through his Bible to concoct

[1]Quoted by Iain H. Murray in *D. Martyn Lloyd-Jones: The Fight of Faith 1939–1981* (Edinburgh: Banner of Truth, 1990), p. 65.

an emergency sermon. But he never let me down. It was with a sense of real relief I would observe the door at the rear of the chapel silently open. He would walk quietly up the aisle to the front seat, sit for a moment bowed in prayer, then relieve me at the pulpit with the welcome words, 'I'll take over now'.

As I grew older, he asked me to take some preaching engagements for him. At first this was in small country towns. Once, when compelled by a double booking, he rang the organizers of the service at the last minute and told them he was sending me instead. It was some special occasion – I think in aid of the local Red Cross. He gave me his notes, but allowed me a free hand. The service was in another of those big old Georgian churches in the centre of Bristol. I went round to the vestry door and introduced myself. The elders did not seem overjoyed to see me. However, there was nothing for it. They sent me, alone, fifteen steep steps up a straight, dark staircase. At the top was a door which I opened and found myself looking down from the high pulpit onto a sea of faces in the body of the chapel, which had a crowded gallery on three sides. Meanwhile, in the other pulpit below, someone was announcing that unfortunately the advertised speaker had been prevented, etc., etc. For the only time in my life I felt my legs give way, and my knees knock together. What amazed me was how painful it was on the inner side of the knees. But this sharp pain had the effect of pulling me together.

I noticed that in none of these places of worship was I ever asked to speak a second time!

When I started preaching my father gave me some advice. He told me, 'If you can't say anything else, tell a Bible story in language so simple that a child can understand, and the Holy Spirit will do the rest.' How I wish that young theological student I heard the other Sunday had been told the same thing. Instead, he attempted to expound an obscure text which his professor had lectured on the previous week.

Another admonition was, 'Never speak from a written script, but always from notes. If necessary write out your opening and closing sentences.' It is because he followed his own advice that almost none of his sermons exist in manuscript form, but only in notes. I have found but one exception to this rule – an occasion on which he spoke to a Scripture Union gathering at the Albert Hall, London. At that time, so he told me, the Hall was notorious for its poor acoustics and inadequate public address system.

I have followed my father's advice meticulously, and have never spoken from a script either in lecturing or preaching. A problem with the method, however, is if one is subsequently asked to provide a manuscript for publication. Only once or twice have I regretted not having a prepared manuscript.

One such occasion was many years ago when television was in its infancy in Australian country towns. Fairly late in the evening, I arrived to give a lecture on parenting. I enquired how long I should speak for. To my surprise I was told that it didn't really matter as I was the last speaker of the day. The station would close down after I finished.

I was ushered into the studio. There was only one TV camera, placed straight in front of me. The rest of the place was in darkness. I spoke for what seemed like a long time, but no one stopped me. There were no teleprompters in those days and as I was speaking from notes which I scarcely needed to glance at, I did not take my eyes off the camera. I discovered that as I looked fixedly at it, I could see my face inverted in the lens. I went on lecturing. How could I know when to stop? I dared not look around for a clock. Everything was still and quiet in the studio. At last I summoned up courage, bade my inverted friend goodnight, and slid out of my seat. The studio was empty! All the technicians were in the control room watching a football match relayed from the rival station. They told me it had not mattered much what I said as no one would have been listening. The whole town were tuned in to the match.

13

POVERTY AND AMBITION

In his younger days, life must have been difficult for my father, squeezed as he was between poverty and ambition. In one of his slim Day Books, commenced in 1908, ARS noted some of the formative influences in his life. He ends, 'From St Francis of Assisi, I learned the sweetness of Holy Lady Poverty, and the love of all created things.' This reference was no hyperbole.

As a medical student in London, he and a friend searched around for the cheapest café near the London Hospital. The one they selected had the advantage that 'it provided chess sets, and we could have a game over our lunch. One day we noticed the waitress blow her nose in the cloth she used to wipe the dishes. We changed to another café.' But the longer walk, greater expense, and the call of a free game of chess, took them back. They reckoned that with summer approaching, she probably no longer had a cold.

As a junior surgeon on the staff of the Bristol General Hospital, ARS found himself 'on call' night after night. The hospital paid for a cab. But he seldom availed himself of this luxury, because he could not afford the tip.

Once in his early days of private practice, he operated on the wife of an antique dealer. Afterwards her husband confessed he could not afford the fee. Instead, he offered a pair of Queen Anne silver candlesticks. My father refused. He needed the cash too badly. The next day the dealer and his wife decamped to Canada. My father received neither money nor candlesticks.

The habit of frugality remained with him throughout his life.

I have his sermon notes. None are written on new sheets of paper. Most are on the back of old notepaper. Our home was comfortable but unostentatious. He never flaunted a show of wealth even when earning a big income.

Nevertheless, ARS was richly generous. His gifts were usually disguised; he strictly followed the injunction, 'Do not let your left hand know what your right hand is doing' (*Matt.* 6:3). So much was this so, that in some medical circles he had the reputation of being stingy. But I have his early accounts. Even when they record a tiny income, he gave liberal gifts to individuals and church causes. Each year, on 31 December, he would tot up his list of benefactions, and if he had not given the sum he had set himself, he would post off some more cheques. He preferred to give several small gifts anonymously, rather than one or two big ones.

But there are other forms of 'poverty', as the world counts poverty. Many people did not appreciate his firm Christian stance. Once, when I thought to apply for a medical post in the west of England, I was advised not to waste my time. 'Why ever not?' I asked. My friend replied frankly, 'Because they don't like your family's type of religion down there.'

A Christian Heritage

My father had the inestimable advantage of a staunch Christian background, extending back, as far as I can ascertain, over many generations. In another early Day Book he recorded the names of several men whose words and example had most influenced him. There was George Müller, 'from whom I learned the power of simple faith in God, to derive all practice and all principle from the word of God, and to obey in simplicity, whatever the consequence.'

And he writes of his father, Edward Rendle Short:

From him I learned nearly everything. Best perhaps a transparent honesty of godliness in every word and work, a freedom from narrowness, pettiness and self-seeking, and a character happy, strong, capable and loveable in a Plymouth Brother.

'I learned'. That is they [these men of God] lived so before my eyes. If only they might one and all become part of myself, my character and my life in the presence of God and man. Amen.

I can confirm that this prayer was truly answered.

Four months later, after he became engaged to my mother, Helen Henrietta Case – Nell – he added an addendum in the Day Book, 'From Nell I learned unselfishness, and love made manifest.' At that time she was a nursing sister at the Mildmay Mission Hospital. This was a General Hospital with an evangelical Christian foundation situated in the slums of London's East End. The building still stands. It is now a specialized hospice for AIDS patients. 'Ren.' was at University College Hospital, some miles away in central London.

The Academic Life

As a student at the University of London, ARS gained first class honours and Gold Medals in Physiology, Materia Medica, Anatomy, Medicine, Obstetrics, in the Doctorate of Medicine, and also in Geology. Scholarships and awards came to him in abundance. It is reported that after he had qualified there was a move in the University to change the rules so that no one individual could obtain all the prizes in any one year. In addition he taught himself Hebrew, as well, of course, as learning compulsory Greek and Latin at school. Someone, congratulating my mother on her engagement remarked, 'I hear you are marrying the *Encyclopaedia Britannica*.'

Throughout his life, besides books on Christian apologetics, ARS authored books and articles on physiology and surgery. He was surgical editor of the world-famous *Medical Annual* from 1919 until his death in 1953. ARS was a man of immense intellect and tireless energy, but this did not come without hard work. He would quote the aphorism, 'Genius is the ability to take infinite pains.'

The Call of Overseas Missions

Despite this academic potential, from early life my father had resolved to do Christian work overseas. He writes:

From my teens I had built a kind of castle in the air that I might one day be a medical missionary. This idea was probably based on hero worship. Two aunts had been in the foreign mission field; I had often heard missionaries speak. It seemed a noble enterprise. But when I was well launched on my medical studies, and was beginning to do well, and prospects opened at home, the vision faded and I came to hate the thought of going abroad. It sounded a lonely, squalid, poverty-stricken existence.

I can vouch that an early aspiration after missionary service is not rare among young men and women brought up in a Christian environment. Many young people, under the heady influence of some thrilling missionary presentation, in all sincerity offer their lives for service overseas. But not infrequently, as time flows by, a successful career opens up in this country, marriage supervenes, and the missionary glamour fades. Should they be bound by a hasty decision made years ago?

I believe every earnest young Christian should, at some time, prayerfully consider the call to full-time Christian service, perhaps as an overseas missionary. When a young man, David Sitton responded to the call to serve in Papua. He writes: 'The mindset I shared with my missionary co-workers was that this world is going to hell, and it was our responsibility to snatch a few souls from the fire. We did not state it in that way, but it was the driving force behind most of our endeavours.' He tells of his great love for the Lord and compassion for the lost, but believes he was driven by the motives of fear and guilt: 'Thousands are dying and going to hell every day, and part of the reason is because you are not out there saving them.'[1]

In the past, I too have been subjected to similar guilt-feelings, but I thank God that early in my life it became obvious I had no aptitude for foreign languages. For me, there was no hard decision: the foreign mission field was never a serious option.

A strange hierarchy has developed in evangelical Christianity. Full-time overseas missionary service often heads the list, and a humdrum life as a Christian at home is often at the bottom. But is this always the will of God?

Despite his growing disinclination, ARS decided to equip himself fully for overseas missionary service. For this reason, he obtained the Fellowship of the Royal College of Surgeons and

[1]David Sitton, 'Never say Never', *Evangelical Times*, Darlington, September 1992, p. 21.

the Diploma in Tropical Medicine. Thus well prepared, so he thought, he applied to a missionary society – but to his chagrin he was rejected as too highly qualified for the post. Seeing an advertisement from a Presbyterian missionary society for a trained surgeon in Formosa, he tried again. This time he was turned down when it was found his views on baptism differed from theirs.

Nothing daunted, he set out alone for Naples to see if he could commence medical practice there. But it was not to be. The authorities proved intransigent and the difficulties insurmountable. Years later someone remarked of these abortive efforts, 'Thank God he never made it.' But I think the Lord said, 'You did well in that it was in your heart' (2 Chron. 6:8). In an autobiographical fragment my father candidly confessed:

The trouble was, I wanted a decently equipped hospital where surgery could be done. I felt no vocation to go out as some of my friends did, on what is called 'faith lines', without any guarantee of support. Whether this was due to lack of faith, or to divine guidance, I have never been able quite to decide.

Ambition

Is it wrong for a Christian to be ambitious? This was a topic my father discussed with me, particularly when, after my demobilization from the Royal Army Medical Corps, I was considering my own future career. He then told me how at about my age he had been plagued by doubts when applying for high hospital and university posts.

In April 1908 he confided meditatively in his Day Book an entry which he entitled, 'Ambition': 'I will not write what I ought to want, but what, in better moments, I *do* want.' He depicts a path to academic fame, concluding, 'But what shall it profit to be the leading authority on some disease all unknown and unnamed before? Jealousy, jealousy and distraction, then – oblivion. . . .' By contrast, he dreams that perhaps, '. . . somewhere, sometime, a few poor folk should say to themselves in half-realized thought – "If *he* had not come, my misery would be with me still – if *he* had not spoken, my life would have been lived in selfish dullness and gone out in blank despair" – were this not worth while?'

The youthful ARS summarized his life's ambition thus – in old age to be able to say:

I have not been great nor good, but I have shown a little of the kindness of God to some in need, and He has given me the continual heart rest of a loving fellowship born, with all His ideals for me, in Heaven. This is my ambition, and may all the powers of a man's will resolutely, determinedly seek it, for this is the will of God.

So is it wrong to be ambitious? That the question haunted him, I can tell by the fact that he so frequently preached on the topic in later life.

One day, so he records in his Day Book, these persistent questionings came to a head, and unexpectedly. He noticed a passage in the book of Jeremiah, 'Seekest thou great things for thyself, seek them not' (*Jer.* 45:5, AV). He was devastated. What a verse for a man with the highest university honours in medical subjects which England could offer! Did this mean that, after all, academic preferment was forbidden? Slowly, he read the verse again, savouring a different emphasis on the words: 'Seekest thou great things for *thyself*, seek them not.' Great things for oneself – no! But great things for God! That surely could never be wrong. To think and do God's will to the peak of one's ability – yes!

My father's understanding of that verse from Jeremiah calls to mind another ambitious academic – the apostle Paul. He proffers his *curriculum vitae* – 'circumcised the eighth day, of the stock of Israel, of the tribe of Benjamin, a Hebrew of the Hebrews; concerning the law, a Pharisee; concerning zeal, persecuting the church; concerning the righteousness which is in the law, blameless . . .' But, he concludes, 'Not that I have already attained, or am already perfected; but I press on, that I may lay hold of that for which Christ Jesus has also laid hold of me' (*Phil.* 3:5, 6, 12).

This surely is the correct fulfilment of godly ambition, with the advantage that it can be undertaken irrespective of outward circumstances or geographical location.

There is another form of ambition which attacks young and old under the guise of spirituality; but it has an uglier name:

spiritual pride. John Bunyan knew this. One evening after preaching in a village church, a man came up to him and said, 'That was a mighty fine sermon you gave us tonight, John.' To which Bunyan replied, 'Yes; I know. The devil told me that as I was coming down the pulpit steps.'

Every preacher must have had the temptation to spiritual pride from time to time. I think the corrective is to be found in the Litany of the Church of England Book of Common Prayer: 'From Pride, Vain-glory and Hypocrisy, Good Lord deliver me.'

How did my father resolve the priorities in his exceptionally busy life, with the competing claims of surgical practice, Christian vocation and family responsibilities? Which should claim primacy? Regretfully, on reading Christian biographies (John Wesley's, for example) one not infrequently finds that, while they were renowned evangelists and soul winners, their home life left much to be desired. On the contrary, I have the happiest memories of the time I spent with my father – Saturday afternoon walks in Leigh Woods, or, if wet, down to the Bristol Art Gallery. Then there was the annual four weeks summer holidays in Cornwall. I fear for 'preacher's kids' today, when the question of priorities is even harder to resolve. But surely God does not desire us to neglect our own wife and children in order to save other people's?

A CRISIS OF FAITH

Some years ago, among a jumble of my father's old papers, I came across a ragged snippet of a newspaper obituary. He was not accustomed to keeping newspaper clippings and this is the only one I have found. In a corner he had written the single word, 'Romanes'. I had not heard the name before, but subsequently I observed that my father referred to him not infrequently in sermons and books in his early days.

The obituary recorded that after the death of a sister whom he dearly loved, George Romanes had determined, 'torture though it was, to remain utterly true to reason and not abandon his agnostic beliefs.'

Desmond and Moore in their book *Darwin*,[1] refer the episode to 1878. This was about four years after Romanes had joined the Darwinian set, and his 'head belonged to evolution, but his

---

[1]Desmond and Moore, *Darwin*, p. 633. In her *Life of George Romanes*, Ethel gives further details. She writes, 'Early in 1878, a great sorrow fell on the Romanes family. The elder of the two sisters, Georgina, died in April, and to her brother, her junior by two or three years, her loss was very great. She was a brilliant musician, and had done much to prevent her younger brother from becoming too entirely absorbed in science, and in keeping alive in him the passionate love of music which was always one of his characteristics.' Georgina was a great friend of Gounod, and she used to sing to him. Ethel quotes a letter which George wrote to Charles Darwin on 10 April 1878: 'Many thanks for your kind expressions of sympathy . . . The blow is indeed felt by us to be one of dire severity . . . My sister did not pass through much suffering, but there was something painfully pathetic about her death, not only because she was so young, and had always been so strong, but also because the ties of affection by which she was bound to us were more than ordinarily tender. And when in her delirium she reverted to the time when our positions were reversed, and when by weeks and months of arduous heroism she saved my life by constant nursing – upon my word, it was unbearable.' (Romanes refers to his attack of typhoid fever in 1873.)

heart would not follow. He was a perambulating paradox.' To make matters worse, he was courting, and would soon acquire a devout wife – Ethel. With his faith faltering and his sister delirious on her deathbed, Romanes yearned for some assurance they would meet again. 'Looking drained and cut up . . . He sought out an eminent spiritualist . . . and poured out his awful doubts. He wanted conviction, pleaded for facts, but went away empty-handed.' A few days later his sister died.

George resorted to his friend Darwin for encouragement. Darwin talked of his own moral outrage at the doctrine of eternal damnation. But all they could agree upon was that Christianity was no use to either of them. 'Romanes simply could not believe in God or in immortality either.'

In despair, Romanes turned for consolation to his evolutionary creed and composed *Gloria Mundi* with its bland assurance, 'Eternal matter reigns as Nature's queen':

> The flower fades while yet the grass is green;
> The trees are standing with their blossom shed;
> The child I loved has drooped her lovely head,
> While reptiles crawl which Milton may have seen:
> The higher life that everywhere hath been,
> To lower life returns ere it be dead;
> And, when all remnant of the life hath fled,
> Eternal matter reigns as Nature's queen.
> Man is the blossom of the Tree of Life,
> And mind the subtlest fragrance he doth bear;
> So all that I have known and thought and felt,
> Of love and hope, and fear, and peace, and strife,
> Before my very eyes ere long shall melt,
> As melts a morning mist into the air.

I am not surprised that the tragic story of George Romanes affected ARS deeply. They had much in common, especially a Christian background and an intense interest in science. I suspect Romanes may have been the trigger which aroused in him a realization of the dilemma which loomed before him: head or heart, science or Scripture, and more specifically, geology or Genesis. His sense of personal crisis was probably accentuated by his membership of the unconventional Christian Brethren. Unlike the majority of their members he was an academic with a brilliant, well-trained mind. He could have made his mark in almost any profession. His family vowed he could talk knowledgeably on any topic except motor cars and film stars. In his youth he was an avid reader with a wide spectrum of interests. Apart from science, medicine and religion, he had a deep knowledge of ancient and modern history. His particular interest was in the English Reformation, and Bunyan's *Pilgrim's Progress*.

In later life he had little time to relax in a novel. In fact, he only allowed himself one per year, on our annual summer holiday. This was carefully chosen for him by his children. John Buchan was a favourite. He did not go to films, rarely to a concert, and never to the theatre. There was, of course, no TV. His relaxation was (accurately) listed in *Who's Who* as 'naturalizing.' ARS had excellent health; an ability to work long hours; an intense, carefully curbed ambition, and throughout his life the self-imposed discipline of financial stringency.

To return to his crisis of faith. This was not concerned with his conversion, an episode I never heard him discuss. I suspect he could never remember a time when he was not a believer. So although nothing could threaten his eternal relationship with his Saviour Jesus Christ, yet he certainly came under attack. Looking back in later years, he wrote:

It is difficult to be quite sure as one turns over the pages of memory nearly fifty years ago, that one correctly evaluates the most significant directives of one's own life. It may be that something really important has been forgotten. But it seems to me, has always seemed to me even when memory was fresher, that there were two intertwined Ariadne threads to lead through the maze of those most formative years, the late teens and the early twenties.

One thread he tells us was vocational – this we have already discussed. It related to his choice of career. Should he become an academic in England, or should he cast all that away and throw in his lot with native peoples in some fever-laden swamp in Africa or Asia? We have seen in a previous chapter how this problem was resolved for him. The second thread was intellectual, and was mainly concerned with his view of Scripture and science. But before we consider this, we must look at the culture and theological climate of his day.

The Turn of the Century

The jubilation which marked New Year 1900 found ARS finishing his studies as a clinical medical student. The previous century had bequeathed a legacy of religious controversy to the opening decades of the new, and this was directed squarely at the authority of Scripture. Most acutely it was aimed at the Pentateuch (the first five books of the Bible), and also at the person of Christ. The attack was two-pronged: The Bible was trapped between evolutionary science, which was the main agent in bringing about the abandonment of the older theology, and biblical criticism which was largely the application of the evolutionary hypothesis to the sacred writings. The scientific 'overturn' of the first chapters of Genesis fuelled the Higher Criticism debate, and the German theologians egged on the scientists.

The great Baptist preacher Charles Haddon Spurgeon called the scientific and theological attack the Downgrade Movement and it was to result in his separation from the Baptist Union in 1887. The Baptists were among the first to be concerned but by 1900 the principles at stake were being debated by all who called themselves Christian. In his book *Who Moved the Stone?*, Frank Morison describes the effect the religious controversy of those days had on him:

When as a very young man, I first began seriously to study the life of Christ, I did so with the very definite feeling that, if I may so put it, His history rested on very insecure foundations.

If you will carry your mind back in imagination to the late 'nineties you will find in the prevailing intellectual attitude of that period the key to much of my thought. It is true that the absurd cult that denied even the historical existence of Jesus had ceased to carry weight. But the work of the Higher Critics – particularly the German critics – had succeeded in spreading the very prevalent impression among students that the particular form in which the narrative of His life and death had come down to us was unreliable, and that one of the four records [St John's] was nothing other than a brilliant apologetic written many years later.[1]

The wrangling which was going on over Scripture, says Morison, 'largely coloured my thought.' Particularly was this

[1]Frank Morison, *Who Moved the Stone?* (London: Faber and Faber, 1958), pp. 6, 9–10, 12.

so because he took a deep interest in physical science, 'and one did not have to go very far in those days to discover that scientific thought was obstinately and even dogmatically opposed to what was called the miraculous element in the Gospels. Very often the few things the textual critics had left standing Science had proceeded to undermine.' Morison did not attach much weight to the conclusions of the textual critics, 'but that the laws of the Universe should go back on themselves in a quite arbitrary and inconsequential manner seemed most improbable.' Had not Huxley stridently declared, 'miracles do not happen'?

Morison continues: 'For the person of Jesus Christ, however, I had a deep and even reverent regard. He seemed to me an almost legendary figure of purity and noble manhood. A coarse word with regard to Him . . . stung me to the quick.'

To resolve the matter in his own mind, Morison decided to write a critical monograph on the events surrounding the resurrection. But it became 'The Book that Refused to be Written'. As originally planned it 'was left high and dry, as a Thames barge when the river goes down. . . .'

One day the writer discovered that, not only could he no longer write the book as first conceived, but he would not if he could.' His research had 'effected a revolution in his thoughts'. The end result was the publication of *Who Moved the Stone?*, the finest apologetic for Christ's resurrection I have read.

But voices such as Morison were rare, and by the time my father was old enough to enter the fray, the battle had been largely decided in favour of evolution.

It was not only liberal Christians who succumbed to Darwinism. Many thinking evangelicals accepted the theory too, although of course they rejected atheism. James R. Moore in *The Post-Darwinian Controversies* [1] tells us of a succession of well-known theologians who held the chair of Didactic and Polemic Theology at Princeton Theological Seminary. He commences with Charles Hodge (1797–1878). The last book Hodge wrote was entitled *What is Darwinism?* [2] After a 'perceptive and even-tempered analysis of Darwinism', Hodge concluded 'It is atheism' .

[1] James R. Moore, *The Post-Darwinian Controversies: A Study of the Protestant struggle to come to terms with Darwin in Great Britain and America 1870–1900* (Cambridge University Press, 1981), Charles Hodge, p. 204; A. A. Hodge, p. 241; B. B. Warfield, p. 71.

[2] Charles Hodge, *What is Darwinism?* (New York, Scribners, Armstrong and Co., 1874).

His son, A. A. Hodge (1823–1886), the next holder of the chair, left more for 'the possibilities of evolution than did his father' though remaining definite on the immediate creation of man. In an introduction to Joseph Van Dyke's *Theism and Evolution*, he concluded, 'Evolution considered as a plan of an infinitely wise Person and executed under the control of His everywhere present energies can never be irreligious'.[1]

The third holder of the chair was Benjamin B. Warfield (1851–1921). He went further. While A. A. Hodge adhered (in 1878) to the chronology based upon the information contained in the genealogies of Genesis, chapters 5 and 11, Warfield (in 1911) held that those genealogies were not intended to be comprehensive and that Scripture did not require us to regard the life of the human race on earth as 'only six thousand years or so.' 'The question of the antiquity of man', he believed, 'has of itself no theological significance. It is to theology, as such, a matter of entire indifference how long man has existed on earth.'[2] Further, while Hodge the younger did not believe that

---

[1]A. A. Hodge in Joseph Van Dyke, *Theism and Evolution: An Examination of Modern Speculative Theories as Related to Theistic Conceptions of the Universe* (New York: A. C. Armstrong and Sons, 1886), 'Introduction', p. xviii. For further discussion see David B. Calhoun, *Princeton Seminary*, vol. 2 (Edinburgh, Banner of Truth, 1996), pp. 79–82.

[2]Compare A. A. Hodge, *Outlines of Theology* (1879, repr. Banner of Truth: Edinburgh, 1972), p. 297 and B. B. Warfield, *Studies in Theology* (1932, repr. Banner of Truth: Edinburgh, 1988), p. 235. Yet the difference between Hodge the younger and Warfield should not be overstated and Warfield's often quoted words, repeated above, need to be read in context. Neither man accepted an age for mankind anything like that required by Darwinism – 'ten or twenty thousand years' conjectured Warfield. How far 'we may hold to the modified theory of evolution and be Christians' he left 'an open question'. Calhoun, *Princeton Seminary*, vol. 2, p. 257.

Both A. A. Hodge and Warfield were concerned with the 'time' of creation, whether 6,000, 10,000 or more years ago. But this is not the crucial point for the gospel. More important is whether or not there was violence, bloodshed and death before Adam sinned (Romans 5:12; 1 Corinthians 15:21, 22). Whether, in fact, the world was created in six days from first light to the creation of man and woman. Only so could it be rightly labelled 'very good'.

A. A. Hodge states, quite correctly, that 'The Bible . . . was written for the purpose of history of redemption'. But he continues, 'the history of redemption begins with Abraham: after that we have biography, we have appointed times, we have history – a history that goes back only to the birth of Abraham. All before that is simple introduction crowded into some ten or twelve chapters, designed to teach us these tremendous facts . . . creation . . . the fall . . . the dealing of God with men in preparation for redemption to come, but these facts are dropped in . . . as an introduction merely to the history beginning with Abraham. Everything back of this is piled up like the background in front of which history stands.' *Evangelical Theology* (1890, repr. Banner of Truth, 1976).

[118]

the body of man had a genetic connection with some lower animal, Warfield considered that it was 'possible' and that man only became man when God supernaturally created his soul.[1]

Please do not conclude that I quote these words in any way to disparage these great men of God. But, as with us all, they were men of their times, and theirs were times when evolutionary belief seemed to be victorious and carrying all before it. While none of these Princeton men accepted Darwinism as such, they were hesitant in the face of alleged facts of science. A. A. Hodge speaks of the 'relief' his father expressed at hearing the opinion of Dr Green, one of Princeton's foremost interpreters of Old Testament, who wrote, 'The time between the creation of Adam and ourselves might have been, for all we know from the Bible to the contrary, much longer than it seems.'[2]

Not until the second half of the twentieth century would facts of science, unknown a century ago, demonstrate the errors in Darwin's original theory. In our day we are seeing increasing evidence pointing to the creation model.

Like all Christians, then and today, my father had to decide the issues for himself. With his love of physiology, geology, and later archaeology, he was particularly concerned with the influence of liberalism on the Pentateuch. After all, if the first chapters of Genesis are suspect, what about the rest of the Bible, especially its record of miracles, for example the crossing of the Red Sea, Jonah and the big fish, the feeding of the five thousand, the Virgin birth of Christ, and above all, as Morison recognized, the resurrection of our Lord?

ARS knew the Bible must be his anchor – but was it really trustworthy? Edmund Gosse's *Father and Son* was not published until 1907, but he surely would have known the tragic story of that fellow-academic member of the Brethren, Philip Gosse; indeed, I glean hints from his writings, that he had read *Omphalos*.

Half a century later, the founder of the L'Abri Fellowship, Dr Francis Schaeffer dedicated his commentary on the Book of Joshua[3]

[1] Yet at the same time, as Calhoun points out, 'Warfield admitted that "the very detailed account of the creation of Eve" presented a serious problem in attempting to harmonize the Bible and evolution' (*Princeton Seminary*, p. 258).

[2] *Evangelical Theology*, p. 150.

[3] Francis A. Schaeffer, *Joshua and the Flow of Biblical History* (Downers Grove, Ill.: InterVarsity Press, 1978).

To all those younger men and women
of the next generation who
are faithful to
the first changeless factor, the written book –[1]
especially as they take seriously
that it is what it claims to be,
the written Word of God without error,
including all that it teaches
concerning history and the cosmos.[2]

Reading this dedication I ask myself, would ARS in his twenties have been able to say 'Amen' to it? Particularly the last two lines? I think his reply would have been, 'Yes, but . . .'

[1]Italics Schaeffer.
[2]Italics J. Rendle-Short.

15

CAN WE TRUST THE BIBLE?

From his teens, my father had been aware that the whole Bible which he loved so much was under attack on two broad fronts: the scientific, aimed at ridiculing its miraculous element, and the theological, disputing the text of the Scriptures. Together they threatened to crush the church. That he regarded the subject of biblical criticism as extremely important is apparent from the fact that he devoted over eighty pages of a Day-Book to the history of the origin of the text. This is far more than on any other subject, even his beloved geology.

*   *   *

The Old Testament Text

One of the first books he studied on the topic was *An Introduction to the Old Testament* by George Salmon, which was published in 1904. From this he learned something of the extensive work on biblical criticism by scholars in German universities in the eighteenth and nineteenth centuries. The ideas of earlier philosophers like Kant and Hegel had been followed by theologians such as Bauer, who called the New Testament 'a beautiful myth', and Julius Wellhausen (1844–1918), who questioned in particular the historical and scientific accuracy of the Old Testament.

Basic to Wellhausen's so-called Higher Criticism[1] was his

[1] I have found the terms German biblical criticism, textual criticism (lower criticism), higher criticism are not used uniformly by various authors. When in doubt therefore I have resorted to the general term Higher Criticism (see *The Fontana Dictionary of Modern Thought*, 1983).

attack on the Mosaic authorship of the Pentateuch. Instead of this he postulated four unknown authors whom he designated by the letters: J, E, D and P. In his early sermons ARS occasionally referred to these presumed authors, although with little enthusiasm.

The desire of the German scholars was to drive a wedge between the Pentateuch and the rest of the Bible, with the following motives:

1. To present the first eleven chapters of the Genesis as non-historical, consisting mainly of myths, allegory or poetry.

2. To undermine the miraculous element which appears in all five books of the Pentateuch, in particular, targeting the story of creation, the great ages of the patriarchs, Noah's flood, the events surrounding the Passover, and God's care of the children of Israel in the wilderness.

3. To destroy the authoritative absolutes of the law, written with the finger of God on Mount Sinai (*Exod.* 31:18).

Many years later, in 1947, my father was thrilled by the dramatic discovery of the Dead Sea Scrolls,[1] and sometimes used to lecture on the subject. Their importance is that they highlight the amazing accuracy achieved by the Massoretes who copied the Hebrew text down the centuries. For example, the age of the oldest manuscript of the Massoretic text of Isaiah previously possessed by scholars was around A.D. 1000 but the corresponding complete Dead Sea scroll was dated around 125 B.C.. This scroll, therefore, is more than 1,000 years older than any copy of Isaiah previously known. When the two are compared however, the skill of the copyists is demonstrated. For example, consider the well-known fifty-third chapter of Isaiah, consisting of 166 words: 'There is only one word (three letters) in question after a thousand years of transmission – and this word does not significantly change the meaning of the passage.'[2]

---

[1] Josh McDowell, *Evidence that Demands a Verdict* (San Bernardino, CA: Campus Crusade for Christ, vol. 1, 1972), pp. 58–59. The relevant section on the OT texts in McDowell's book is well annotated and very valuable.

[2] Ralph Earle, *How We Got Our Bible* (Baker Book House). Quoted by McDowell, p. 60.

The renowned archaeologist, Sir Frederic Kenyon, maintained that the Massoretes counted everything that could be counted, so that 'not one jot or tittle' of the law should be lost. Kenyon considered the extreme care devoted to the transcription of manuscripts to be the major reason for the disappearance of earlier copies.

When a manuscript had been copied with the exactitude prescribed by the Talmud, and had been duly verified, it was accepted as authentic and regarded as being of equal value with any other copy. If all were correct, *age gave no advantage to a manuscript*; on the contrary age was a positive disadvantage, since a manuscript was liable to become defaced or damaged in the lapse of time. A damaged or imperfect copy was thus at once condemned as unfit for use.[1] (italics by Kenyon)

At the age of twenty-eight, in a reflective mood, ARS noted in another Day-Book some of the 'formative influences' in his early life: 'Books first, then men.'

He states that, 'Books on religious and medical studies, with geology, taken together, colour all my thought. They taught me the world of old, and the world of today.' In particular he singled out, 'Bishop Westcott for the historical setting of the New Testament and the early church.' [2]

While Regius Professor of Divinity at Cambridge University, Bishop B. F. Westcott (1825–1901), and his lifelong friend Bishop F. J. A. Hort (1828–1892) had together revised the Greek text of the New Testament. These two bishops worked at a time when theological, philosophical and scientific thought in England was in a state of flux. Darwin's *Origin of Species* had just been released, and anything ancient was fascinating, especially old manuscripts of the New Testament such as the Codex Sinaiticus, which had been found under extraordinary circumstances.

As with all educated men of their time, both bishops had studied Darwin's work. In April 1860, about six months after the publication of the *Origin*, Hort wrote a letter to the Rev.

[1]Sir Frederic Kenyon, *Our Bible and the Ancient Manuscripts*. Quoted by McDowell, pp. 58–59.
[2]Some books ARS studied and quoted at the time were: Westcott, *On Hebrews*; – *History of the Canon of the New Testament*, 4th ed.; – *Bible in the Church*, Part I; – *Contents of the New Testament* (1866); Authors unknown, *The Shepherd of Hermas and other heretical scriptures*; Miller and Burgon, *Traditional Text of the Gospels* (1896).

John Ellerton, discussing interesting books he had recently read: 'But *the* book that has engaged me most is Darwin. Whatever may be thought of it, it is a book that one is proud to be contemporary with. I must work out and examine the argument more in detail, but my present feeling is strong that the theory is unanswerable, if so it opens up a new period – I know not what.' [1]

And in a letter on Old Testament criticism to Edward Benson, the Archbishop of Canterbury, dated 4 March 1890, Westcott comments:

I am quite sure that our Christian faith ought not to be periled by any predetermined view of what the history and character of the documents contained in the O.T. must be. What we are bound to hold is that the O.T., substantially as we receive it, is the Divine record of the discipline of Israel. This it remains, whatever criticism may determine or leave undetermined, as to constituent parts. No one now, I suppose, holds that the first three chapters of Genesis, for example, give a literal history – I could never understand how anyone reading them with open eyes could think they did. [2]

Aided by these and other authors, ARS made a detailed analysis of the Greek New Testament, and in researching the ancient texts, it was natural that he would give special consideration to those manuscripts which Bishops Hort and Westcott had used extensively in their 1882 revision of the New Testament: the Codex Sinaiticus and the Codex Vaticanus.

The Search for New Testament Manuscripts

With his Brethren connections, ARS was particularly fascinated by a prominent textual scholar, Dr Samuel Prideaux Tregelles (1813–1875). He recorded some details in a small book on the 'Open Brethren', published in 1911. [3]

Tregelles was born in Falmouth, of Quaker parents, but later joined the newly formed Christian Brethren. He had made it his life's work to recover the original text of the New

---

[1] *Life of Hort*, vol. 1, p. 416.
[2] *Life of Westcott*, vol. 2, pp. 68, 69.
[3] *The Principles of Christians called the 'Open Brethren'* by A Younger Brother (Glasgow: Pickering and Inglis, 1913), 2nd ed., p. 92.

Testament.'¹ 'He laid the foundations on which the Greek text underlying the Revised Version was restored.' His endeavour was to prepare 'a Greek text *drawn entirely from ancient sources.*' From 1857 to 1872 he studied to write a 'critical edition of the Greek New Testament.'

Unfortunately, so my father tells us, the text which Tregelles eventually produced with such labour, 'had limitations. The Codex Sinaiticus was only discovered late in his life, . . . and he was barely allowed to look at the great Codex Vaticanus, his pockets being searched by Papal authorities for pen or pencil, and the book was snatched out of his hands if he examined it too intently.' Furthermore, according to the *Encyclopaedia Britannica* a photographic facsimile of this work did not appear until 1889–90.

The discovery of the Codex Sinaiticus in 1844 by Count Lobegott von Tischendorf (1815–1874)² reads like detective fiction. German-born Tischendorf, a lecturer in biblical studies in Leipzig, was convinced that somewhere in the world there must exist further ancient MSS of the Greek New Testament. So at the age of twenty-eight he set out in search. His journey took him to the Middle East, to one of the most uninviting places in the world, the Monastery of Saint Catherine, situated on the northern foot of Mount Sinai. In the summer it is intensely hot, yet the relative humidity is high. The oldest continuously inhabited monastery in the world, it was founded in A.D. 530.

Some years ago, a friend of mine, Dr Joseph Shelley, recounted to me how during the 1914–1918 war he was stationed in the Middle East. While on vacation, he and a friend borrowed a car and set out to cross the desert and visit the monastery at Mount Sinai. Unfortunately, at about the half-way point the car broke down. Repairing it proved a

¹Of Dr Tregelles, William Burgon (not a man given to plaudits) writes, 'Of the scrupulous accuracy, the indefatigable industry, the pious zeal of that estimable and devoted scholar, we speak not. All honour to his memory . . . Be it only stated that Tregelles effectually persuaded himself that eighty-nine ninetieths of our existent manuscripts and other authorities may safely be rejected and lost sight of when we come to amend the text and try to restore it to its primitive purity.' (John William Burgon, *The Revision Revised*, 1883 [Paradise, Pa.: Conservative Classics Edition, Undated, p. 22: 343]).

²Tischendorf, *Narrative of the Discovery of the Sinaitic Manuscripts*, p. 23. Quoted by J. W. Burgon. For further information see also *New Encyclopaedia Britannica*, 15th ed.

lengthy process. They then had to make the agonizing decision as to whether to continue their journey in the searing heat or return to base. Meanwhile their water supply was almost finished. They struggled on, and eventually arrived at the monastery, tired out, sun-blistered and grossly dehydrated. Dr Shelley described in graphic terms how in the cool of the ancient building they spent the first twenty-four hours alternately drinking vast quantities of lukewarm water, sleeping, then waking to drink again.

Such was the place where about half a century before, Tischendorf had searched for ancient biblical manuscripts. He writes that while in the great library he 'perceived a *large and wide basket* full of old parchments; and the librarian told him that two heaps like that had already been *committed to the flames*. What was his surprise to find amid this heap of papers, discarded old parchment leaves' which he immediately recognised as being of great age.

Tischendorf was permitted to take forty-three leaves back to Leipzig for examination. Then in 1853 he undertook a second journey to the monastery, but searched in vain for the precious document. Just as he was about to give up hope, a steward showed him where the rest of the manuscript was hidden. After much haggling he was able to purchase it for Tsar Alexander II of Russia for $7,000.

In 1933 it was bought by the British Government for £100,000, and was housed in London in the British Museum. I was only fourteen years old at this time, but I well remember the thrill in my father's voice as he told me of the happening, and its significance. He made a special journey from Bristol to London to see the Codex.

According to the *Encyclopaedia Britannica* this manuscript (like the Vaticanus) dates from the fourth century and comes from Alexandria. 'It is probably by three hands and several correctors . . . The later corrections, representing attempts to alter the text to a different standard, were probably made in the sixth and seventh centuries at Caesarea.' The Vaticanus is incomplete.

Why have these ancient documents survived in relatively good condition? ARS pondered this question and made notes on authorities he consulted. One book in particular impressed him, *The Traditional Text of the Gospels* (1896) by Miller and Burgon. Summarizing the message of this and other books, he came to the conclusion that 'Antiquity is not a good test of the truth.' In this statement he echoes the words of Kenyon, 'that age gave no advantage to a manuscript'.

My father almost invariably used the Authorised Version. True, the Revised Version (RV) had been available since the end of the nineteenth century. I have a tattered copy of the 1924 edition myself. It is inscribed by my mother on the flyleaf, 'John Rendle Short, Oct. 24 1935 from his Father and Mother.' The occasion was that of my baptism in Bethesda Chapel, Bristol.

In the last year of his life, my father was presented with a copy of the recently published Revised Standard Version (RSV) inscribed, 'With grateful appreciation, Shaftesbury Men's Bible School, December 11, 1952.' This gave him great pleasure.

16

AN INTELLECTUAL IMPASSE

'To Darwin's *Origin of Species* I owe more than I can say.' My father was twenty-eight years old when he made this surprising admission. For one brought up in an evangelical home, it is totally unexpected, and constrains me to ask two related questions: Why was the *Origin* so important to him? And why, for an extra academic subject, did he elect to study geology?

It is not uncommon for a bright medical student to read a non-compulsory subject in the early years of their medical course, but usually it is one which is at any rate vaguely related to medicine: zoology or psychology are common, or nowadays, computer science, or even for relaxation, music. But to take a subject remote from medicine such as geology is most unusual.

During his medical course ARS had already taken a special interest in zoology and physiology. In later life he would write two textbooks on physiology[1] and lecture on the topic for twenty years at Bristol University. So he was already well-grounded in the biological aspects of evolution. But Darwinian biology is really only a part of evolution theory. Darwin had to build on a foundation. His thesis could never have stood on its own.

And what was this foundation? It was, as we have seen, Lyell's geological uniformitarianism, by which it was possible to allow as much time as necessary (billions of years) for chance

---

[1]A. Rendle Short, *The New Physiology in Surgical and General Practice*, 1911, and *Synopsis of Physiology*, 1927. Both published by John Wright and Sons, Bristol. For a number of years ARS was an examiner in physiology in the primary Fellowship for the Royal College of Surgeons (Eng.).

variations to produce new species, account for the fossils, bury the idea of a universal flood and, most importantly, reject any need for a supernatural agency.

As we considered the beliefs of Philip Gosse in the nineteenth century, it was apparent that he was battling not against *one* new scientific concept, but against *two*: the age of the earth, and the origin of living things, and of these Lyell's geology was the more important to him.

But by 1908, a very old earth – even millions of years – was accepted as indisputable fact and Lyell's contribution had been virtually forgotten and thus the two parts of the evolutionary theory were lumped together and known collectively as Darwinism. For about three decades the idea of the six-day Genesis creation had been abandoned in scientific circles – and increasingly in theological and lay circles too. So this was where science and Scripture clashed and geology was an obvious subject for ARS to study.

But why did Darwin's *Origin of Species* help my father so much? I am not certain, but I suppose the *Origin* provided a way whereby biology and geology could be reconciled. As Thomas Huxley had exclaimed: 'It's so simple. Why didn't I think of it myself!' Christians like my father had no doubt that the spiritual part of man was special, created in the image of God (*Gen.* 1:27). And now, with new Darwinian insight, man's *body* could be fitted into the evolutionary picture. Perhaps the human body was the result, not of direct creation, but of millions of years of imperceptible change. Thus reconciliation between biology, geology and Genesis seemed at last possible.

Nevertheless, Darwinism continued to present my father's religious beliefs with an acute conflict. In an autobiographical remnant, written fifty years later, he explains why:

I was cast for education in the school of science. I do not recollect that chemistry or physics much influenced my thinking, but zoology and physiology and geology did, and disturbingly. Everything was to be brought to the test of the laboratory, to personal observation, to experiment.

It was the era of triumphant Darwinism. Modern doubts as to the sufficiency of a self-working theory of Natural Selection, to account for the origin of all living things had scarcely achieved a hearing among men of science.

He continues:

> Wellhausen's theories about the Old Testament, and Bauer's about the New Testament were accepted, even by theologians, as pretty well proven. Some people seem to be able to hold on to a religious faith by turning a Nelson's blind eye on conflicting facts and theories. But I was not made that way. I could not follow 'cunningly devised fables' however glamorous. Things were moving on to an intellectual *impasse*. Some working hypothesis had to be found, or something would have to be thrown overboard.

Unfortunately ARS lacked the friendship of like-minded Christian academics with whom to discuss and argue. Doubtless his own father was a tremendous support in the study of the Scripture, but he had no scientific training. My father explains:

> I owed very little to sermons in coming to a conclusion as to whether the fundamentals of the Christian faith were credible or not. I did not sit much under a scholarly ministry. Even if it were occasionally scholarly, the preacher's education was not my education, nor his mind my mind.

What was the *impasse*? All his school and university training was based on the *fact* of evolution. But from his cradle he had been instructed in the truth of the Holy Bible. If God also wrote the Book of Nature, then surely no conflict between the two books should be possible, or if there was a conflict, it should be reconcilable. Yet apparently this was not so.

'Fortunately,' he writes, 'I was preserved from the folly of a precipitate decision.' Clearly, he was contemplating the desperate choice that either one or the other, science or Scripture, must be abandoned, or at least severely modified. Intellectually he appeared to have reached a dead end.

Let me remind you again how carefully he had prepared himself so that any decision would be well informed: Firstly, by ascertaining that the whole Scripture was trustworthy. Secondly, by an in-depth study of physiology and zoology. Thirdly, by what he describes as 'the whimsical step' of adding a BSc in geology to his undergraduate curriculum. He passed the examination with flying colours: first class honours and the gold medal. Years later he wrote of that examination: 'I proved most conclusively to the satisfaction of the examiners that the world was 100 million years old. That was the teaching in 1899.

But now the dates have changed and my poor little essay is a back number.' [The present date quoted is more like 4,600 million years.]

Elated by his success in the BSc, he later attempted the DSc in geology. But here he was unsuccessful – the only examination he ever failed. To obtain research material for the thesis, my father had himself lowered by a rope from the top of Aust cliffs on the banks of the river Severn. Years later, one blistering hot Saturday afternoon we cycled together to Aust, and he showed me the spot. I thought he was very brave.

The Impasse Resolved?

My father eventually found a resolution of sorts to the dilemma which had long plagued him in a book by Henry Drummond entitled, *Natural Law in the Spiritual World.*[1] It did so by 'linking together my science and my faith'. In his mature years he wrote:

I do not think the first reading of any book has ever given me such a thrill. The modern reader will be at a loss to understand this . . . It showed me, for the first time, that a synthesis between natural science and the Christian message was not impossible, and that the Designer of the world might very well be the God of the Christian.

Judging by the many copies which I have observed on second-hand book stalls, both in England and Australia, the book must have fulfilled a universal need. First published in 1883, it had reached thirty-three editions by 1897, and was still quoted approvingly as being of value to 'multitudes of orthodox theologians in all the churches', forty years later.[2]

Henry Drummond, FRSE, FGS (1851–1897) is described by James Moore as 'a well-known evangelist and Professor of the Free Church College, Glasgow.'[3] He was a 'Scottish naturalist [who] abandoned the experiments in mesmerism for the 'enquiry room' of D. L. Moody's revivals.' According to Moore, Drummond's book was 'a collection of sermons which

---

[1] Henry Drummond, *Natural Law in the Spiritual World*, 1st ed. 1883. Hodder and Stoughton, London.

[2] *The British Weekly*, July 1924. Quoted by Iain Murray, in *D. Martyn Lloyd-Jones: The First Forty Years 1899–1939* (Edinburgh: Banner of Truth Trust, 1982), p. 148, fn. 3.

[3] James R. Moore, *The Post-Darwinian Controversies. A study of the Protestant struggle to come to terms with Darwin in Great Britain and America 1870–1900* (Cambridge University Press, 1979).

supplied the basic doctrines of the spiritual life as interpreted by evangelical Christianity with proof texts from *Synthetic Philosophy*.' (I have failed to find the author of this book.) Moore notes that Drummond was 'twice subject to charges of heresy before the General Assembly of the Free Church of Scotland'.

In the introduction to *Natural Law*, Drummond tells us that regularly each week he addressed two very different types of audiences on different themes: 'On weekdays I lecture to a class of students on the Natural Sciences, and on Sundays to an audience consisting for the most part of working men on subjects of a moral and religious character.'

As I read Drummond's book today, it seems to me a bizarre amalgam of Darwinism, Christianity, metaphysics and Teilhard de Chardin philosophy. Consider this extract:

What is required therefore, to draw Science and Religion together again . . . is the disclosure of the naturalness of the supernatural. Thus as the Supernatural becomes slowly Natural, will also the Natural become slowly Supernatural, until in the impersonal authority of Law men everywhere recognize the authority of God.[1]

*　　*　　*

As we have seen, my father's early creed was Darwinism – there was virtually no alternative for a man of his scientific training. Yet he viewed it through the eyes of a Christian with a deep love of nature and a profound knowledge and reverence for Scripture. He fully appreciated the words of Saint Paul: 'Since the creation of the world His eternal attributes are clearly seen, being understood by the things that are made, even His eternal power and Godhead. So man is without excuse' (*Rom.* 1:20).

The synthesis he arrived at seems to have been that God used and controlled the evolutionary process to produce an ape-like creature then breathed into it the breath of life, thus making it human. In 1910 he wrote,[2]

---

[1]*Drummond*, pp. vi & xxiii. It is only fair to add that A. R. Simpson (Professor of Midwifery, Edinburgh, from 1870–1905) in an article titled 'The Year of Grace in Edinburgh 1884–85', tells us that Professor Drummond was a speaker much used by the Holy Spirit. Simpson, himself an eye-witness, writes: 'Starting 25 January 1885 – when Professor Drummond spoke to an audience of some 1,000 students – he led the series of addresses for the next ten years. During these meetings many students and post-graduates were brought to Christ'. Quoted in *Journal of Christian Medical Fellowship*, October 1987, pp. 7–9.

[2]In a Day-book.

An Intellectual Impasse

It was according to His settled plan that He made the worlds and their elements, that He cooled the nebulous, the molten globe, that He gave the sun to give light and heat, that He made the earth, endless ages ago as habitable places for life. He was *preparing a place for us* . . . into some favoured dust He elected to breathe the breath of life. Happy dust! To triumph over the whole inanimate creation – raised into another world – yet for no virtue of its own.

Ten thousand times the developing life of the world was called to go forward to nobler, fitter things; the many chose the lower path, the few responded to the call. The many left their bones in the record of the rocks . . . till the advent of the fullest fruition of earth: man in God's own Image.

The West Country Influence

My parents proudly called themselves 'Bristolians: Citizens of no mean city.' But the West of England and particularly Cornwall was always beckoning them. For a while during the second World War my mother lived in a house we owned in Padstow.

Happy holiday memories of the north Cornish coast with rocky sunlit bays, but also its rugged inhospitable cliffs, and fierce Atlantic storms remained with my father (and myself) throughout his life. Shipwrecks were common. As a boy I had learned the couplet, 'From Hartland point to Trevose light, a watery grave by day or night.' I remember standing, one late September afternoon, heeled over against the wind, on the cliffs above Land's End. Beneath us three coastal vessels battled against the gale.

Every now and then one or other would be hidden in the trough of a huge wave. Then we noticed only two were visible. The third had foundered before our eyes. All the crew were lost. Mrs Magor, a local woman who looked after our holiday home in Padstow, told us the Cornish did not like to place a cut loaf of bread on end. It reminded them too much of a sinking ship. The hymn I always wanted when the family sang round the fire on a Sunday evening, went:

> Fierce raged the tempest o'er the deep,
> Watch did thine anxious servants keep,
> But Thou wast wrapped in guileless sleep,
> Calm and still.

And the last stanza:

> So, when our life is clouded o'er,
> And storm-winds waft us from the shore,
> Say, lest we sink to rise no more,
> 'Peace, be still.'

To increase the terror of the storms and rocks, until early in the last century, ships were sometimes lured onto the rocks by lights held aloft by wreckers. Before the days of coastguards, little sympathy was shown for the sailors.[1] When news of a wreck reached the local pub, the first question would be, 'What's the cargo?'

In about 1900, a wreck occurred when my father was holidaying with his family at Perranporth. The cargo was white china – plates and cups which were strewn all over the beach. Many found their way into local homes. Then the word went around that the police were going to search all the houses in the district. The next morning, so my father told me, neat piles of plates were to be seen dotted about the sand, all just above high water mark.

I give this Cornish interlude as a background to a soliloquy, composed by my father at the age of twenty-six while sitting on a cliff overlooking the much loved three-mile stretch of sand and wild Atlantic breakers of Perranporth beach:

A Summer Day's Reverie
To the left the endless moaning tossing irresistible sea. My Father made it all. Those stars declare His glory; that sea and these hills, and valleys and cliffs, His power. Look at the rocks and see the shores and seas of long ago. Look around and see how slow change is, then think what endless ages are in the rocks beneath you. See the life preserved in those rocks, relics of the preparation He made for man. If the rocks spell ages, the fossils spell eternity. And all this was to provide and prepare the way for man. It is defiled now. Those wonderful rocks could unfold a sorry story of wreckers and wrecked. The animals these wilds belonged to have been brutally treated and enslaved. The earth is downtrodden and ruined by those who were not worthy of it, and its glorious beauties defiled and defaced. The whole creation groans for the liberty of the glory of the children of God [see Romans 8:19–22]. It was made for them. It shall by and by be theirs alone. The seas and

---

[1] See, for example, *Jamaica Inn* – a novel by Daphne Du Maurier.

the hills, the heather and the gorse – these shall be for the children of God in their glory. The animal creation longs and groans for it, that emancipation. Then, and then alone, shall the human race be truly free 'from vice, oppression and despair'.

Constantly in his early writings the same themes recur: the wonder and beauty of nature; the sovereignty and power of God; the puniness and sin of man, the glorious salvation in Christ, and withal a glad anticipation of a future heaven and earth in which righteousness shall dwell.

Yet always there were evolutionary overtones: the cooling of the 'molten globe'; the 'favoured dust' into which God 'elected to breathe the breath of life'; 'the life preserved in the rocks, relics of the preparation He made for man. If the rocks spell ages, the fossils spell eternity.'

I am in no way surprised that ARS, bombarded by evolution theory from fellow-scientists and fellow-Christians alike, could not fully understand the biblical story of creation. But at least, instead of a precipitate decision, he managed to arrive at a compromise position (which would today be called progressive creationism[1] or theistic evolution). He did not possess the increasing amount of data now available to refute evolution and to substantiate the scientific feasibility of the creation model. By the grace of God he did not lose his faith like poor George Romanes, nor did he become permanently blinkered by some false theory like so many modern-day Christian evolutionists. Instead, as a true scientist, he possessed a research mind. He was ever anxious to discover new facts and absorb new ideas as long as they seemed to be consistent with the revelation of God.

Recently I read a book, *Did God Use Evolution?*, by Werner

---

[1]An active present-day proponent of the progressive creation camp is Dr Hugh Ross. See for example *Creation and Time*. Briefly, Ross's position can be summarized as:
'The earth and universe are billions of years old.
The days of creation were overlapping periods of millions and billions of years.
Death and bloodshed have existed from the beginning of Creation and were not the result of Adam's sin.
Man was created after the vast majority of earth's history of life and death had already taken place. The flood of Noah was local, not global.
The Key – The age of the earth is "a trivial doctrinal point".'
(See Mark Van Bebber and Paul S. Taylor, *Creation and Time: A Report on the Progressive Creationist Book by Hugh Ross* [Arizona: Eden Productions], pp. 12, 15.)

Gitt.[1] It links up-to-date science, particularly in the realm of information theory, with a deep understanding of Scripture. Constantly, as I did so I thought of my father and wished he was reading it with me. ARS concluded the *Reverie:*

Every science fades into mystery. What is under the crust of the earth, and why? . . . What is life? . . . What is mind? Every page of physiology, pathology and medicine merely raises a dozen unanswerable questions. History, too begins in mist and is full of 'why's'. Yet God was so great that He planned it all, and His power that He made it all. We are utterly incapable, apart from what He has told us, even to conceive His objects, His principles . . . it is our part just to trust and say, 'It is the will of God'.

[1]Werner Gitt, *Did God Use Evolution?* For further details see Appendix 1.

17

THE FACT OF CHRIST

In an autobiographical manuscript quoted in *The Faith of a Surgeon*,[1] my father describes his difficult early days. Having first assured himself of the textual accuracy of the biblical records, he then asked, 'What ought one to think of the Person whose story they tell?' He listened to preachers who proclaimed that the writers of the Scriptures were inspired; if so, 'their testimony that Christ is a Divine Person must be true. And we know that they are inspired because Christ, who is a Divine Person, says so . . . But this is surely arguing in a circle.'

Later, in his twenties, ARS came across *The Fact of Christ* by Carnegie Simpson:[2]

It was Simpson's little book that broke the circle. The true grounds for believing in His Deity are found in His character. Added to this are His teaching, His practical wisdom; His miracles; His resurrection, and His influence on history. He is too wonderful for the four evangelists to have invented Him.

So impressed was he, that when he came across the book again in 1952, he arranged for it to be republished. He tells us in the foreword, that when he first read it,

It opened up to me a kind of trunk road of thought. It showed [by] the most convincing evidence that Jesus Christ, our Lord, is worthy of the highest honour, an honour which indeed is quite inadequate if it does not amount to worship . . . His purity of holiness, love for all

---

[1]Capper and Johnson, *The Faith of a Surgeon*, p. 37.
[2]P. Carnegie Simpson, *The Fact of Christ* (1st ed. 1900, repr. 1953). Foreword by ARS.

mankind, forgiveness of wrongs suffered and humility, well exemplified by His readiness to give time and attention to quite unimportant people, were virtues which He introduced almost new into the world.

When I read *The Fact of Christ* myself forty years later, I found it interesting for three reasons: the intrinsic merits of the book; the insight it gives into the religious viewpoint of Simpson's times, and in particular, the light it shines on my father.

On the first page, Simpson quotes the question asked by Jesus of His disciples, 'Whom say ye that I am?' (*Matt.* 16:15, AV). He comments, 'It was a question simply about Jesus Himself. It was neither theological nor ethical, but personal.' And it was upon the answer to this question, Jesus declared, that His church would be built.

Simpson explains that in his day, unbelief had settled into a rooted agnosticism, rather than frank atheism; there were no serious rivals to Christianity:

Vagaries such as Neo-Buddhism, make few converts . . . But these facts do not mean that the age is agreeing with the Christian faith. They mean rather a settled refusal of it. An opposition that contends, however fiercely, that Christianity is false might possibly be overcome; but an unbelief which submits, however courteously that Christianity is futile, because the whole topic of religion is beyond human ken, is a far subtler foe.

Simpson asks:

Why this uncertainty, this agnosticism? The reason is that men more than ever feel the difficulty, the impossibility, of answering all the great questions of God and the soul. The origin and meaning of the universe is something so far and vast, and life is something so complex, that we can not say much more about them on the religious side. Nature we can know, but though Nature stretches out into the Infinite, we cannot see what meets her [sic] there. The battle of faith and unbelief was always an inconclusive one, and now less than ever are men able to take as decided in the affirmative the problems of God, of revelation, of freedom, of immortality.

*   *   *

In *The Fact of Christ*, Simpson cut through what he regarded as the tangle of New Testament philosophical/theological questions to consider Jesus Christ himself – the Jesus who,

[138]

calls us from the inscrutable to the positive. To everyone – be his agnosticism intellectually self-satisfied, sensually self-indulgent, or neither of these, but only sad – comes the great Master of the soul with His revolutionary restatement of the problem of religion . . . 'What is your attitude toward Me?'

Clearly Simpson's objective was not to present Jesus historically, but to demonstrate his overwhelming superiority of character, and record its impact on men and women throughout the centuries. Instinctively, says Simpson, we do not class him with other men. We talk of Alexander the Great, or Charles the Great, but never of Jesus the Great. Simpson excels when he is discussing the character of Jesus. He lists four main elements:

1. Christ's *purity and holiness:* '[Christ] made virtue a wholly new thing – an inward refining passion of the soul. He taught His people to pray: "O God, make clean our hearts within us." Clean, transparent, pellucid as a hillside spring in which all that is turbid and foul has sunk . . . Who before had suggested to the sin-befouled soul of man such a thought of virtue as this?'

2. Christ's *love* for all mankind: Simpson wrote, 'If the ancients knew love at all, they did not know its universal realm. [Love] that will do anything, and that is recognized as life's first law, . . . dates from Him who has re-created the name of love in the world.'

He explains this last statement in a footnote:

The word 'love' [Gk. *agape*], to us one of the most elevated in the language, had an ancient classic usage of very different reputation, and even in the fourth century, Jerome, writing the Vulgate (in Latin) could not use the ordinary word *amor* to express the Christian grace of love, and had to recourse to the unusual *caritas*. Hence the use of the word 'charity' [instead of 'love'] in our AV [e.g., 1 Corinthians 13].

'Thus', he concludes, 'Jesus introduced *a new concept of love into the world* . . . He was love.'

3. Christ's *forgiveness:* Again from the classics, Simpson shows that forgiveness was a virtue of little value. 'But Jesus made the law of forgiveness operative. [Was it not Jesus who cried],

"Father, forgive them; for they know not what they do"' (Luke 23:34, AV)?

4. Christ's *humility*: Humility is the opposite of self-esteem, self-pride. In some versions of the Bible it is translated, meekness. I prefer meekness. It means strength. It means pity in action. Jesus taught, 'Take my yoke upon you, and learn of me; for I am meek and lowly in heart: and ye shall find rest unto your souls' (*Matt.* 11:29, AV). Today, meekness is virtually unknown among non-christians, and uncommon even among Christians – certainly in the sense that Christ intended by his words 'Blessed are the meek, for they shall inherit the earth' (*Matt.* 5:5).

My father absorbed these four virtues personally. Throughout his life he made them particularly his own. A few days after his death, I happened to meet one of his colleagues: a specialist in venereal diseases, a man certainly not known for his concern for Christian matters. He remarked, 'Your father was the most extraordinary person I have ever met'. He told me that on one occasion he had taken a female patient in the Bristol Royal Infirmary to see ARS for a surgical consultation. He described the woman in lurid terms: an old hag, filthy, smelly and disgusting. 'And yet,' he ended as he turned away, 'Short treated her like a princess.'

As I knew him, meekness was one of my father's most endearing characteristics. He had suffered the lash of words from many sources. Miss Esther Lloyd, who entered our household at about the time of my birth and remained with us as parlour-maid and eventually, after my father's death, as my mother's companion, recalled how he once said to her, 'Remember, Esther, you and I are nothing, we never have been anything, and we never shall be anything.'

Conclusion

I find it very strange that *The Fact of Christ* was so helpful to my father. I think he loved the book because he loved the Saviour and strove to emulate him. He ends his foreword to the 1953 edition: 'The reader must finish it himself. We shall be greatly surprised if he is not a better worshipper as a result of doing so.'

There may have been other reasons ARS so often mentioned *The Fact of Christ* in early sermons. In a career given to contending for the Scriptures mostly on inadequate scientific and historical evidence, Simpson's book helped him to concentrate on the centre of our Faith: the Lord Jesus Christ himself. Yet Christ is only fully knowable as the long-awaited historical Messiah (see *Acts* 17:2–3). Could Simpson's attitude be because nineteenth-century evolutionary science and Higher Criticism had dulled his belief in the authenticity of the early chapters of the Bible? Yet Christ himself frequently quoted the Old Testament (e.g., tellingly in Matthew 19).

Revealingly, Simpson not only ignores the Old Testament, but he also omits reference to the virgin birth, many miraculous episodes in Jesus's life, his death, resurrection and ascension; not to mention all references to him in the rest of the New Testament. And this is not accidental as Simpson reveals on the last page: 'In these lectures I have not argued from the authority of Church or Bible, I have tried to state Christ, who, if He be the truth, is His own authority.'

I believe such an approach enabled my father to bask in less contentious issues for a time. But there are dangers. In fact, if the truth be told, this book distils the essence of Higher Criticism – the idea that something can be spiritually true but historically uncertain at the same time. Liberal scholars, committed to the historical-critical approach to Scripture, now divide the writings of the Bible into '*Heilsgeschichte*' (salvation-history) and '*Historie*' (the actual events that took place and the facts concerning them). 'Salvation-history' indicates the message intended is true even though the events recorded may never have occurred.

The Christ of Simpson's book is revealed only as a great example. The miraculous elements of the gospel are downplayed. Do not misunderstand me. Not for a moment am I minimizing the beauty of Christ's matchless life. The story lifts us – we are indeed 'better worshippers' from contemplating him. But there are great dangers in removing the story from its historical background. Only yesterday, I was told by a Christian friend: 'Why bother about creation? Just stick to Jesus Christ and the essentials of the Faith. Look to Jesus. Preach love and unity. Don't rock the boat.' But is this really enough? After all, where do we find the information about Christ's exemplary life?

* * *

The Younger Brother

The intellectual impasse which had faced ARS was fundamentally a failure to find reconciliation between Christianity and science. They seemed irrevocably opposed. But his reading of Drummond had shown that a compromise might be possible. Then in the *Fact of Christ* he found spiritual strengthening. Now the time had come to consider in further detail the scientific problems which worried Christians. I have no doubt that he searched for books to help. But he found none. In 1913 they didn't exist.

However, this was only part of a greater lack. The Brethren are a non-confessional church. That is, they possess no written manual of doctrine and practice, comparable to, say, the Westminster Confession of Faith of the Presbyterian churches. It was in an endeavour to fill this gap that ARS decided to write a small book. It was entitled, *The Principles of Christians called the 'Open Brethren'*,[1] and was published in 1913. He arranged for it to be printed anonymously, preferring to sign it, 'A Younger Brother'.

Mostly it is concerned with church matters, but the book contains an important chapter entitled, 'Problems of Inspiration'. This might well have been called, 'Scientific difficulties in Genesis.' This chapter seems out of place in a book of this type, being more a highly personal *credo* of a thirty-three-year-old academic, than an authoritative statement of Open Brethren beliefs. ARS, however, may well have regarded it as the most important chapter in the whole book.

By now he was well qualified to write on the vexed topic of science and the Bible. But such a hot topic as science could cause problems with the church hierarchy, and it may perhaps have been this reason, rather than modesty, which decided him not to reveal his true identity.

[1] *The Principles of Christians called the 'Open Brethren'* by A Younger Brother (Glasgow: Pickering and Inglis, 1913).

Be that as it may, the biblical/scientific section provides us with a valuable insight into my father's views at the time. We also find that this chapter was particularly addressed to younger Christians.

ARS held strong views on Noah's flood, which he believed could not have been worldwide (see Appendix 2). This is a topic on which he has frequently been quoted. He wrote:

Some years ago the Deluge might have been adduced as a difficulty, but a very ordinary acquaintance with geology, or even with geography, will convince anyone that the flooding of an immense area is one of the common-places of our world's history.

He cites evidence of widespread flooding from the Middle East, England and even mentions Naples. (A contemporary prayer-list shows that he was still very interested in that city.) From this evidence he concluded that, 'the area submerged in the Noachian Deluge included no more than the *then-known* world' .

According to the 'Younger Brother', the main scientific problems in Scripture cluster around 'the origin of the world and of the human race.' In a passage with obvious autobiographical overtones, he continues, 'It is highly unfortunate that nearly all defenders of the Bible . . . lack scientific training, and thereby stumble young Christians who have had scientific training.' He complains that the apologetics advanced by these teachers is often '. . . full of misstatements of well-ascertained facts of science.' How much I agree! Many times I have cringed when listening to some well-meaning but scientifically naive Christian explain to an evolutionist a speculative idea which has confirmed his own faith, but which is scientifically most improbable.

Near the end of the chapter there is a passage which gives some inkling of my father's mental and spiritual struggle at this time; a struggle which was to continue unabated until the year of his death:

When we who have been taught that the Scriptures are inspired from cover to cover come into real touch . . . with evolutionary and other doctrines of the biological and anthropological sciences, we are strongly tempted to jump to the conclusion that the whole Bible is shaken from its throne. The scientific facts and theories are put before us in dogmatic form, as established truths . . . we see the force of their illustrations, and can not escape the grip of their logic. So we think they are all right, and the Christian revelation must be all wrong.'

What help could he offer his readers? Only to appeal to 'some of the very princes of science [who] have found it possible to be earnest Christians and believers in the Word of God. We recall with pride . . .'. Observe carefully the only three names he lists:

The incomparable Lord Kelvin, mathematician, physicist and humble man of God. No one can quibble at his right to be included;

James Dana (1813–1895), Professor of Geology at Yale University, who although an orthodox Christian is said to have boasted that he had made Yale a stronghold of evolutionary science to 'correct the false dogma of the theological systems.' Today we would call him a militant theistic evolutionist;

And 'even G. Romanes, the zoologist, in the evening of his days'.

So at that time (1913), my father was unable to point to any scientific evidence refuting the Darwinian theory, or to name any contemporary scientist who held to a creationist position.

Failing firm evidence, he can only beg for perseverance and humility. 'After five to ten years of study and research into the underlying facts, when we begin to think for ourselves and teach others, we find that around every island of knowledge there is a wide ocean of ignorance . . ., all science is edged with mystery . . . Truth can always afford to wait. The quest is not in vain. "In the latter days you will understand" ' (*Jer.* 23:20).

At the end of the chapter the 'Younger Brother' lists his references. They comprise:

Three old masterpieces by Bishop Westcott: *The Bible in the Church; Introduction to the Study of the Gospels; History of the Canon of the New Testament.*

A critical analysis of the Old Testament by James Orr.

An introduction to the New Testament, by Salmon.

The Philosophy of the Plan of Salvation by an American ex-sceptic [anon.].

You notice there is nothing of a scientific nature. My father was a lonely voice crying in a very dry place. Darwin stood victorious.

18

SURGEON AND TEACHER

My father lived two public lives. By saying this I do not wish to imply that he separated his Christian profession from his practice of medicine. On the contrary, these two major interests were fully integrated. ARS lived a full life as a medical man, but also had a ministry as a Christian, often speaking at two or three meetings in a week. This duality was recognized by Dr Martyn Lloyd-Jones in the 1974 Annual Rendle Short Memorial Lecture to the Christian Medical Fellowship. Lloyd-Jones commenced, 'Rendle Short was known as a Christian doctor. This is now a fairly common term, but thirty, forty, fifty years ago it was uncommon. There were two men, Rendle Short in this country, and Dr Howard Kelly in America, who were known in religious circles as Christian doctors.'[1]

ARS was also a rarity among doctors, and especially among surgeons, in that he had a profound knowledge of physiology. More commonly the road to surgery lies via anatomy.[2] But he early appreciated the importance of physiology to his chosen specialty. The first textbook he wrote was entitled *The New Physiology in Surgical and General Practice*. It was published in 1911 by John Wright and Sons of Bristol, and went to five editions. Lectures on physiology given at the University of

[1]Martyn Lloyd-Jones, 'Annual Rendle Short Memorial Lecture', Christian Medical Fellowship, 1974. Audio tape distributed by The Martyn Lloyd-Jones Recording Trust, Barcombe Mills, East Sussex.
[2]As a broad generalization, a surgeon is more concerned with the anatomical position and structure of the various parts of the body, rather than the physiology, that is, the science of the normal (or abnormal) function of the body.

Bristol later formed the basis of *A Synopsis of Physiology*.[1]

In February 1914 ARS combined his interest in physiology with surgery when he was appointed to lecture as Hunterian Professor before the Royal College of Surgeons, London, on 'Surgical Shock', a topic which was to assume great significance during the two World Wars.

From 1914 to 1917, while most of his colleagues were in France, ARS accepted a punishing surgical workload to keep the Bristol hospitals functioning. His iron constitution enabled him to see out-patients and in-patients, and to operate for long hours both day and night. He did the same during the Second World War, especially at the time of the Bristol blitzes. He confided in me that he was able to operate continuously, without sleep, for three days, and up to two nights, but that he must have rest on the third night. He records that at one period in 1916 he performed fifty-four operations during a period of three successive days.

In 1917 ARS was posted to France, while a fellow surgeon took over from him in Bristol. He worked mainly in Casualty Clearing Stations just behind the allied lines. Here he continued his research into surgical shock and gave the first blood transfusions ever performed in the front line. By the sophisticated standards of today, it was a crude performance. Knowledge of blood groups was rudimentary, and severe reactions common. Needles were bulky and blunt. It happened that I commanded a small Blood Transfusion Unit in Burma during the Second World War, and later worked in Siam, at Kamburi, near the infamous bridge over the river Kwai. The needles we used then were little better than they had been in my father's day. They had to be sterilized by boiling and sharpened again and again. During my father's early days in France, the donor and recipient were positioned side by side, and blood syringed direct from donor to patient. In the 1940s we had rubber tubing, but inadequate facilities for cleaning and sterilization meant that infection and fever often followed.

In France, sandwiched between days of hectic drama, were periods of supreme boredom. My father was fortunate to meet a fellow doctor who was an excellent ornithologist. In lulls

---

[1] A. Rendle Short and C. I. Ham, *A Synopsis of Physiology* (Bristol: John Wright and Sons, 1927).

between battles, they would walk and cycle the Flanders countryside, during which ARS learnt to recognise birds by their song. This skill gave him great pleasure throughout his life. On country walks he would stop and ask me, 'Do you hear that willow warbler . . .?' or whatever the bird might be. When I replied 'No', he would say, 'I'll lift my stick next time it sings.' A young lady walking with us, once asked, 'What bird is that?' She borrowed the stick to indicate when it next sang. 'That, my dear,' he answered gently, 'is a sparrow.'

Return to Civilian Life

After the 1918 armistice, ARS returned to Bristol, and resumed a busy round of activity which persisted until long after he retired. An early memory I have is of him eating hasty meals with his gold watch and chain propped up in front of him. In 1920, surgical work in the public hospitals, a growing private practice, with an especial interest in acute appendicitis coupled with his love of medical history, formed the basis of a paper on 'The Causation of Appendicitis'.[1] He wrote:

The facts with regard to the history of appendicitis and its racial distribution are so clearly defined and unusual, and the disease is so common and plays such an important part in modern surgery, that it is passing strange that we have come to no settled conclusion as to its causation.

The problem looks so simple. When a disease leaps into extreme prominence within a decade or two, becomes an everyday occurrence in the hospitals of certain more civilized countries, and leaves the rest of the world alone, surely the riddle of its causation should not be hard to read. Yet it has proved so.

ARS was impressed by the steep rise in incidence of the disease at the beginning of the twentieth century. He reviewed the historical and geographical data, compared the cases in developed and underdeveloped countries, and, with the help of the Bristol Zoological Gardens, observed that even apes in captivity sometimes suffered from appendicitis. (Although he acknowledged that his comparative figures for animals in the

[1]A. Rendle Short, 'The Causation of Appendicitis' (1920), *British Journal of Surgery*, **8**, 171. Also a book of the same title published by John Wright and Sons, Bristol, 1946.

wild were sketchy!) This data he compared with the changing patterns of diet. Finally he concluded that 'the main cause of appendicitis is the removal of much of the cellulose [or fibre] content of our food.'

Soon after the close of the Second World War, his friend Dr Douglas Johnson drew Dr Denis Burkitt's attention to the article.[1] Dr Burkitt, FRS, who as a missionary surgeon in Uganda had previously risen to fame by his research into the Burkitt tumour in Uganda, immediately became interested. In an article written in 1971, he states that it was Rendle Short's seminal observation which stimulated him to begin his own research into the medical importance of fibre in food.[2] Thus it is no exaggeration to say that an article written by my father on the aetiology of appendicitis in 1920 provided the impetus for research which has revolutionized the food habits of the Western world to the present day.[3]

Surgical Practice

Over the years, my father developed a considerable private practice which took him all over the West of England. With a newly acquired driving licence it was often my delight to drive him into the country to see patients. My father did not like driving. He had come to it too late. A medical student whom he was taking to assist him at an operating session in Weston-Super-Mare during the Second World War told me he drove the twenty miles entirely in second gear, because, he said, 'I have better control of the car that way.'

We travelled faster when I was driving. Sometimes he would say as we started out, 'Don't let grass grow under your feet.' This was the signal that a surgical emergency awaited him. Occasionally we would return to Bristol with the patient in the back of the car for immediate operation. It was quicker than sending for an ambulance. In particular I remember a hazardous winter journey of about 150 miles from Bristol to Bude in 1941. For many years ARS was surgeon to Clifton

---

[1]Douglas Johnson, personal communication (March 1976).
[2]Denis P. Burkitt, 'The Aetiology of Appendicitis' (1971), *British Journal of Surgery*, **58**, 695.
[3]Science Report, 'Role of appendix in fighting infection' (1986), *The Times*, April 22.

College, and the school had been evacuated to Bude during the war. On this occasion we had to return after blackout time. There were no street lights, and car lighting was reduced to about the equivalent of today's side lights. Much of the road was hilly and winding. Fortunately there was almost no traffic at that time of night. The journey was punctuated by the groans of a Clifton College boy suffering from acute appendicitis on the back seat. It was because of these occasional high speed dashes that my father purchased a large Humber limousine, quite a spacious and fast car in those days.

Fast driving in icy conditions could be dangerous. I must say I loved it. Unknown to my parents I would take the car out on frosty days to practise skidding. I learned how to control a back-wheel skid by driving into the direction of the skid. My ambition was to skid the car round 180 degrees on a narrow road without hitting the curb. I never succeeded. This was before the idea of using the hand-brake for the exercise had been thought of.

Rain and fog presented another peril. In the winter we would set out with hot-water bottles on our knees and rugs for our feet. There were no car heaters in those days.

One night on Foss Way in Gloucestershire – the straight old Roman road – when visibility was poor, we suddenly came upon the rear of an elephant. It was the back member of a circus trudging through the sleet. Someone had thoughtfully tied a lantern to its tail, but it had gone out.

There was beauty, too. One perfect January day during the war years, when petrol was rationed and country trips a rarity, my father was called to see an elderly gentleman in a lovely eighteenth century country house in the Cotswolds. Usually, on such occasions I masqueraded as the chauffeur and waited in the car. But that day it was bitterly cold, and the lady of the house kindly invited me to wait inside. She took me into a beautifully appointed upstairs drawing room. As I looked out of the window at the blue sky, with crisp white snow and pendants of ice, sparkling like a chandelier from the bare branches, the lady told me how, a few days previously, there had been the crack of a gun, and a wounded pheasant fluttered down onto the snow-covered lawn. The tranquil scene was spoiled by the convulsions of the dying bird and the spreading red carpet on the snow. She went out to remove it, then returned to gaze out of the window. But, so she told me, the beauty was destroyed. True, the bird had gone, and the blood-stains covered, but the track of feet to and fro and the tramped snow still told their story of lingering death. But last night it had snowed again, and as I looked down, the marks were totally obliterated. Death might never have intruded.

My father was considered a fine surgeon. His small, strong hands enabled him to explore crevices in the body inaccessible to other operators. He was fastidious with his hands, and well aware of their value. For example, although he knew the Latin name of the flowers in the hedgerows and his garden, his practical gardening skill was confined to nipping an occasional dead rose off a bush. He would hold out his hands to each new group of medical students and tell them, 'These hands have not touched pus for . . . [whatever the current figure might be] . . . years.' He told them to visit the hospital chapel, which had been founded in the eighteenth century, and look at the plaques in memory of the doctors and nurses who had died of infection contracted from their patients. This was in 1941 before penicillin and other modern antibiotics were freely available. He never carried an insurance on his life, but his hands were well insured. 'If my hands are damaged, I lose my surgical livelihood', he said. But it was as a diagnostician that he earned especial fame. Presented with conflicting evidence, he prided himself on his ability to weigh the pros and cons. 'I don't mind who does the operation,' he once remarked, 'as long as I make the diagnosis.'

The Professor of Surgery

As a teacher of the didactic style, ARS was pre-eminent. His weekly 'surgical grinds', held uncomfortably in the museum of the Bristol Royal Infirmary, were a 'must' for all students in the Bristol medical school. They were freely laced with memorable anecdotes, delivered with dry humour, and prefaced with 'I well remember on one occasion'. Often he would dictate notes: 'Start a new line . . .'.

At the bedside he was a master of the Socratic method of teaching, based on the question and answer method. He also used this form of teaching in discussions at Christian student conferences. In his biography of Dr Lloyd-Jones, Iain Murray recounts that in the IVF Conferences in 1940–1941 informal discussion groups were held on such topics as, 'The Biblical Doctrine of the Fall', and 'How Should We Combat the Spirit of the Age?'. These meetings were chaired by Lloyd-Jones, but, Murray continues:

It is noteworthy that the influence of the medical men was strong in all these conferences; the 'chiefs' Blair[1] and Rendle Short were there . . . and Douglas Johnson,[2] holding his usual place in the background, was also always present. The informal 'meetings' were invariably led by the medical men, introducing the students to the Socratic method of questioning to which they had become accustomed in student days. In handling this form of instruction and debate, Lloyd-Jones was the only minister who could match the two 'chiefs'. There was no experience in the normal ministerial training which resembled the grilling which a medical professor's students were put through on ward rounds, and sometimes it was the other conference speakers (as well as the students) who were shaken by the interrogation involved in this method.[3]

How I wish I had been present at these battles of the giants!

As with all doctors in those days, ARS never charged a fee to fellow doctors, medical students or nurses. In addition he also included missionaries, clergy of any of the main-line denominations, and many others whom he sensed to be in financial need. To some he took a Robin Hood approach. His consulting room was in his study in our home, the patients waiting in the dining room where copies of *The Illustrated London News* and *Punch* would be placed on the long mahogany table. We children were warned to keep out of the way. Sometimes we watched the action by hanging over the banisters. When I was older, my father would occasionally ask, as a patient drove away, 'What sort of a car was that?' Or, to a female member of the

[1]Duncan McCullum Blair (1896–1994) was formerly Professor of Anatomy at King's College, London, and later Regius Professor of Anatomy at Glasgow. Described by Lloyd-Jones as 'a truly giant speaker', he was one of the very few academics to appear on the platform of the IVF in those days.

[2]Douglas Johnson (1904–1992) was General Secretary of the IVF for fifteen years. An indefatigable organizer in the background, he would, however, never appear on the platform, or even if he could help it, in official photographs.

[3]Iain H. Murray, *D. Martyn Lloyd-Jones: The Fight of Faith 1939–1981*, p. 69.

household, 'Was that fur coat real mink, or just rabbit?' But usually he took the advice of the referring General Practitioner in deciding the fee.

*   *   *

The Inter-Varsity Christian Fellowship

It was soon after World War I that my father developed an interest in Christian work in the universities. As a student, he had been a member of the Student Christian Movement. But that organisation, although commencing with evangelical zeal, succumbed after only a few generations, to Darwinism and Higher Criticism. By 1920 its creed was unabashed liberalism.

It was with a heavy heart that ARS witnessed the apostasy of an organisation which had once helped him so much. But now, with others, he recognised the need for a new, conservative witness in the universities. And slowly, one by one, all over the country, there arose small evangelical unions. My father assisted in the beginnings at Bristol, Exeter, Glasgow and some others. These groups, and others, later banded together to form what was to become the Inter-Varsity Fellowship of Evangelical Unions (IVF). Twice he became president, and for many years he was one of the senior treasurers. Until the end of his life he was in demand as a speaker at University Evangelical Unions all over the British Isles; so much so that he was affectionately known as 'The Senior Travelling Rep.'

'Dings'

My father's Christian interests were by no means confined to instructing fellow doctors and sophisticated university students. In 1912 he had been asked to take charge of a Bible school in the Shaftesbury Workman's Institute, known later as The Shaftesbury Crusade, or more affectionately, 'The Dings'. This was situated in the centre of Bristol, near Temple Meads station. The work grew strikingly to a weekly attendance of between forty and fifty. My father conducted the school himself about thirty weeks in the year, visiting speakers being found for the other meetings. The regular leader always had a spare talk in his pocket in the event of a last minute phone call from ARS to say he had been delayed by some urgent surgical case.

My father loved 'my men', as he called them, many of whom were old or unemployed. After a hymn, prayer and Bible reading, he would expound some passage of Scripture in an informal, conversational manner. Questions, comment and humour were welcomed. His method was to take a Bible book or subject and devote several evenings to a discussion on it. He was frequently amazed at the depth of knowledge and biblical insight shown by men who, in the eyes of the world, were uneducated, even illiterate. The Holy Spirit seemed able to use the 'Old Book' to instruct them. Unfamiliar words like 'salvation', 'propitiation', 'justification', or 'sanctification' had to be explained and, if important, the meaning learned. This seemed to present no insurmountable problem to men thirsty for knowledge. Sometimes when he went to speak on a Thursday night my father was told that one of the men was ill. If possible he would visit the sick man after the class. With only unavoidable absences he continued conducting the 'Dings' Bible School until his death in 1953.

ARS had a great love for the Word of God. He had learned Greek at school and taught himself Hebrew. His prodigious memory enabled him to give chapter and verse for almost any passage quoted to him. Added to this was a knowledge of theology and church history, particularly the Reformation. The last time I heard him speak in public was at a lecture for the British and Foreign Bible Society.

19

WAITING FOR LIGHT

Not until he was forty-four did ARS feel free to speak publicly on the subject of creation and evolution. True, he had written incidentally on the topic as 'A Younger Brother' in 1913, but that was over ten years before. The scientific and theological world had changed greatly since then, and his personal views, matured by the horrors of war in the trenches, had matured too. (In parenthesis, I add that my father never referred to those dark days except to tell with delight of 'bird song walks'.)

The forum he chose for this lecture was the 1924 annual IVF conference in Swanwick, Derbyshire. I have his sermon notes before me, written in legible handwriting on the back of 'A Notice of Meeting' of the Clinical Board of the Bristol Royal Infirmary. The notes are markedly fuller than those he used in later days. There are several alterations, in one place a flat contradiction and a polemical note is detectable. The title of his address was 'Genesis and Geology'. The notes commence:

One man's meat is another man's poison. Therefore I have been silent till lately – publicly.

Those who deal with this subject usually fall into one of two classes. They say –

(a) 'Of course, it's part of the Bible; world and everything created 4004 B.C. in six days, so if science and archaeology don't agree with this interpretation, scientists and archaeologists are all a pack of liars.' Well, I won't discuss that attitude.

For you, charges of wholesale lying may be satisfying, for me – for many of us – they aren't. My whole education discounts that idea. (Here he mentioned his training in Geology, culminating in a BSc.)

They may have interpreted their facts wrongly; perhaps you may have interpreted your Genesis wrongly.

(b) 'Modern discovery absolutely contradicts Genesis, so Genesis must be only a myth.'

At this point, ARS digressed to discuss Higher Critical theories, such as the Documentary Hypothesis of the Pentateuch, concluding this section with the exclamation: 'No, thank you. I'm not following. I think, if it were not such a technical subject I could direct you to important reasons for refuting the P theory.'

Having thus disposed of contrary arguments, ARS stated his own position frankly:

I accept Genesis as the inspired word of God –
(i) All documentary evidence shows that it is part of the Bible, & the Bible, taken as a whole, bears obvious marks, in its unity, moral power, prophecy, of divine authorship.
(ii) Christ accepted & quotes from Genesis. See Mk. 10:6, 7. Christ must be intellectual King as well as Moral King; 'Full of grace & truth.' If you are wrong re Genesis, how right re *God, salvation & eternal life?*
(iii) The Fall. *An impasse.* Lots of problems in science bring us face to face with seemingly irreconcilable facts. *We can only wait patiently,* comforting ourselves that perhaps traditional theology has not been free from mistakes in interpreting Genesis; or science & archaeology in interpreting their facts. *No final solution possible today.* (my italics)

Having come to a conclusion essentially similar to that in his 1913 book, ARS proceeded to provide 'some temporary suggestions for alleviation of the present apparent clash'.

His first suggestion was negative: 'Not to teach science.' By this he meant that the Bible was not a scientific textbook and therefore Christians without qualifications should not attempt to teach something they know little about.

His second suggestion was positive, namely that the Bible was given, 'To teach One Creator God.'

Then comes a spell of confusion. ARS lists 'Some remarkable confirmations of the Genesis story.' But the original list – five lines of them – are all crossed out! More strangely still, some of them, such as: 'The age of the fossils; of animals; of man,' are repeated later on the bottom of the last page, under the heading, 'Difficulties!' A new list of 'Confirmations' is given later.

Alternative suggestions are provided, for example: 'Catastrophe Theory [the Gap theory]. Some of us don't think it the best.' [However], 'Will serve for those who know no science.' But this too is crossed out.

Several more suggestions are proposed only to be crossed out, until we come to a strange entry: 'Palaeolithic Adam Theory. Cainan, son of Arphaxad. Gen. 11:12; Lk 3:36.' The notes go on, 'Please don't attach too much importance to these speculations. I am not advocating a theory – only trying to show that a clash is not inevitable – *a little more light & we shall be clear about it.*' (my italics)

The sermon ends with: 'Confirmations: The Genesis record and geology. Day = Period of time (proposed by Dana, Dawson). Origin of man from one pair. Mesopotamia. The flood . . .' 'Difficulties: The age of fossils – of animals – of man. Godless theory of evolution by natural selection.' ARS concludes with a plea for: '*Concessions each side.*' 'Sorts of dog, wolf, fox etc.';

'Natural selection inadequate. A Divine Supervisor necessary. Special creation of man: mind, spirit.' (Not however, *body,* mind and spirit.)

* * *

What do you make of all this?

I see a man squeezed between a rock and a hard place. He was steeped in physiology and geology, yet on the other hand he retained a deep reverence and love for the Word of God. Nowhere else in his writings, sermons, or in my personal memory of conversation with him, do I ever remember him so irresolute. It is almost as though he had met some persuasive academic in the train journey to Derbyshire and altered his notes at the last minute.

Review

Let me bring together some strands of my father's thoughts as they appeared in 1924. That he remained shaken by the evolution/creation conflict is obvious. Darwinism was still triumphant. Yet he was prepared to say, 'I accept Genesis as the inspired word of God.' He called the Fall, 'An Impasse', which, of course it must be to anyone who tries to equate millions of years of 'Nature red in tooth and claw' with an earth created *good* by a loving God in six days.

Lastly, my father's closing comment – 'Natural selection inadequate. A Divine Supervisor necessary. Special creation of man: mind, spirit.' – shows that he was still assuming a dichotomy between man's body which evolved, and his mind, or spirit which was specially created in the image of God. This idea had first been proposed toward the end of the nineteenth century.

Meanwhile, all he could do was to hope for more evidence, and accept by faith what little light he had. Patiently he waited for an answer.

Other Interests

After what I think we must call the debacle of 1924, my father seems to have heeded St Paul's dictum, 'If the trumpet makes an uncertain sound, who shall prepare himself for battle?' (*1 Cor.* 14:8). While waiting for 'a little more light' on the Bible and science he temporarily dropped the topic. Meanwhile, he discovered a new interest. Some years later, while browsing among books in the Medical Library of Bristol University, he found on an obscure shelf, an old volume, *The Medical Language of St. Luke* (1882) by W. K. Hobart. He writes:

I knew enough Greek to be able to follow it. It was a convincing demonstration, derived from a close comparison of the language of the author of the fourth gospel and the Acts of the Apostles, with that of Greek medical writers, Hippocrates, Galen, [and others] that whoever wrote these two books of the New Testament was a medical man. He uses twenty-three technical medical expressions not found in the other New Testament writers. Four of these, diagnosis, dysentery, thrombi, syndrome have been taken over into modern medical English. All this started me off on a line of study with eminently satisfactory results, confirming the reliability and date of the four Gospels.

Some time later in a second-hand book store, he found

another book which fascinated him. I have his copy here before me; he often referred to it in sermons. It was entitled, *The Voyage and Shipwreck of St Paul* by James Smith, first published in 1848.[1]

Smith, a man of wealth, was an ardent yachtsman and amateur geologist, much encouraged by Lyell. Owing to the poor health of members of his family, he lived for some years in Malta. There he researched his *magnum opus*. According to the prologue of the fourth edition published in 1880, a copy my father obtained, Smith died in 1867, 'in full possession of his faculties and in humble yet firm trust on "Jesus Christ alone"'.

My father's interest in St Luke stimulated him to move to other apologetic topics, resulting in a whole succession of books: *The Historic Faith in the Light of Today.* 1922; *The Bible and Modern Research*, 2nd edition 1933; *Modern Discovery and the Bible*, 1942, eight editions and reprints, the last in 1957; *Archaeology gives Evidence*, 1951; *Wonderfully Made*, 1951; *The Bible and Modern Medicine*, 1953; *Why Believe?* 1938, 5th edition 1951; *The Rock Beneath*, 1955, a posthumous collection of writings. In addition there was a book on Isaiah and an abbreviated biography on George Müller. On physiological and surgical topics he wrote five books. In addition, from 1919 to the end of his life he was surgical editor of the *Medical Annual*, with Sir Letherby Tidy as the medical editor. He also published articles in surgical and religious journals.

When you take into account regular University teaching; membership of the Medical School Faculty Board, and University Senate; long operating sessions on public and private patients; preaching at least twice per week in Bristol, and throughout Great Britain; eldership of the local church – the wonder is that he managed to fit it all in! I think the key lies in his phenomenal memory, and meticulous timing. He never seemed to waste a moment, and was almost never sick.

Although he rarely travelled overseas, his influence extended worldwide. Ten years after his death, and only a few months after I had arrived in Brisbane, I was invited to visit the University of Sydney. On the way in I was introduced to the

---

[1]James Smith, FRS, *The Voyage and Shipwreck of St Paul: With a Dissertation on the Life and Writings of St Luke, and the Ships and Navigation of the Ancients* (London: Longmans, Green, 1880).

porter at the gate. He seemed surprised to meet me, and remarked, 'That's a very famous name, Sir'. Not infrequently in Christian circles I am thanked for writing some book. I always enquire which one: usually I find I am being credited with one of my father's.

Modern Discovery and the Bible[1]

This book was first published in 1942. Since it became so popular, and reflects my father's mature views, I have selected it for more detailed study. In the Prologue, he wrote:

The reasons Christians hold their faith in God, and in Jesus Christ and in the Bible, are quite remote from the type of evidence discussed in this book. There were believing Christians long before any of our modern discoveries were made. The Hebrew prophets and the New Testament missionaries did not argue that there must be a God from the facts of science or history, or at least this argument is only sparingly used. Paul does say that 'the invisible things of Him from the creation of the world are clearly seen being perceived through the things that are made, even His everlasting power and divinity' (*Rom.* 1:20). But the writer to the Hebrews declares that it is 'by faith we understand that the worlds have been framed by the word of God'; he does not argue that the earth, sun and stars prove that there must be a divine Creator (*Heb.* 11:3). Jesus Christ quietly assumes that His hearers will believe in God and the life to come, and His teaching is on that basis. The knowledge of Himself, He says, is a divine revelation to the soul (*Matt.* 16:17). But many men and women with a modern education shrink back from the call.

ARS lists a number of questions he was often asked by enquirers: 'If I come to believe in God', they think almost subconsciously, 'will not modern science confront my faith, and say, "I can disprove that he ever existed"?'

'If I accept Jesus Christ as Lord of my thinking, will he not require me to accept as true a book, the Bible, which I have been taught to regard as wholly contradicted by geology, biology, history, archaeology, literary analysis, and I know not what other branches of knowledge?'

'Has not modern learning gone over almost entirely into the other camp?'

'Will not Christian faith lead eventually, either into an

[1]A. Rendle Short, *Modern Discovery and the Bible* (London: Inter-Varsity Press, 1942).

intellectual impasse, or into obscurantism – a compulsion to shut the eyes to unpleasant opposing facts for the sake of maintaining a theory?'

It is on grounds such as these, ARS suggests, that many hold back from committing their lives to Christ. And it is this type of argument, I suggest, which is still advanced today against those who accept the Bible in its natural sense with a six-day creation and a young earth. Such people are told, 'Your old- fashioned views put people off.' 'Who would ever become a Christian if it requires belief in such rubbish?' 'Don't rock the boat.' Or, 'Teaching like that is anti-evangelistic. You are putting a stumbling block in the way of young, thinking people.' And so on.

ARS continues:

Modern research bearing on the Bible has wandered into many fields, so far removed from one another, that it may well be asked . . . what possible qualifications a mere surgeon, or indeed any one person, can possess to write on subjects so many and various. The last thing in the world we claim is to write with any personal authority about the subject of any chapter in this book. But if we are to read books only by experts, we shall have to find them by the score, one or two for each subject, and that is difficult. The hope is that what follows may save the reader some of the labour. We are not concerned to argue that natural science, archaeology or any other branch of learning *proves* the facts of the Christian religion, but only that it does not necessarily disprove them.

He ends the Prologue, *'Happily, the years to come are likely to bring yet more evidence to light.* Rightly and fairly interpreted, it can but strengthen what is true in our beliefs, and winnow out the false.' (my italics)

In *Modern Discovery*, ARS refers to a number of contemporary writers. For example, [Sir] Fred. Hoyle, who at that time was still advocating the 'Steady State' theory. Later he was to abandon this in favour of the 'Big Bang' theory.[1]

He also quotes Dr Albert Einstein,[2] 'greatest of living scientists', who wrote:

[1]As I write the Big Bang is also considered suspect.

[2]Hawking, a noted evolutionist, writes of Einstein that he objected very strongly to the introduction of 'an unavoidable element of unpredictability or randomness into science . . . Einstein never accepted that the universe was governed by chance; his feeling was summed up by his famous statement "God does not place dice."' Stephen W. Hawking, *A Brief History of Time* (London: Bantam Books, 1991), p. 60.

My religion consists of a humble admiration of the illumination of the superior Spirit Who reveals Himself in the slight details we are able to perceive with our frail and feeble minds. That deeply emotional conviction of the presence of a superior reasoning power, which is revealed in the incomprehensible universe, forms my idea of God.

Referring to agnostic scientists, ARS suggests they may ask: 'Why not concentrate attention on the ordinary and well understood? Why worry about origins?' To which we reply that, as Pasteur pointed out long ago, it is by the study of the unexpected, and the exceptional, that progress in understanding nature has been made. M. Becquerel found that radium carried in his waistcoat pocket burnt his skin. That observation opened up the whole field of radiotherapy.

With the professional interest and expertise of a biologist ARS devotes considerable space to the origin of life, and particularly to the idea that life evolved from some primordial slime. But even in those days, there were those who doubted. For instance Dr J. Gray, a leading experimental zoologist, giving the presidential address to the zoological section of the British Association in 1933, took as his theme the mechanical origin of life, and decided against it. He said,

The spontaneous origin of living from inanimate matter must be regarded as a highly improbable event, and as such can be assumed not to have occurred.

We conclude, then that science is unable to put forward any satisfactory explanation as to how life arose in the first place. We must therefore accept the Bible doctrine that God created life, or go on making improbable speculations.

Fifty more years of experimental science has amply confirmed that view. In fact the findings of modern molecular biology have shown that the spontaneous origin of life is virtually impossible. In *Evolution: a Theory in Crisis*[1] (1985), a molecular biologist Michael Denton describes something of what is now known about the simple cell: 'Perhaps in no other area of modern biology is the challenge posed by the extreme complexity and ingenuity of biological adaptation more apparent than in the fascinating new world of the cell.'

[1]Michael Denton, *Evolution: a Theory in Crisis* (Bethesda, USA: Alder and Alder, 1985).

Denton concludes his book:

The influence of evolutionary theory on fields far removed from biology is one of the most spectacular examples in history of how a highly speculative idea for which there is no really hard scientific evidence can come to fashion the thinking of a whole society and dominate the outlook of an age . . . One might have hoped that the Darwinian theory was capable of a completely comprehensive, and entirely plausible explanation for all biological phenomena from the origin of life, on through all its diverse manifestations up to, and including the intellect of man. That it is neither fully plausible, nor comprehensive, is deeply troubling . . . [One might have expected that] a theory that has literally changed the world, would have been something more than metaphysics, more than a myth.

Ultimately, the Darwinian theory of evolution is no more or less than the great cosmogonic myth of the twentieth century.

David Attenborough's fascinating television pictures of the life of animals and plants has wonderfully confirmed Denton's assessment of Darwinian evolution. (I say 'pictures' because the script of these films is, as might be expected, freely laced with atheistic evolutionary jargon, which fits ill with what our eyes are actually observing.)

* * *

Micro- and Macro-evolution

In *Modern Discovery and the Bible* ARS gave his views on the origin of species:

Let us make it plain at the outset that we are not disposed to argue that species, or genera, were created at the beginning exactly as they are now, and that no changes or variations have taken place. It seems that large variations have as a matter of fact occurred. It is very likely indeed that the lion, the tiger and the wild cat all came from one stock. Also the thrush, the missel-thrush and . . .

[With his love of birds, my father then devoted a whole page to further examples (!) and concludes] Having conceded so much, let us add we do not believe Natural Selection is an adequate explanation for the origin of species.

With the above I entirely agree. Let me sum up this passage: While not using the actual words, it is apparent my father believed in what today we call 'microevolution', but not in 'macroevolution.' I can explain these terms as follows: Micro-evolution is illustrated by the changes commonly seen in breeding animals or plants, whereas macroevolution is the idea that one type or species can evolve into another quite different one: cows to whales; ape-like creatures to man, and so on.

In 1980, the journal *Science*,[1] under the heading *Evolutionary Theory under Fire*, reported that, 'An historic conference in Chicago challenges the four-decade long dominance of the Modern Synthesis.' The article commences:

Overheard at breakfast on the final day of a recent scientific meeting: 'Do you believe in macroevolution?' Came the reply: 'Well, it depends how you define it.'

[Later, the reporter concludes], the central question at the Chicago conference was whether the mechanisms underlying *microevolution* can be extrapolated to explain the phenomena of *macroevolution*. [This was essentially Darwin's contention. He experimented with breeding pigeons.] At the risk of doing violence to the positions of some of the people at the meeting, the answer can be given as a clear 'No'. (my italics)

In a later chapter of *Modern Discovery and the Bible*, ARS probed further into the problem of man's origin. Most of his material is long outdated. For example, he gave careful consideration to Piltdown man, which he regarded as probably the most important 'missing link' ever found. But he did suggest that 'There is no proof that the skull and the jaw came from the same creature.'

In the 1957 edition of the book, published after his death, the publishers appended a footnote: 'This warning is now seen to be fully justified. In the *Geology Bulletin* . . . Weiner and Oakley, "reach the conclusion that the jaw [of Piltdown man] was that of a modern ape which had been faked to give the appearance of great age."' In fact the skull was later found to be that of a modern man. But this discovery was first publicised in December 1953. My father had died in September 1953.

The Danger of Incorrect Scientific Evidence

Scientific evidence which is later proved to be false can be

[1]'Research News', *Science*, November 1980.

highly destructive to faith. Not only if it refutes Scripture, but perhaps even more so if at first sight it, wrongly, seems to support it. In his books and some sermons, ARS makes much of a 1929 discovery by Sir Leonard Woolley. While excavating in Ur of the Chaldees, Woolley found 'a layer, eight feet thick of water-laid clay, evidently deposited by a deluge of stupendous proportions.' Woolley believed no ordinary flood could have given rise to such a deposit which had obviously cut off the previous culture. ARS quotes Woolley as saying, 'There could be no doubt that the flood was the flood of Sumerian history and legend, the flood on which is based the story of Noah.'

Confirmation was soon forthcoming. A few days later Professor Langden announced that he had made exactly the same discovery at Kish, hundreds of miles away. Langden wrote, 'When we made these observations two months ago we were loth to believe that we had obtained confirmation of the Deluge of Genesis, but there is no doubt of it now.'

ARS accepted that both these reports referred to Noah's Flood. But he considered that, although they described an inundation of 'stupendous size', there was no reason to believe that it was more than local in extent. So he concludes:

If it were reasonable to interpret the Bible as teaching that the whole world as we now know it, including South America, Antarctic and the like was submerged at one time, and that every one of our million species of animals was represented on the ark, which was only 150 yards long, the difficulties would indeed be formidable. This is just the sort of artificial difficulty that some types of minds love to raise against the Bible. It is an outrage on the use of words to talk like this; words in the Bible, as in any other old book, are used in the sense that they bore at the time of writing, and not in the sense they have come to bear today. It was the *then known world* that went under the Deluge, and the then known animals that were preserved alive (see Appendix 2).

I have found this passage of my father's quoted by so many authors since, that it is important to see what conclusions we can draw from the Woolley episode.

Certainly Woolley found evidence of a huge local flood, but there is no reason to connect it with the Flood of Noah. That Flood, beside being universal (as we are told many times in

Scripture), was associated with a vast outpouring of subterranean water; mountains were covered, and everything on earth was destroyed except for the eight souls and creatures saved on the boat. It was a catastrophe the like of which has never occurred before nor will ever occur again. It was God's punishment for sin. The episode surely illustrates how careful we must be not to place our faith in dubious scientific data.

What about the Fall?

In his Swanwick address in 1924 ARS had called the Fall 'an *impasse*', and commented, 'We can only wait patiently.' What was the difficulty? Simply this: For the biblical Fall of man (and indeed of the entire creation [*Rom.* 8:20–23]) to have taken place, demands a previously good world. This is precisely what we read about in Genesis 1 and 2 and it is precisely what is denied by evolutionary theory, with its dependence on uniformitarianism and survival of the fittest. In no way can 'nature red in tooth and claw' be equated with the statement in Genesis 1:31 that 'God saw everything he had made and behold it was very good.'

'Why, Why, Why?'

These emotive words were found on the metal wall of the lift which serviced the oncology (cancer) ward of a large children's hospital. Presumably they had been scratched there by a distraught mother whose child was dying.

In 1938, in his highly successful paperback for students, *Why Believe?*, ARS tells his readers that no question is more frequently asked of him than, 'How can pain and disaster be reconciled with the Christian view of God?' He replies:

This question does not really affect the argument from nature that the evidence of purpose and plan and craftsmanship which we see everywhere must bespeak a divine Creator, or the argument from history that there is a guiding Power behind the powers of earthly empires, controlling the fate of nations. We should have to accept such evidence if there was no other available, and take the Deity as we find Him. It is to the teaching of Christ and His apostles . . . that we owe the conviction that God loves us as a father loves his children. So we must look to Christ to solve our problem, not to nature or history.

ARS explained that the cause of the problem is that there is an enemy, the devil, who sows tares among the wheat; that he is a murderer and a liar, and we do his will. 'That is the root cause of human misery':

The love of God is shown, not by dragooning man's will so that the world is peopled by nothing but yes-men, but by sending His own Son to the rescue, to suffer the extremes of human cruelty and wickedness, so that those who have turned aside to their own selfish ways, and have come to misunderstand and hate Him might be won back. Eventually His purpose will be accomplished, the devil rendered harmless and His kingdom established.

But to me this answer skates around the very question which the students and the mother scratching on the lift had asked, viz., 'How can pain and disaster be reconciled with the Christian view of a loving God?' It is a question asked in substance, although not in these exact words, by Romanes, Darwin and Hoyle, to name but a few. What are they all implying? That God is either love, but impotent; or he is all powerful, but a sadist.

Tennyson described the dilemma in this way: Man –

> Nature's last work, who seem'd so fair . . .
> Who trusted God was love indeed
> And love Creation's final law –
> Tho' Nature, red in tooth and claw
> With ravine, shrieked against his creed.
>
> (*In Memoriam*)

I believe the answer to the question 'Why, Why, Why?' lies in the story of Adam and Eve. In *Modern Discovery and The Bible* ARS asks 'Where do Adam and Eve come into the picture?' He deplores the readiness to discard everything in the Bible which does not fit 'with the passing ideas of our own day'. What was 'once thought incredible', he maintains, 'is often found to be historical':

That the story of the Fall of man may be presented to us in pictorial form, suitable for the comprehension of a primitive people, may possibly be true, but the doctrine of man's Fall from innocence to sin, and the doctrine of the Tempter are both basic for Christian teaching as set forth in the New Testament. So too, the Christian doctrine of marriage is based by Christ on the union in the Garden of Eden . . .

However, ARS continued to promote the idea that there may have been a pre-Adamic race. He seemed baffled by 'the Genesis story of the origin of woman [which] certainly sounds strange in the ears of those brought up in the atmosphere of modern science'. On these topics he is not prepared to speculate but ends the chapter with this expression of his current (1949) opinion: 'The reverent Bible student must wait further for the light, and meanwhile hold steadfastly to the doctrines of man's divine creation, his distinction from the beasts that perish, his fall into sin, and the divine institution of marriage.'

So we find the impasse concerning the Fall of man, the creation of woman and, incidentally, the question of why God allowed suffering, still remains.

As I have re-read *Modern Discovery and the Bible*, I empathize strongly with my father's constant cry for more light. All he could do was to hope for more evidence and in faith wait patiently for an answer. As far back as 1913 he had written, 'It is we who are short-sighted. Truth can always afford to wait . . . The quest is not in vain.'

20

LATER YEARS

Evolution remained victorious in academic England in the 1930s and 1940s. Almost all Christians in Great Britain held some sort of compromise position. Two major organizations had been formed to fight atheistic evolutionism. By far the older was the Victoria Institute.

The Victoria Institute

The Institute was founded in 1865, six years after the publication of Darwin's *Origin*. One of the three founding vice-presidents was Philip Henry Gosse – that 'honest hodman of science', as Thomas Huxley disparagingly called him. The stated objects of the Institute were:

First: To investigate in a reverent spirit important questions of Philosophy and Science, especially those bearing on the Holy Scriptures.

Second: To arrange for addresses from men who have themselves contributed to progress in Science and Religion, and thus to bring Members . . . into direct touch with the latest advances.

Third: In humble faith in one Eternal God, Who created all things good, to combat the unbelief now prevalent by directing attention to the evidences of the Divine care of man that are supplied by Science, History and Religion.

Papers read before the Institute had to be either original contributions to knowledge, or essays on important questions of philosophy and science. The Institute was still an important scientific and religious forum at the commencement of the Second World War. ARS was a member and occasional contributor. In 1938 the illustrious Sir Ambrose Fleming, MA, DSc, FRS, etc. (1849–1945), Emeritus Professor of Electrical Engineering in the University of London, was president. Inventor of the thermionic valve which made radio possible, he had been nominated for the Nobel Prize.

Sir Ambrose had embraced evangelicalism in later life and resolutely defended its teachings. He accepted the miracles and prophecies of the Bible unquestioningly. In addition to many scientific books and articles, he had also written two books on creation.[1] However, in the mid-1930s his views on creation were somewhat idiosyncratic. According to Ronald Numbers[2] they can be summarized as follows:

1. Pre-Adamic humans, clearly distinguishable from animals, had inhabited the earth prior to 'the arrival of Adamic man at the approximate date of 5500 B.C..'
2. 'The creation of Adamic man, who was to convert existing humanity to a belief in a Creator, produced 'a being, more eminently endowed with psychical faculties of initiative, authority, and powers of intercommunication than before.'
3. 'Because Adam and Eve were not parents of the whole human race, the Bible reveals only a small, but central segment of human history.'

The Gunning Prize Essay

In 1938 the winning essay for this prestigious prize was read by the Rev. D. E. Hart-Davies, MA, DD, under the title 'The First Two Chapters of Genesis Considered as a Basis of Science'. The President, Sir Ambrose Fleming, was in the chair, and the Essay was reported in the *Transactions* of the Victoria Institute.

I quote from this communication because it gives an idea of

---

[1]Sir Ambrose Fleming, *The Origin of Mankind* (1933); *Evolution or Creation* (London: Marshall, Morgan and Scott, 1938).

[2]Ronald L. Numbers, *The Creationists* (New York: A. A. Knopf, 1992), p. 144.

[169]

the views commonly held at that time, in particular as they relate to my father. In a section entitled, 'Duration of the Period of Creation', Hart-Davies states:

[It is] difficult to determine the precise duration of the 'days' of Genesis 1. Dr Rendle Short, whose opinion as a scientist and student of Scripture ranks very highly in this connection, thus testifies, 'Many eminent conservative Bible scholars resolve the difficulty, more satisfactorily we believe, by interpreting the "days" as periods of indeterminate length. It seems fair to regard them as representations of God's time, periods of rest with alternating periods of activity . . .' (*Transactions*, p. 9).

Later, Hart-Davies refers to the 'Gap or Ruin/Restoration Theory.' He states that he, personally, cannot accept the theory. 'Few Hebraists, I am convinced, would be willing to translate the Hebrew in the manner suggested.' For further confirmation of this view, he refers to:

Dr Rendle Short, no mean authority, comments thus upon the theory in question: 'When Geology was a young science and these difficulties were perceived, a comparatively easy way of escape was propounded by conservative theologians. They introduced what may be called the catastrophe theory, which seems to have been promoted by Dr. Thomas Chalmers.'

Chalmers had suggested that the proper translation of Genesis 1:2 should be, 'And the earth *became* without form and void'. Hart-Davies continues:

A great catastrophe occurred, which put an end to all life known to the geologist, and left an empty world which the Almighty replenished with life in six ordinary days. We do not think the catastrophe theory is likely to commend itself to persons with a scientific education . . . The theory creates scientific difficulties greater than those it was intended to resolve.

Dr Chalmers (1780–1845) was Professor of Divinity at Edinburgh University. A founder of the Free Church of Scotland, and a staunch evangelical, he became known as 'the father of modern sociology,' because of his outreach to the poor and destitute. As early as 1814 he anticipated the possible inroads the new field of geology might make into the historicity and authority of Scripture. He therefore suggested that 'the

detailed history of Creation in the first chapter of Genesis
begins in the middle of the second verse'. [1]

The gap theory is now discredited, but before we leave it let
me make three points:

First, it was an ingenious, but misguided attempt on the part of
Chalmers to reconcile geology and Scripture.

Secondly, the gap theory would have died an early death, like
Gosse's somewhat later *Omphalos* idea, if it had not been
actively promoted in this century by the Scofield Reference
Bible. Personally, I distrust Reference Bibles. They so easily
come to invest the speculations of fallible man with a cloak of
biblical authority.

Thirdly, God can, nevertheless, overrule man's faulty beliefs or
explanations to his glory. A friend told me how, in his teen years
his Christian belief was almost destroyed by evolution. Then he
discovered the gap theory. He said, 'Although I now know that
there is no truth in it, I thank God for the theory. Once it saved
my faith.'

The Evolution Protest Movement (EPM)

The EPM was founded in 1932, also under the presidency of
Sir Ambrose Fleming. The longest serving president was Sir
Cecil P. G. Wakeley, Bart., KBE, CB, KStJ, DSc, LLD,
FRSEd, PRCS, etc., (1892–1979). Sir Cecil was Professor of
Surgery in the University of London, President of the Royal
College of Surgeons and, during the Second World War, a
Surgeon Rear Admiral.

I had the honour of meeting him twice, and both occasions
were memorable and pleasant. The first was when he came to
speak at a meeting in war-torn Bristol. He travelled from
London resplendent in his admiral's uniform. If I remember
correctly I was deputed to meet him at Temple Meads station.
He was bubbling with amusement. Apparently, when the train
stopped, an old lady called him to get her case from the
overhead rack. Being a Christian gentleman he willingly did so.
He told me, 'She must have thought I was a porter, but a very

[1]Taylor, *In the Minds of Men*, p. 363.

superior one, for she tipped me half-a-crown. [A big sum in those days.] I wondered if I should say, "Pardon me, madam, I am a Surgeon Rear Admiral".' But he thought this might embarrass her. So he pocketed the tip! My second meeting with Sir Cecil was at my final viva examination in surgery at Cambridge University.

In the past, the EPM has been supported by people favouring divergent theories on Creation: The long day-age, successive creations, the Gap, progressive creation, a young earth, and so on. The mix has varied. Early pamphlets published by the EPM mainly concentrated on criticism of atheistic evolution, stressing the impossibility of the natural world coming into being by chance, rather than on positive scientific evidence in support of creation. This is scarcely surprising as such evidence was virtually unknown in England at the time.

I do not think ARS ever joined the EPM, although he was good friends with Sir Cecil and other members of the movement. In 1980 the name of the organisation was altered to The Creation Science Movement, and with it the character of the movement changed.

What did Evangelicals Believe?

'Let us now praise famous men and our fathers that begat us.' At the risk of underestimating our forefathers in the Faith, let me attempt to summarize the beliefs of most evangelicals with a scientific interest up to the end of the Second World War. [I must stress that the belief pattern given below refers to Great Britain and Australia, and differs markedly from that found in the United States if Noll[1] is anything to go by. Also that they are my personal reflections. I have not undertaken detailed research.]

1. Evangelicals all maintained that creation did not occur by chance. Both the origin of the cosmos and the initial creation of life demanded the intervention of a Creator.

2. There was a difference of opinion as to whether or not the

---

[1]Mark A. Noll, *The Scandal of the Evangelical Mind* (Grand Rapids: Eerdmans, 1994).

creation of man was *ex nihilo,* out of nothing. After all, are we not told man was created from dust?

3. They saw the importance of 'the argument from design and beauty', but had little scientific evidence with which to underpin it.

4. Most understood the difference between micro– and macro-evolution, although not by those names, which had not then been coined.

5. They had absolute acceptance of Lyell's theory of geological uniformitarianism based on the fossil record. From the above flowed the possibility of (a) The Day-Age Theory; (b) Pre-Adamic man; (c) Progressive creationism; (d) Death occurred before Adam sinned, including the death of Adam's immediate ancestors, and so on . . .

6. The word 'good' in Genesis 1 referred to the incredible design and beauty of nature, and to the anatomical and physiological perfection of all living creatures, not to the moral perfection of creation in its original form.

7. They did not understand how altruism could have come into the world (if indeed they ever thought of it).

8. The Fall remained an unsolvable enigma.

9. The creation of Eve from Adam (woman from man) was inexplicable.

10. Noah's flood was local, and only covered the then-known earth. It had little to do with the deposition of fossils.

*   *   *

Changing Views

As might be expected, my father's views gradually changed during his life. Let me remind you of some of his statements which I have quoted previously:

1906, at age 26: From 'A Summer Day's Reverie'.
'Every science fades into mystery . . . History too, begins in mist and is full of "Why's?" . . . We are utterly incapable, apart

from what He has told us, even to conceive His objects, His principles . . . it is our part just to trust and say, "It is the will of God." '

1913, at age 33: From *The Younger Brother.*
'It is we who are short-sighted. Truth can always afford to wait. . . . The quest is not in vain'.

1924, at age 44: Sermon at the IVF Conference.
'A little more light and we shall be clear about it.
'The Fall, an impasse. We can only wait patiently.
'No final solution possible today.'

1942, at age 62: Prologue, *Modern Discovery and the Bible.*
'Happily the years are likely to bring more evidence to light.'
    ARS was fond of quoting from Jeremiah 23:20, 'In the latter day you shall understand'. The full quotation ends '. . . perfectly' (or 'clearly'). Strangely, ARS almost always omitted this last word. Perhaps he did not feel able to see that far.

1947 to 1953: After the end of World War II, ARS recommenced preaching on the topic of creation. I have beside me as I write notes of several addresses given in these years. Each time he followed the same pattern, commencing the address with: 'The Old Idea' (that is, prior to the Darwinian revolution); followed by 'The New Idea' (modern evolutionary theory); and lastly 'The True Idea', which I take to be his assessment of the current situation.
    In each sermon the Old and New Idea remain substantially the same, but changes occur successively in 'The True Idea'. In 1947, for example, he addressed the Irish IVF and posed the question, 'What is *The True Idea?*' His reply: there are 'many unanswered questions'.

In 1948, at Devizes, he summarized *The True Idea* as, 'Best of both [ideas]. Science changes. Bible not.'

In 1949, another address is inscribed, 'For a Popular audience.' Here under the heading: *The True Idea,* the notes are fuller and read: '?4004 B.C.. Man ?ex nihilo. (Genesis. 2:7) . . . Bible does not tell us whether man's body direct from dust or any intermediate stages.'

In 1953, a few months before he died, ARS flew to Dublin. (As

far as I know this was the only occasion he travelled by plane.)
He used the same formula, which I here give in full:
A. *The Old Idea* 4004 B.C.. Six days. All species separately
created. *Ex nihilo.*
B. *The New Idea* Earth 2,000 million years old. Man a million.
Darwinism: evolution self-working, depends on chance. Atheistic.
C. *The True Idea* Belief of scientists. Einstein? Kelvin, Ambrose
Fleming . . . On 4004; 6 days; separate species. Living things
change. Races of man. What does species mean?'

Some new sections follow listing such scientific problems as:
'1. Origin of life; 2. Precambrian; 3. Absence of ancestors; 4.
Valueless characteristics, e.g., peacock's tail; 5. Origin of
organs, feathers, eye, colour vision; Mind and speech in
animals.' ARS added separately, in note form: 'Man's intellect; Calculating machines. Sherrington on mind and brain.'

His final new section is the one of greatest interest to me:
'*Back to the Book.* Order of Creation: 'Man in His own image.'
Not enough just to believe in God: ? *Why* 7 days – Sabbath; ? *Why*
origin of woman – Otherwise mankind might be just like
animals: meet, mate, part; ? *Why* The Fall – Rom. 5'.

This 1953 address ended with the words: 'All we like
sheep . . .'

I wish I could have discussed this sermon with my father, but
I did not see the notes until 1971. In any case, in 1953 I was
totally uninterested in the creation. I can only recollect one
occasion on which I conversed with him on the subject of
creation: that was during my student days. We had little
opportunity for deep conversation during the last years of his
life. I lived in Cardiff, my parents lived in Bristol. Although the
cities are quite near 'as the crow flies', before the opening of the
Severn bridge it was a tedious journey.

Those closing words spoken in Dublin appear to me to
express a greater certainty than had been evident in any of his
previous writings. Most importantly, the Fall is no longer an
'*impasse*'.

An aphorism he was fond of quoting runs like this: 'God,
stooping, provides sufficient light for me in my darkness to rise
by, *and I rise.*'

*　　　*　　　*

One Sunday in early September 1953, I was called out of Evensong to be told my father had been hospitalized in Hereford where he and my mother had been staying with old friends. In the morning he had taken part at the Breaking of Bread service in the local assembly as was his custom, but in the afternoon started to feel ill.

I drove to Hereford as early as I could the next day. I was greeted at our friend's home by the General Practitioner. He explained my father had had a severe heart attack; the prognosis was grave. He very kindly offered to pray with me. I found this very moving and helpful.

I went on to the hospital and found my mother alone with my father. He was sitting, propped up in bed. He appeared amazingly normal, and completely rational. There were none of the paraphernalia associated with modern intensive care. I doubt if he had any treatment other than morphine. At that time he gave no indication of pain or distress. But very soon after he suffered another massive heart attack.

*　　　*　　　*

The opening words of *The Faith of a Surgeon* tell the story of a doctor in Bristol telephoning a close friend in the North of England on the evening of 14 September 1953. 'I have bad news for you,' he said, 'Professor Rendle Short died suddenly today'. A few minutes later the bell in the North rang again and a voice from the exchange said apologetically, 'When I was transferring the long-distance call, Sir, I could not help hearing your friend's first words. I am deeply moved. I feel as if I had lost my own father. I grew up in the St Philip's ward of Bristol [The site of the 'Dings']. If ever there was a Christian, that man was. Some of us owe everything to him. He made my father a Christian.'

The funeral was held in Alma Road Chapel, Bristol, where my parents had been married. It was crowded to overflowing. During the service we sang the *Nunc Dimitis*. It had been a special favourite of my father. Often as he operated in the Pembroke Road Nursing Home, (a Church of England foundation), he would listen to the staff and patients singing

Evensong. He was always comforted by the words, 'Lord, now lettest Thou Thy servant depart in peace, according to Thy word.' Unlike poor George Romanes, he could continue triumphantly, 'For mine eyes have seen Thy great salvation . . .'

As the cortège wound slowly up steep Blackboy Hill on the way to the cemetery, there was quite a crowd on the footpath. Watching, I assumed they were normal morning shoppers, until I saw one elderly man go down on his knees on the pavement in prayer. I was very moved by this demonstration of obvious affection. Many times in the years since there have been other occasions on which men and women have told me how much they owed to him.

The verse my mother chose for the funeral notice was from Malachi 2:6, AV: 'The law of truth was in his mouth, and iniquity was not found in his lips: he walked with me in peace and equity, and did turn many away from iniquity.'

I would like to conclude with this personal tribute to my father:

'In the latter days you will understand' (*Jer.* 23:20).

'These all died in faith, not having received the promises,
but having seen them afar off
were assured of them [and] embraced them . . .
therefore God is not ashamed to be called their God' (*Heb.* 11:13–16).

PART FOUR

JOHN RENDLE-SHORT

21

CHILDHOOD

Earache, *earache,* **earache**. Earache in the left ear, earache in the right ear, earache in both ears! My early memories are dominated by the throbbing, lancing, crescendo pain of earache. Mostly it would start in the evening; the distress building up as I struggled for sleep. At last it would be bad enough for me to steal sleepily downstairs to the warmth of the sitting room fire and the comforting arms of my mother. Then would come the familiar battle as I was forced, resisting vigorously, to swallow a crushed aspirin tablet thinly disguised in jam.

Huddled on mother's knee, a rubber hot-water bottle applied to the worse ear, I would wait for the relief which followed when the drum burst. The pain subsided as the sticky pus oozed out, allowing me to slide into sleep.

Sometimes surgery was required to lance the drum, relieving the pressure. What I hated most was the sickening, suffocating smell of the chloroform. There was a moment of terror as I stared up at the familiar, inverted face of the anaesthetist a few inches from my eyes, and inhaled the heavy breath of a confirmed pipe-smoker. Then the mask was suddenly and firmly clamped over my mouth and nose and, so it seemed to my drugged consciousness, instantly metamorphosed into the tight bandage which held the wad of dressing over the offending ear. Simultaneously, the hated face of my arch-enemy changed into the anxious gaze of my mother telling me to wake up.

On the other hand, I loved the Ear, Nose and Throat surgeon, Dr Angell James (the Angel I called him), then a young man who later rose to the top of his profession. He was gentle and kindly even when painfully cleaning pus from my ear.

Eventually, with much apprehension I have no doubt, he decided it was essential to perform a bilateral mastoid operation. In those pre-antibiotic days – about 1930 – this was a considerable undertaking. It involved chipping away infected bone from behind both ears with a hammer and cold chisel. The infected material must be removed while not penetrating the near-by brain coverings, or damaging the delicate hearing ossicles. This procedure, like all my ear operations, was performed in the nursery on a portable operating table belonging to my father.

The operation was a success. My hearing was preserved, and the attacks of earache dramatically decreased. However, I had lost more than a year of schooling, a disability which dogged my footsteps throughout my educational years. Try as I might, I never quite managed to catch up the time lost.

Another educational problem, probably linked to the intermittent deafness, was the disorder now known by the grandiose diagnosis of 'dyslexia'. Then it was thought to be laziness, lack of attention or plain stupidity. With me it was manifested by right/left disorientation and an almost total inability to spell. I have samples of my spelling from those early days and find I even spelt my own name 'Jhon'.

Exasperated, people would shout, 'There is no excuse for bad spelling. Why don't you look it up in the dictionary?' They fail to understand that a modicum of spelling ability is required even to locate the word in a dictionary.[1] In addition my handwriting was bad, 'atrocious', my teachers called it. But in part this was purposeful. I discovered that grown-ups have a strange hierarchy of importance; they regard bad spelling as more culpable than bad writing. After all, don't doctors have awful writing? So I learnt to write illegibly in order to disguise my poor spelling. It is easy to slur an 'a' into an 'e' if you are uncertain which it should be.

Needless to say, I had difficulty in passing examinations and failed on the first occasion almost every examination I have

---

[1] I have found the best place to look up the spelling of a word is in the index of Roget's *Thesaurus*.

taken, even including my last, the MD. I wrote a thesis on the life of an eighteenth century physician, Dr William Cadogan (1711–1797), whom I called the 'Father of Child Care'. Needless to say, it was returned by the examining board of Cambridge University for spelling correction. They pointed out that I had even spelt Cadogan's name inconsistently.

I write this to comfort fellow sufferers. Bad spelling does not necessarily mean you are stupid. It may be a specific and exasperating disability. Now I use a word processor with a 'spell' attachment.

Christian Experience

An episode important to my religious growth occurred when I was about six years old. I had been given a big inflatable rubber duck for my birthday. I was allowed to play with it in the shallows during a summer holiday in Cornwall. One day the wind blew softly off shore and the duck drifted out to sea in the clear, calm water. I never could swim well, but I set out to catch it. Always it was just in front of me. If only I could get my arm over it, I could rest till I had regained my strength. I was aware of people on the shore shouting, and I knew I was out of my depth, but by now I was too tired to swim back. Desperately I cried to God, promising that if he would save me I would serve him all my life. I didn't even see the rowing boat glide up behind me. Suddenly I found myself plucked out of the water to safety. That night, Esther (Miss Esther Lloyd, whom I have referred to before) said as she tucked me up, 'Remember, Master John dear: "Saved to serve; saved to serve".'

The duck was rescued too, but to my disappointment I never saw it again! Then one Easter when I was about eight years old, my sister and I were taken by the faithful Esther for a week's holiday to the little town of Burnham-on-sea, in Somerset. It was not an exciting holiday venue. I had expected beaches and sea like in Cornwall. But no. Burnham-on-sea must have been so called to remind people that the sea had once been there.

However, the occasion was notable for quite another event. On Easter Sunday evening we went to the local gospel chapel, and listened to a sermon, nothing of which I now remember. But I date my conversion with certainty from that night.

The next day we climbed a hill, I think called Brent Knoll, and walked down again through a field covered with sweet-smelling yellow cowslips. I have rarely seen a cowslip since, but I still remember the glory of that scene. I always associate Easter with the colour yellow. I'm so glad that even in the topsy-turvy seasons of Australia, the wattle with its profuse yellow flowers and sweet perfume is there to remind me of Easter.

I recount these early events because, when I now tell people that for well over forty years I was a Christian who believed in evolution, I am sometimes asked incredulously, 'Are you sure you really were a Christian?' The answer is, 'Yes, certainly.' If I had doubts in my teen years, I would ask the leader at a youth camp how I could be certain I was saved. The answer I usually got was, 'Well, if you are not quite sure, just accept Jesus into your heart now.' 'Just in case,' they almost added, 'just in case you didn't do it right last time.' So I accepted Jesus again – and again, lots of times. At last someone wiser than the rest told me it didn't depend on my feelings, but on God's promise. 'If you confess your sins' (which I had, many times) 'God is faithful and just to forgive us our sins and to cleanse us from all unrighteousness' (*1 John* 1:9).

I think my problem lay in the fact that although brought up in a Christian home, I had little appreciation of the character of God as just and sovereign. In those days the subject of creation and the Creator were seldom mentioned in sermons or private conversation. Jesus I knew, but who was God? Nor did I have much realization of sin. Sin was playing with toys on Sunday. One birthday I was given a present of a Hornby train set. But the birthday happened to fall on a Sunday. Someone pleaded for a special dispensation that I might be allowed to try it out briefly in the afternoon.

I can't remember the words the preacher in Burnham had used to present the Gospel, probably something like 'Accept Jesus into your heart', or 'Open your heart to Jesus', using the illustration from Revelation 3:20: 'Behold I stand at the door and knock, if anyone opens the door, I will come in . . .'. As a boy I had been taken to see Holman Hunt's famous picture of Christ outside the fast closed door in St Paul's Cathedral, London. Someone had explained that the door had no handle on the outside, 'but there was one on the inside'.

The problem was that my acceptance of the gospel was self-centred. I don't remember anyone explaining to me that it was not I who had to do something for Christ – like opening a door –but that Christ had done everything for me. Peter tells us, Christ 'bore our sins in his own body on the tree' (*1 Pet.* 2:24). More than that, Paul writes that God made Christ, 'who knew no sin, to be sin for us that we might become the righteousness of God in Him' (*2 Cor.* 5:21). Jesus had given his life, his very being in my place, and we had Easter to celebrate his resurrection.

The difference between these two messages is that the first is subjective and puts the emphasis on what man must do. The other is objective and puts the emphasis on what Christ has already done.

My lack of understanding of these principles was to cause me endless problems in my student years and after.

Natural History

My father always took a great interest in nature. On sunny Sunday afternoons he would sometimes take us for a walk round the garden. He knew the Latin names of all the flowers, but he never did any practical gardening, preferring to employ Mr Wiltshire, who came once a week. I was not allowed to touch the garden.

I took only a superficial interest in natural history until one Christmas when I was given a toy microscope for a present. I was thrilled. However, everyone was too busy to show me how to use it, or give me any slides to use with it. After examining a few bits of dust, I put the point of a pin on the stage. I was amazed at how blunt it looked. So I went out into the cold winter garden and hastily picked a leaf from a holly bush and carried it upstairs to study. Behold the sharp prickle of the holly! What a difference from the bluntness of the pin! I was amazed. I don't think at that time I thought of it as a comparison between God's perfection and man's crude copy. But so, of course, it was.

22

UNIVERSITY

After much educational turmoil, I left Clifton College and Bristol, took the tedious cross-country train journey to Cambridge, and enrolled in Corpus Christi College to study medicine. I greatly enjoyed my time at Cambridge, although, being perpetually a year behind my contemporaries I had to work extra hard to keep up. Thus I missed many of the extra-curricular activities which are the essence of university life.

During 1938, my first year at university, Corpus Christi College still retained many of the traditions it had inherited during its six hundred or so years of existence. The food was superb. Jugged hare was a favourite. All the cutlery was heavy silver with the college crest. But living facilities were spartan in some rooms, especially in Old Court (built about 1350). Coal fires in the sitting room only; no heating in the little attic bedrooms and only cold water to wash in. One morning I woke to find the ewer in my basin had frozen solid, splitting the jug neatly in two from top to bottom. With the two halves encasing a solid core of ice, it resembled an opening tulip.

My second year coincided with the start of World War II. We were warned that failure in examinations would result in immediate drafting into the Forces – a smart incentive for even the laziest student. Two of my close friends joined the Royal Air Force and both were shot down over Germany within months.

In my day, Cambridge was male and Anglican dominated. College Chapel was, of course, Church of England. It was only in the middle of the last century that nonconformists and Roman Catholics had even been allowed to enter the university as students, and as for girls – in my year, despite two women's colleges, very few studied medicine. When I joined the Cambridge Inter-Collegiate Christian Union (CICCU) in 1938 it too was strictly men only. Women received full membership of the university in 1948, and after much debate, the Women's Inter-Collegiate Union was permitted to amalgamate with CICCU. But this was long after I had 'gone down'.

The activities of CICCU centred round College Bible studies, daily prayer meetings in the Henry Martyn Hall and the CICCU sermon on Sunday evenings in Holy Trinity Church. There I heard many of the well-known evangelical preachers of the day.

However, like my father before me, I started to have doubts about Christianity. But whereas his anxieties were theological and academic, mine were mainly hedonistic. One seemed to miss so much by being a follower of Jesus. I therefore felt the importance of examining carefully the basis of my beliefs.

Bible Miracles

As I was studying for the Natural Science Tripos, the topic of miracles loomed large. Did I really believe in them? Was the Bible true? Or did everything have a naturalistic explanation? Although I was thinking like this it never even entered my mind to query the creation narrative. That wasn't a miracle. It was just a story. To me evolution was fact.

I soon decided it was pointless going through each miracle in detail. Surely if the Bible was truly the Word of God, then *all* the miracles must be true. But if the Bible were not God's communication to man, then nothing could really be trusted. A particular biblical narrative might be right, or it might be wrong. Who could tell?

I felt that there must, of course, be a physical explanation for some miracles, although I would not have gone as far as Albert Schweitzer who considered the feeding of the five thousand (*John* 6) as a mere story of a boy's food being enough for every person who took a crumb.

My favourite miracle is recorded in Joshua 3:11–17. How the children of Israel crossed the Jordan. Joshua told the children of Israel, 'As soon as the soles of the feet of the priests who bear the ark of the Lord, rest in the waters of the Jordan, the waters of the Jordan shall be cut off.' Later we read, 'it was harvest time, and the Jordan overflows all its banks at that time of year. The waters that came down from upstream stood still, and rose in a heap very far away at Adam, the city that is beside Zaretan.' I surmised that the river was in spate, and a landslide occurred upstream temporarily blocking the river, and damming back the water. So the miracle was partly one of timing. The blockage had to occur some hours earlier, so that at the exact moment when the feet of the priests dipped in the water, the waters ceased to flow, and the people crossed the river dry-shod, opposite the town of Jericho.

If a naturalistic explanation was valid on this occasion when we are told the mechanism, might not similar explanations account for other miracles too?

Here is another example: the first man, we are told, was created 'from the dust of the ground'. Now, when a creature – any creature, man or ape – dies, it returns to dust. Therefore, following the evolutionary scenario, man evolved from some dust-returning, ape-like creature into which God breathed the breath of life. This suggestion would harmonize biology and Scripture. I spent quite a time working out ingenious explanations for Old and New Testament miracles in this way.

But there are dangers in this type of reasoning. It is possible to rationalize the supernatural clean out of Christianity, including eventually Christ's resurrection.

Here I found the road blocked. Could this have a figurative explanation too? But if so then the whole of Christianity collapses, and my salvation would be void. Paul states categorically: 'If Christ is not risen, your faith is futile, you are still in your sins' (1 Cor. 15:17).

On the other hand, if the resurrection really did occur in space and time, improbable though it might seem, then my faith was on sure ground. Furthermore, if this, the most spectacular and improbable miracle was true, there should be no difficulty in accepting other lesser miracles.

So I studied the historicity of the resurrection story in as much detail as I could. This was long before I knew about Morison's book, *Who Moved the Stone?* If I had found it I would have been saved a mint of trouble.

I don't think I appreciated the importance of the grave clothes. That insight, which came much later, I now find compelling. The apostle John tells us that as he followed Peter into the tomb he was immediately arrested by the sight of the linen cloths which had encased the embalmed body of the Lord, still lying on the stone slab. Particularly, he noticed the 'handkerchief', or headgear which had been around his head. This was lying separate from the other grave clothes (*John* 20:6–9). John, Matthew and Luke all use a unique Greek word to tell us this headpiece was 'wound up' or 'entwined'. Under the action of the spices used for embalming, the linen strips had probably set solid, so retaining, undisturbed, the shape of the head which the linen had recently encased. It lay there like a helmet. John Stott likens it to 'a discarded chrysalis case'. And if this was so, there was no physical way the Lord's head could have left the helmet without damaging it. St John, an eye-witness, tells us it was the singular appearance of the grave cloths which convinced him that Christ had risen: 'he saw and believed'.

But in my early days, the evidence which as much as anything convinced me, was a chance remark from an elderly teacher at Clifton College – 'Fluffy' Thomas, so named on account of his truly spectacular beard. I only had one lesson by him throughout my whole time at Clifton. How the class got on to the subject I do not know, but I remember him telling us that what convinced him of the truth of the resurrection was the dramatic change in the disciples before and after the crucifixion. Before, they all forsook him and fled – Peter scared of a servant girl, denying his Lord, then running, weeping out into the night. Yet afterwards, they were as brave as lions; the foundation stones of the church of Christ, still a mighty force nearly 2,000 years later. These were the unlearned and ignorant men who boldly confronted the subtle philosophy of the Greeks and silenced its advocates by preaching the cross and resurrection of the Lord Jesus.

Nothing but a really dead Lord Jesus, who really returned to life as a man, who ate and walked and talked with them, could account for this dramatic change in their behaviour. So, during my student years, whenever my belief in Christianity started to waver, I rehearsed to myself again and again the reasons why the resurrection must be historically true. And if so, then my faith *was* founded on solid ground; I *was* a Christian.

Restrained by lack of time, and the unavailability of helpful books, my reading on religious topics had so far been of the muscular-Christianity, schoolboy variety; that is a punchy, Arminian-based evangelism of no great depth. I should have learned the danger of this form of evangelism early on from an episode which occurred soon after I joined Corpus. Looking out of my window, I happened to notice a college member, obviously 'drunk and disorderly'. I enquired who he was. A friend told me his name, and added, 'He is often like that, yet he was the dramatic conversion at the University Mission last year.'

Cambridge Inter-Collegiate Christian Union

I greatly valued my contact with CICCU. True, it largely elbowed out regular church attendance, but many of the members were men of great spiritual depth, who in later life left their mark on the Body of Christ in England and overseas. John Pollock writes of this time, 'The consciousness of Christ as Saviour and as Friend was the dominant feature of the CICCU man's life; to evangelize was the first aim of the Union.'[1]

Apart from special missions, evangelism consisted mainly of persuading a friend to come with you to the CICCU sermon at Holy Trinity on Sunday evening; afterwards inviting him to your rooms for coffee and 'sticky Fitzbilly buns', to chat about Christianity until late into the night. What mortal can tell the eternal consequences which may have resulted from these encounters?

But coupled with this activity there was a horrible shallowness. We had not thought through the place of the Christian in the world. CICCU life for me was a legalistic discipline. For instance, it was 'not done' in CICCU circles to go to the cinema. So for fear of being seen, I never went to a 'flick' while in Cambridge. However, I usually managed to arrange the train time of my journey to and from vacation in Bristol so that I could see a film in London. Once, in a West End cinema

---

[1]J. C. Pollock, *A Cambridge Movement* (London: John Murray, 1953), p. 248.

during the war, the lights suddenly came on and the audience was told the air-raid sirens had sounded. We were invited to leave or stay as we wished. Some people left. I stayed at first. But for me the film (the innocuous 'Colonel Blimp') had lost its charm. What if the cinema was bombed and my mutilated body discovered among the ruins? What would my Christian friends think? I crept out and did not see the rest of the film for forty-five years!

Presuppositions

Recently I wrote:

When I was a student and used to talk to fellow students about Christianity, I could assume their basic viewpoints, their presuppositions were much the same as mine. They believed there was a God, although perhaps he had started the world off aeons ago and then left it to its own devices. They knew about Jesus Christ, even if they thought of him as a mere man, not the Son of God. They believed in goodness and badness. They used such words as 'honest', 'decent' and 'gentleman' – even 'patriotic' and 'chastity'. In short, they subscribed to the Judeo-Christian ethic.

In those days the task of the evangelist was to tell men and women about sin and point the way of salvation through Jesus Christ. It was assumed, correctly, that everyone believed in God, had heard of Jesus and recognized themselves as sinners.[1]

Of course, at the time I never analysed the current evangelical scene like this. Probably about the only person to do so was Dr Lloyd-Jones. In his biography, Iain Murray describes how Dr Douglas Johnson tried to persuade the Doctor to become involved in student Christian work through the IVF.[2] According to DJ (as he was always called):

He had clearly made up his mind not to be drawn into what he thought to be a shallow, American-type evangelistic and activist society . . . He began by asking questions on our doctrines, aims, methods and ecclesiastical outlook, and watching me like a hawk! But we also had a tyrannical, Socratic-method teacher at King's College Hospital, so I was quite used to coming back at a forceful questioner.

[1]John Rendle-Short, *Reasonable Christianity* (Darlington: Evangelical Press, 1991), p. 9.
[2]Murray, *D. Martyn Lloyd-Jones: The First Forty Years*, p. 296.

Nevertheless, Douglas Johnson was hard-pressed until he managed to divert the conversation from the IVF in general to his own views and personal beliefs in particular.

Then and Now

Over the decades I, and others in my age group, have witnessed an amazing and complete turnover in basic presuppositions (or world-view) in Western Society. If you are under forty-five years old, you will find it almost impossible to appreciate the difference in moral consciousness between the days of the Second World War and now. One way to check this is to watch a war-vintage movie, such as *Mrs Miniver*, or *The Best Days Of Our Lives*, and compare it with modern films. In those days even kissing on film was sanitized, there was no sex and violence was 'not on'.

Today the scene has completely changed. Why? For ordinary people, science has proved – not that God is dead, but that there never has been such an individual. At most there is a supernatural 'force' of the New Age variety. Jesus was probably a 'good man' who lived years ago. The phrase 'act of God' beloved by insurance companies, is just that, a phrase. It has nothing to do with the Deity. Given time, scientists will probably discover the cause of all natural phenomena. If Genesis-type creation is a fairy story akin to Santa Claus, what reason is there to believe the rest of the Bible? So the Ten Commandments are optional, just suggestions by ancient philosophers, on a par with those of Confucians. Morality and ethics are man-made. Truth is relative. The word 'sin' has disappeared from our vocabulary, so there is nothing for a saviour to do.

We are compelled to ask, what has caused this dramatic change? Theologically, I guess, one can point to the remnants of the liberal, Higher Criticism movement. But that is strictly for the theologians. The ordinary man and woman do not read theology. For them, the change has come mainly from the almost universal acceptance of evolution by both non-Christians and Christians alike, resulting, of course, in a loss of absolute values and spawning such secondary philosophies as Freudism with its advocacy of free sex. The greatest surprise is that the sociological effects of a revolution as profound as Darwinism have taken almost 150 years to mature. At Cambridge I absorbed evolution in the usual way. I do not remember anyone, Christian or not, ever questioning the theory. It never occurred to me that the 'days' of Genesis 1 might be literal days, or that Noah's flood was anything more than local. To me evolution was a fact, the 'days' long periods of time, and the world millions of years old. *Finis*.

On one occasion, I had to write an essay on evolution for a biology assignment. I propounded a vaguely progressive creationist[1] viewpoint; that is, evolution proceeded as per science text books, except that God, not chance, was in control, and perhaps from time to time he created further creatures as required (the God of the gaps idea). This was accepted without question by my tutor. I showed the essay to my father. He agreed with what I had written. Not till then did he tell me that evolution/creation was a subject with which he had wrestled all his life.

While at university my interest in art and the humanities was nil. I am ashamed to say I never entered the world-famous Fitzwilliam museum, or even visited the Corpus Christi library, full of priceless medieval manuscripts, including the Latin Bible read by little Thomas Bilney and carefully annotated the night before he was burned at the stake.[2] I had heard of the Reformers and of John and Charles Wesley, but I knew little about such stalwarts as John Newton, Whitefield, Jonathan Edwards or Bishop Ryle. There was no Banner of Truth Trust. Dr Lloyd-Jones started to preach in Westminster Chapel in 1938, but his name meant nothing to me, even though I was once asked to drive him somewhere when he was in Bristol. Our conversation in the car revolved around why he wore a gown in the pulpit. With teenage smugness I disapproved! I did not bother to stay and hear him preach.

C. S. Lewis

Then I discovered the world of C. S. Lewis. From Lewis I learnt a new type of 'popular' Christianity. The first Christian book I

[1]Now sometimes known as 'Old Earth Creationism.'
[2]Isa. 43:1-2 were the verses marked.

read with delight was *The Screwtape Letters*. Then in 1942, during the dark days of the war, I found *The Problem of Pain*, and some years later, *Miracles*.[1]

When I came to write my own book, *The Five Essential Miracles*, I was careful not even to open Lewis' book for fear of being influenced by him. However, when my book was eventually finished, I read *Miracles* again. I was amazed to discover how much I had plagiarized Lewis even after an interval of twenty years. Some sentences were almost identical with his. I tell this cautionary tale to illustrate how greatly our philosophy is influenced by what we read.

I think *The Problem of Pain* was probably the first book I read in which evolution is discussed from a religious viewpoint. Lewis writes, 'When the saints say that they – even they – are vile, they are recording truth with scientific accuracy.' But how, Lewis asks, can this state of affairs have come about? He replies:

For long centuries God perfected the animal form which was to become the vehicle of humanity and the image of Himself. He gave it hands whose thumb could be applied to each of his fingers, and jaws and teeth and a throat capable of articulation, and a brain sufficiently complex to execute all the material motions whereby rational thought is incarnated. The creature may have existed for ages in this state before it became man . . . Then in the fullness of time, God caused to descend upon this organism, on its psychology and physiology, a new kind of consciousness which could say 'I' and 'me'.

Lewis' beliefs on the mechanism of the Fall, I find confusing. Here is a sample:

The story of Genesis one and two is about a . . . magic apple of knowledge. . . . I have the deepest respect for even the Pagan myths, still more the myths of Holy Scripture. I therefore do not doubt the version which emphasizes the magic apple, and brings together the tree of life and knowledge. . . .

Yet Lewis was even-handed; he could parody evolution too. Here is the first stanza of his Evolutionary Hymn:[2]

[1]C. S. Lewis, *The Problem of Pain* (London: Geoffrey Bles, 1940); *Miracles* (Geoffrey Bles, 1957).

[2]C. S. Lewis, *Poems*, ed. Walter Hooper (Harcourt Brace Jovanovich, 1964).

Lead us, Evolution, lead us
Up the future's endless stair:
Chop us, change us, prod us, weed us,
For stagnation is despair:
Groping, guessing, yet progressing,
Lead us nobody knows where.

I suppose at one time I agreed with these beliefs of Lewis. But reading them now, they strike me as darkly confused and deeply distressing. How could I have ever accepted such ideas? However, I am certainly grateful to him for many valuable insights in later books.[1]

If there were flaws in evangelicalism as I knew it during my university years, the so-called liberal camp was even worse. This, of course, was really the old Higher Criticism modernised by such theologians as Barth and Brunner. In 1948 Drs Sangster, Soper and Leslie Weatherhead were regarded as the outstanding preachers in London.[2] These men were convinced that it was the old 'stern' view of God which drove people from the churches, and the prime reason for this wrong view of God was 'bibliolatry'.

It is reported that one Whit Sunday, Weatherhead preached on the subject: 'The witness of the Spirits [sic] with our Spirit'. In place of the second reading he substituted a short poem, 'Some call it Evolution and others call it God', thereby illuminating the address that was to follow.

[1]Particularly, I value *Mere Christianity* and *The Abolition of Man*.
[2]Murray, *D. M. Lloyd-Jones: The Fight of Faith*, pp. 61, 189.

23

TRAINING FOR PAEDIATRICS

Before the war, Cambridge University had almost no facilities for the instruction of clinical medical students. Most, therefore, went to one of the great London hospitals. But because of the air assault on the capital, after a war-shortened pre-clinical course at Cambridge, I joined Bristol University and 'walked the wards' in Bristol hospitals, only returning to Cambridge for examinations.

Being a medical student in bombed Bristol had its excitements. There were hours of boredom, sitting on the roof of the hospital waiting to extinguish any incendiary bombs which might fall; this was interspersed with feverish drama on the eruption of a full-scale blitz. During the first major air raid on Bristol, from a vantage point high on the roof of the Royal Infirmary, I watched with awe the mighty conflagration which reduced the centre of the ancient city to rubble and ashes.

Rationing was stringent for food items such as milk, sugar, eggs, meat, and bread; also clothes, fuel and petrol. All travel was restricted. However at some time (I cannot remember quite when), I managed to get away to attend an IVF student conference in Swanwick, Derbyshire. The railway journey was long and tedious, and my conscience was constantly pricked by the intimidating notice plastered on every station, 'Is Your Journey Really Necessary?' Was it, I wondered? At Swanwick the young engine driver overshot the station by quite a distance, and had to reverse back to the jeers of the elderly porter.

I recollect almost nothing about the weekend. I met no-one

I knew. Looking back after fifty years, I cannot recall the name of the speaker, or the topic. But the occasion was made memorable for me because the last talk affected me deeply. Why? I cannot remember. But as I lay in bed in the blacked-out dormitory, I was in a state of ecstasy such as I have never experienced before or since. If it had not been for the dark and cold and the other men in the room, I would have leapt from bed and shouted! Next morning I left early to catch the train back to Bristol. I told no-one what had happened, indeed I never did for forty years or more. But as I travelled home through the spring countryside, the words of the old hymn revolved constantly round my head:

> Heaven above is softer blue,
>   Earth around is sweeter green;
> Something lives in every hue
>   Christless eyes have never seen:
> Birds with gladder songs o'erflow,
>   Flowers with deeper beauties shine,
> Since I know, as now I know,
>   I am his and he is mine.

That was it! Whether or not I had been converted at the age of eight, I certainly was now. I have never had a moment's doubt since.

I recount this story solely because when I tell people that for years I was a Christian who believed in evolution, they sometimes exclaim, 'But were you really a Christian?' I can reply with utter conviction, 'Yes, I was. I know I was!'.

In many respects my medical training in war-torn Bristol was deficient. Take anaesthetics for example. All the anaesthetics I ever learnt was taught me by a repeat student from the year above who had failed his examination. I asked him how I would know when the patient was sufficiently 'under' to be taken from the anaesthetic room into the operating theatre. 'When the porter opens the doors', was his helpful reply.

In my final year as a medical student, I 'did kids'; that is, for five weeks I studied Paediatrics in the Bristol Children's Hospital. Owing to the call-up, few qualified staff were left. This was during some of the darkest days of the war. I remember one evening another student admitted a desperately

[197]

ill baby into the ward, and told the mother it would be all right for her to return to her home in the country. He then went off duty leaving me in sole charge of the hospital. Soon after, the infant unexpectedly died. About midnight the mother rang to enquire how her baby was. As gently as I could, I told her the child was dead. There was a gasp on the phone. Then the noise of the receiver banging to and fro in the call box. Eventually a thin voice whispered that she would come up in the morning. Next day she told me she had fainted at my news. She had been phoning from a call box at a country crossroads, half an hour's walk from where she lived.

It was during that five weeks that I determined to specialize in Paediatrics. Standing one day beside the cot of a severely wasted baby, I said to myself, 'No one has a clue what's wrong with this child, I'm going to do Paediatrics.' With the hindsight of fifty years, I think almost certainly the child suffered from Cystic Fibrosis, a condition not then recognised.

It was more than four years before I could start putting my resolve into effect. First came service with the Royal Army Medical Corps in India, Burma, Thailand (then called Siam) and Malaya. It was in Kuala Lumpur that my wife (Angel Mary Jones) and I met for the first time. She too was an Army medical officer. After demobilization, we were married from her home in Ballycastle, Northern Ireland.

Before commencing paediatric studies, I had to obtain a higher degree in general medicine. So after demobilization, I returned to Bristol to study. Later I obtained Paediatric posts in London, Cardiff and Sheffield.

*   *   *

Frustration

Because of the logjam of ex-service men and women after the war, paediatric consultant positions were hard to obtain. My post as Lecturer in the Department of Child Health, University of Sheffield, was very valuable, but the time came when advancement to a more senior position became essential. By then I was over forty, and I applied for many posts all over the British Isles. I was often shortlisted, but in vain.

Interviews became a routine. I would travel by train to the town concerned – Edinburgh, Hull, Brighton, Belfast, London, or wherever – to look over the hospital in the morning. This was always interesting. Frankly, I was often in dread that I might be offered a position in the hospital to which I was applying. Then, after a lonely lunch, I would turn up at the office at 2.00 p.m. The same old crowd of aspiring applicants would greet me – less one, of course, the person who had been successful on the last occasion we had met, but with the addition of some new aspirant. At last it was over. 'See you next time', we would joke, as the failures left for home.

In those depressing days I took comfort from Psalm 73. 'Truly God is good to Israel, to such as are pure in heart. But as for me, my feet had almost stumbled; my steps had nearly slipped. For I was envious of the boastful, when I saw the prosperity of the wicked' (verses 1–3). I am not suggesting the other candidates were especially wicked, nor that verse 13 really applied to me: it reads, 'Surely, I have cleansed my heart in vain, and washed my hands in innocence.' But I felt frustrated and sorry for myself. I tended to blame the interviewers, who time after time turned me down for someone else. I even felt tempted to blame God.

Eventually I studied two aspects of verses 21 to 24, which I applied to myself: 'My heart was grieved, and I was vexed in my mind. I was so foolish and ignorant; I was like a beast before you. Nevertheless I am continually with you; you hold me by my right hand. You will guide me with your counsel, and afterward receive me to glory.'

What right had I to be grieved and vexed when God had promised to 'hold me by my right hand'? Did those others have the same inner resource? Some certainly did not. I remember one girl bursting into tears when she discovered she had been rejected yet again.

God promised to guide me with his counsel. How? During the interview I studied those men and women sitting on the opposite side of the table, probing me with their questions: 'Why did I want this post?' Frankly, I didn't, but it would be better than nothing. 'Why did I think myself particularly suitable?' etc., etc. As I walked out of the room, my mind said to them, 'You think you are deciding my fate for the next twenty-five years or so. But you are not. You are part of God's will for my life, and the lives of those dependent on me. You are not thinking about that, you may not even acknowledge God exists, but it is so, and I know it is so.' Verse 26 reads: 'My flesh and my heart fail; But God is the strength of my heart, and my portion forever.' So although it was true that 'My flesh and my heart failed', yet I held to the belief that 'God was the strength of my heart and my portion forever'.

To Australia

One lunchtime in October 1960, I crossed the road from the Children's Hospital to the Sheffield University medical library to look at the latest paediatric journals, and glance at the advertisement columns in the *British Medical Journal*. An advertisement for the position of Foundation Professor in Child Health in the University of Queensland, Brisbane, caught my eye. I looked up Brisbane in an atlas and found it was in Australia, half-way down on the right-hand side. I applied to the PO Box number in London, and waited.

But not very long. About a week later, I was invited to an interview in London on the following Tuesday morning to meet the Vice-Chancellor of Queensland University, Sir Fred Schonell. I was informed that if I wished to attend, I must phone the day before (Monday) to be told the time of the interview. It so happened that on that Monday, I had yet another interview, on this occasion in Birmingham. The only time available to phone my acceptance to London was immediately before the Birmingham interview. But all the public telephones were occupied by long-winded callers. At the last moment I found one which was empty. But the coin box was jammed. It would not accept my money. I did not have time to locate another phone. My interview was in half an hour, and if I missed ringing now, it would be too late afterwards. In desperation I managed to get through to the exchange and explained my predicament. Would the girl connect me? I told her the money was in the machine, but I couldn't prove it. She agreed, and I was connected.

Strangely, that afternoon I was offered the Birmingham consultancy, the first such offer I had received. Which should I take? A firm appointment in England, or a possibility in Australia? The Birmingham committee generously allowed me to delay my acceptance by a week. The next day, Sir Fred offered me the Queensland post, but only provisionally. He had to return to Brisbane (no jets in those days), call together the University Senate appointment committee, and let me know by cable. To inform Birmingham on time, I must receive that cable before noon on Saturday.

That Saturday morning I was participating in a regional clinical meeting in Sheffield. My lecture was scheduled to end at midday. Just before the hour struck, I saw someone creep in to the back of the hall waving a telegram. I concluded my lecture very quickly.

All this may seem complex and unimportant to you. But to uproot a family of five children, with a sixth on the way, to travel to a completely unknown country, to a university post and hospitals of which I knew almost nothing, required firm confirmation from God. My wife and I certainly wanted to go. The last year had been one of perpetual frustration. True, the Birmingham job was quite good, but I felt happier working in a university. However, we needed evidence from God that the momentous step was in his will. If so we would step out in faith. I have to confess I had purposely made it as difficult for the University of Queensland as I could by my rigid time frame. Little did I then know the additional problem Sir Fred had in returning to Australia and gathering his committee together in the short time available.

Without doubt the decision to emigrate to Australia was one of the most important my wife and I have ever made. The only thing that held us back was the condition of our mothers. In particular my mother, then an invalid in her eighties, and without any family in England. We agonized over whether to go or stay.

Several things decided me. There was no doubt I had to leave Sheffield: the situation there had become intolerable, and the supply of consultant paediatric posts in the UK was drying up. I had been offered only one position after countless applications – the regional consultancy at Birmingham, but this included almost no teaching component.

Then there were the circumstances surrounding the offer

from the University of Queensland. We had an overwhelming sense that God was directing us as a family to move to Australia. But we had to be sure.

In this context there is an important message in Isaiah 30:21, 'Your ears shall hear a word behind you, saying "This is the way, walk in it", whenever you turn to the right hand or whenever you turn to the left.' Notice, the voice does not come from in front, leading you, but from behind, correcting you. Have you ever taken a dog for a walk in the country? You go on your way, but your dog runs ahead, and goes down a side path, following every exciting smell. When you reach the entrance to that path you whistle after him but keep on walking. Soon he turns round, runs after you and catches you up. Do you get the idea? Often in the Christian walk we make mistakes. We may go ahead of God's will and run down side paths, but if we are sincerely desirous of doing his will come what may, we can trust God to call us back in time.

When my mother heard of our proposed emigration, she sent a telegram, which read: 'He hath done all things well' (*Mark* 7:37, AV). Looking back now, from an age much nearer that of my mother's in 1960, I realize that I greatly underestimated the price she paid. I never considered, for example, the pleasure her grandchildren would have given her.

We landed in Australia in May 1961. Four weeks later our sixth, and last child was born.

24

QUEENSLAND

Life in Brisbane started with a flourish. Quite a group of people from the university, the hospital and the press met us off the overnight train from Sydney. The paediatric fraternity was most helpful. However, our rented accommodation proved to be cold, dirty and crawling with cockroaches. Dr Jim Hood, a paediatric radiologist, came to the house to help us settle in. When he saw there was no heating in the place, he kindly drove across the city to fetch an electric fire from his own home.

In 1961, Brisbane sprawled over a huge area. Most of the houses were made of wood, perched on stumps to save them from the white ants (termites, not really ants). There was only one high-rise building in the whole city. There were no traffic lights. The result for the motorist was chaos. Cars on the right always had priority even if emerging from a minor road onto a main one. I was helped when someone told me, 'You have to remember that Brisbane is really only an overgrown frontier town'. And at that time this was true. What a change today. Now it is an attractive modern city.

As soon as possible we purchased a suitable home not far from the University. It was not sewered – few houses in Brisbane were. But we found septic tanks very efficient.

I discovered that the medical situation in Queensland was quite different from that to which I was accustomed. The State Labor Party, who had been in power almost continuously since 1915, lost office in 1957. One of their proud achievements had been to provide a free hospital service (the only one in Australia) and this tradition was carried on by the Liberal

Party who followed them. Unfortunately the State was not wealthy enough to service it.

In March 1960, Sir Fred Schonell was appointed Vice-Chancellor of the University. He had an affinity with the practice of medicine, and was very helpful to me. He had previously been Professor of Education at Birmingham and had a soft spot for children, especially those who were handicapped.

Soon after he was appointed, he set about recruiting new academic clinical staff, of whom I was one of the first. Emeritus Professor Douglas Gordon[1], who was Dean of Medicine at the time, writes:

Medical education in Queensland benefited greatly from this influx of new blood in the clinical years of the course. Apart from the fact that they were men with the necessary experience in teaching, clinical practice and research, their presence was stimulating. They came from environments in which academic clinical teachers had been respected and successful, whereas in Queensland hitherto they had been barely tolerated in the halls of bureaucratic power. Such men inherently had expectations. They took it for granted that hospital authorities would treat them with respect and that money would be available to support their research interests. Sometimes it was the melancholy duty of the Dean to diminish their expectations . . . At first the newcomers suffered massive cultural shock but they adapted manfully.

I had the task of founding a new department in an unknown university, in an unknown city, in a strange country. Everything was strange.

The Department of Child Health is situated in the Children's Hospital (now the Royal Children's Hospital). This is part of a huge general hospital complex some miles from the university. Everything struck me as primitive. Paediatrics was particularly looked down on. An extremely bright student who after his internship left Queensland to work in a university in a southern State – 'Because I saw there was no future in Queensland' –told me that the night before he left, he happened to meet a senior hospital bureaucrat in the hospital car-park and informed him

[1]Douglas Gordon, 'Coming of Age in Queensland', in *A Medical School for Queensland*, ed. by R. Doherty (Brisbane: Boolarong Publications, 1968), p. 106.

that he was going to do paediatrics. 'You're a fool. There's no future in it', he was told. 'All you need is a few children's cots on the veranda of an adult ward, looked after by adult physicians.'

Visiting hours in the Children's Hospital were one hour on Saturdays and Sundays only. No mothers living in, of course. But fortunately a new ward was being built for the department, and I was given a say in the design. Here we had some accommodation for living-in mothers – the first in Australia. A few years later this was followed by free visiting.

While the department was being built, I was given a temporary office in the 'Grey Cottage'. This was a tiny, isolated, old wooden building incorporating the original hospital mortuary. It has long ago been pulled down to make place for a modern hospital.

I retain an affection for that place. The first Saturday, I sat in my Chair at the desk and savoured my new position. Later I found that very rarely did people find me there, and I could sit and meditate in peace. But that day, just as I was about to leave, I heard a footstep on the veranda and an elderly man entered, dressed in the shapeless khaki uniform of a hospital wards-man. Diffidently, he asked if he could speak to me for a few minutes. He told me he was a Christian and much revered my father although he had never met him. He had heard I was coming to Brisbane, and wanted to welcome me. We had a lovely and most welcome conversation. As he left he turned and said, 'I shall not see you again, I retire this week. Goodbye, Sir, – Brother'.

Thoughts on Evolution

I paid little attention to the theory of evolution until about 1966. Then, in January, I was asked to speak at a Christian convention for overseas students. Another of the speakers was a professional geologist. He took as his subject 'Evolution from a Christian Viewpoint'. I had never heard anyone address the subject before. I was fascinated.

Afterwards I had a long talk with him. Particularly, I asked him about the word 'good' in Genesis 1. We are told that God saw the earth he had made, and it was good (verse 10); similarly with the great sea creatures (verse 21); the land animals (verse 25), and so on. Then, in the last verse we read that 'God saw everything that he had made, and indeed it was very good' (verse 31). Man is not specifically pronounced 'good'; presumably because being made in the image of God, he was of necessity good.

I asked the geologist how the earth on which billions of creatures had died before Adam was created, could possibly be called good? He answered that the word referred to physiological and anatomical perfection. Everything in the world had been perfectly designed, so God could rightly call it good. This explanation satisfied me at the time.

However, the encounter started me thinking. There were books on creation for sale at the convention and I bought one. My idea was to read it carefully myself, then if suitable, to draw it to the attention of my teenage children.

Bernard Ramm

My initial purchase was *The Christian View of Science and Scripture* by Professor Bernard Ramm.[1] According to the 'blurb', Ramm had a wide area of expertise including 'the broad fields of astronomy, geology, biology and anthropology. While giving due weight to the known facts of both science and Scripture, he dealt plainly with the unfortunate religio-scientific literature that fails to meet the issue squarely and is at times an obscurantist's refuge.'

My general impression of the book was that it was detailed, well indexed and had an impressive bibliography. In the preface, Ramm had written:

In research for this book I have discovered that there are two traditions in Bible and science both stemming from the developments of the nineteenth century. There is the ignoble tradition which has taken a most unwholesome attitude towards science, and has used arguments and procedures not in the best traditions of established scholarship. [And there is] a noble tradition in Bible and science, and this is the tradition of the great and learned evangelical Christians who have been patient, genuine and kind and who have taken great

[1]Bernard Ramm, BD, MA, PhD, *The Christian View of Science and Scripture* (Exeter: Paternoster Press, 1st ed., 1955. Second paperback impression, January 1965).

care to learn the facts of science and Scripture. No better example can be found than that of J. W. Dawson[1] (1882; 1887), but we would also include[2] such men as John Pye Smith (1840), Pratt (1872), Dana (1880), Hugh Miller (1857), James Orr (1904), Asa Gray (1876), Bettex (1903), Ambrose Fleming (date unlisted), Rendle Short (1943) and Malcolm Dixon (title and date unlisted).

Ramm continued:

Unfortunately the noble tradition which was in the ascendancy in the closing years of the 19th C. has not been the major tradition in evangelicalism in the 20th C. A narrow bibliolatry, the product not of faith but of fear, buried the noble tradition. The sad result has been that in spite of stout affirmations that true science and the Bible agree and do not conflict, science has repudiated the ignoble tradition. It is our wish to call evangelicalism back to the noble tradition of the closing years of the 19th C.[3]

Ramm wrote as an American. So when he came to the question whether a Christian can believe in theistic evolution, his reply was that,

much bitterness has gone into this controversy . . . The author has been told that many evangelicals in Britain and Germany [and he could have added Australia] have accepted evolution into Christianity as theistic evolution, and have left the controversy alone and gone on to other things. In America we have had such bitter debates that the word evolution is a loaded word, and with many implies something evil, sinister, satanic, and atheistic. The anti-evolutionary literature is staggering in bulk.[4]

Ramm was certainly correct in his appreciation of the picture in Britain from about 1860 to the time of his writing. I am not able to comment on his assessment of the American scene.

Although he writes so disparagingly about those he calls the 'ignoble tradition', or the 'hyper-orthodox', Ramm maintains that he personally 'believes in the divine origin of the Bible and therefore in its divine inspiration; [and] emphatically rejects

[1] J. W. Dawson, *Facts and Fancies in Modern Science* (Philadelphia: American Baptist Publication Society, 1882). Also four similar, the last dated 1887.

[2] Ramm also listed a number of other authors. I have given the dates of their principal publications. Further details are given in the bibliography of his book.

[3] Ramm, *The Christian View of Science and Scripture*, pp. 8–9.

[4] Ibid., p. 197.

any partial theory of inspiration or liberal or neo-orthodox views of the Bible. If what follows disagrees with the cherished beliefs of the reader', he continues, 'be assured that it is not a difference over inspiration but over interpretation'.

Professor Ramm forcefully rejected the concept of a young earth. He stated, 'If the scientist [or theologian] affirms that the Bible teaches creation at 4004 B.C., he needlessly makes science and Scripture conflict through misinterpretation. If the first step toward truth is the removal of error, the Ussher chronology should at this point be abandoned.'

Ramm, of course, held the uniformitarian viewpoint. He believed the theory has been wrongly attacked by the hyper-orthodox who hold to the 'naive-literal view of creation . . . [The importance] of uniformitarianism' he says, 'is underlined by the fact that the entire roll-call of the earth sciences is built on the uniformitarian principle.' Logically therefore, Ramm denied a universal flood, 'or a flood as universal as man'. Also the 'derivation of all races from Noah . . . [since] it is a pious fiction to believe that Noah had a black son, a brown son and a white son.'

Paradise, the Fall, the Curse

This is an important section. You will remember that my father called the Fall, 'an impasse'. Here is how Ramm resolved the problem:

The curse fell upon the man, the woman and the serpent. The two matters of the curse which have received most attention, have been the cursing of the ground and the sentence of death. The answer to both is the realization that man was in Paradise and that too frequently commentators have presumed that the same conditions obtained outside the garden as inside. Part of man's judgement was to be turned out of that park and into the conditions prevalent in the rest of creation. Barrels of ink have been used to describe the effects of sin upon animals and nature. It has been categorically stated that all death came from man's sin. When Paul wrote that by sin death entered the world (*Rom.* 5:12)[1] it was presumed that the word world meant creation, not just humanity. It was argued that before Adam

[1]Ramm does not mention Romans 8:19–22 or 1 Corinthians 15:21–22.

sinned there was no death anywhere in the world and that all creatures were vegetarians. But this is all an imposition on the record. Ideal conditions existed only in the Garden. There was disease and death and bloodshed in Nature long before man sinned.

Ramm insists that: 'Life can only live on life. All diet must be protoplasmic. Are we to believe that the . . . magnificent array of teeth of the lion and tiger were for vegetarian purposes only?' The author also gave attention to the word 'good' which had worried me previously; he writes: 'One might affirm that such a creation could hardly be called *good*, but that is pre-judging what good means. Outside the Garden of Eden were weeds, disease, thistles, thorns, carnivores, deadly serpents, and intemperate weather.'

Over the years I have discussed the Fall with a number of Christians who believe in evolution. Most have found it an area of difficulty. In the words of one much revered Australian Christian, 'You know, John, I have never really understood the Fall'. Of course not, he is an evolutionist.

Another 'impasse' for Christian evolutionists is the narrative of the creation of Eve: Woman from man; instead of the universal, *per via naturalis*, man from woman. But Ramm ignores this. Neither Eve nor woman are referenced in his extensive index.

Conclusion

Rereading Ramm's book recently after almost thirty years, and from such a different viewpoint, I am at a loss to understand why I should have thought it might be suitable for my children. But the fact that I did, indicates that I must have subscribed to most of the ideas in it. There is, of course, much more I could quote, but I hope I have given enough to indicate the kind of thinking suggested by this well-known Christian leader. Like others in the middle of the twentieth century he lacked the scientific and historical evidence we now have.

25

WHO WAS ADAM?

Six years after I had finished Ramm's book, I discovered another book on the biblical aspects of evolution: *Who was Adam?*[1] Written in 1969 by Victor Pearce, an anthropologist and Prebendary of Lichfield Cathedral, it had been favourably reviewed in the Christian press, so I wrote to England for a copy. Pearce commences:

Development in scientific discovery has been so rapid that we are now able to see an exciting connection between the Bible and science. . . . In the field of anthropology, the identification of Adam with New Stone Age man by the use of proper diagnostic principles, is now becoming apparent.

Pearce then amplifies his major thesis: 'In Genesis 1, Old Stone Age man is described [by] the Hebrew collective noun *"adam"* meaning mankind as a whole; but in Genesis 2:4 the second toledoth commences . . . Here the noun becomes "The Adam" or "The Man" [v. 8] with the article referring to an individual, and then becomes a proper name "Adam"' [v. 19]. This, then, is the Adam of Eden who, according to Pearce, was a New Stone Age man.

Commencing from his discipline of anthropology, and linking it with his interest in the Scripture, Pearce sets out to reconcile the first chapters of Genesis with this developing field of science.

I enjoyed the book, and made detailed notes. As I look at

---

[1] Victor E. K. Pearce, BSc, Dip.Anth., *Who Was Adam?* (Exeter: Paternoster Press, 1969).

them today, they make interesting reading, not only because they are a review of Pearce's book, but also for the insights they provide into my own thinking at that time. Pearce, I opined, had advanced a useful theory, well thought of by his contemporaries, and I believed much of it was true. But, again we come to the *impasse* of the Fall, and the meaning of the word 'good'. I wrote:

When we read that, 'God saw everything that he had made and behold it was very good'. This would mean that '*adam*', Pearce's Old Stone Age Man (a hunter) was 'good', which is surprising; one would not have expected a hunter to be designated 'good'. In fact, Romans 8:20–22 makes us think that the travail of the creation came with the Fall, not before.

I decided that there were three major arguments against Pearce's thesis:

Firstly. A minor point: *The great ages at death of Adam and the ancients* do not fit Pearce's hypothesis.

Secondly. *Random selection by struggle would surely not be God's chosen method.* Pearce himself seemed unhappy about this, for he says,

We must now consider whether we are right in saying there is a general harmony between the first twenty-five verses of Genesis and what science knows of the order of events from the beginning of the present universe down to the appearance of Old Stone Age man.
  In doing so we should not forget that Genesis was written with a religious object – not a scientific one. The generalized scientific structure is but a framework for religious truth. We must remember also that it had to be phrased in such terms as would be understood by people of all ages . . . It is so brief, yet so comprehensive, presenting Creation with dignity, order, progression, purpose and goodness. The recurrent phrase 'God saw that it was good' is a lesson much needed by modern geologists, whose horizon is over-filled with the concept of nature red in tooth and claw'.[1] [Frankly, I do not understand what Pearce means by this last paragraph].

Thirdly. *Death before Adam sinned.*
Pearce tells us Scripture was not intended to satisfy our curiosity about other creations; it is only concerned 'with the

[1]Ibid., p. 84.

salvation of our own present race which now occupies this world; . . . which anthropologists agree are descended from one stock, and which need the redemption God has provided in Jesus Christ'.[1]

Against this I wrote in big letters, 'Wrong! Scripture, throughout, is concerned with the restoration of history and ecology too.'

Summary

After finishing the book, I concluded:

Assuming there was no death before Adam sinned (plants excepted), what then?
Therefore no fossils.
Therefore all species of animals would have been alive on the earth at same time. Lots of variation between and within kinds but the essential species would have been present. Therefore man far older than believed now.
Since fossils presuppose death, I asked myself the question,
'Why are there so few fossils of man?'

I noted that Pearce quotes a comment made at a meeting of The Royal Anthropological Institute: 'Evidence of the existence of Old Stone Age man for half-a-million years is more convincing from his tools than from the comparatively few skeletal remains . . . All the [human] fossil bone fragments would only cover two tables'.[2]

Maybe, therefore the so-called 'primitive humans' are degenerates, descended from Cain, etc. Perhaps relics of a pure line have not yet been found. Since Isaiah 65:25 tells us that one day carnivores will become herbivores again; and, since God gave skins to cover Adam and Eve's nakedness, therefore 'death' must have occurred almost immediately after Adam sinned.

*   *   *

It will be seen from the above that I was still muddled, but at least was working in what I now think to be the right direction. At any rate at this time in my life I too was searching.

[1]Ibid., p. 34.
[2]Ibid., p. 35.

On a number of occasions Pearce quotes my father with approval. For example, when writing about the third day of creation he comments:

The land brings forth Plant Life at God's word . . . Plant life had to precede animal life by millions of years, in order to extract from the atmosphere poisonous carbon dioxide and put oxygen into the atmosphere for animals to breathe.

[Then, quoting ARS], 'We have already seen reason to believe that animal life was not possible until there was vegetation to supply oxygen to the atmosphere . . . It is noteworthy that the Coal Measure ferns were seed-bearing. Seed-bearing plants are therefore very old.'

And concerning the sixth day:

The final act of creation was to bring man into the world. 'And God said, "Let us make man in our image, after our likeness".' Fossil man appeared on the earth much later than other mammals, certainly during the ice age, perhaps during Pliocene times. 'These considerations', wrote Rendle Short, 'bring to light a perfectly amazing concordance between the Creation narrative and the discoveries of modern science. When we remember the wild guesses as to the ultimate nature of origin of the earth that were current among other ancient people, the accuracy of Genesis stands out in solitary grandeur. Geology is a young science; the classification of strata is not much older than a hundred years; we may be sure that the author of the Creation narrative derived none of his information from fossil-hunting. Neither guesswork nor intuition taught the writer to arrange events in the correct order. This narrative bears the mark of a divine inspiration.'

My father was certainly correct in pointing to a general concordance between the Genesis account of creation and the fossil record (plants were created before animals, for example) yet if we study the details we find there are really considerable differences

Geology/Biology	**Genesis 1**
Land before oceans	Oceans before land
Life first appeared in sea	Life first appeared on land
Fish before fruit trees	Fruit trees before fish
Insects before birds	Birds before 'creeping things'
Man born from woman	Woman created from man
Death before Adam sinned	No death before the Fall

What about Pearce's personal views on the Flood? He repeats the story of the Flood as an unusually severe inundation of low-lying parts of Mesopotamia. But after providing evidence of widespread travel, he states, 'Stories of local floods would deceive nobody'. Widespread, yes! But Pearce gives no indication as to how far he thinks the Flood might have extended.

Conclusion

It seems that in the early 1970s, when I was about fifty-two, I had arrived at the same *impasse* as all other evolutionary-thinking, evangelical Christians: I was starting to wrestle with the meaning of the word 'good' in Genesis 1; the importance of the Fall, and, to a lesser extent, with the creation of woman from man. As well, I did not understand the importance of the flood. I still believed it to be local. Certainly I did not connect it with the deposition of fossils.

Last, and most importantly, I still thought in terms of millions of years. The possibility of a six-day creation had not entered my mind. Alongside the word 'day' in my Bible I had written, 'Why limit God's 'days' to man's petty days?'

All this time, so my wife tells me, I constantly affirmed that God would never break his own laws of nature. I still reasoned that all miracles must have some scientific explanation. I am ashamed to say I even thought up ingenious, but improbable, hypotheses to account for them. For example: I too had walked on water – on ice. Did Christ walk on an ice-floe?

Lastly, you must understand that although earlier in this book I quoted extensively from ARS's daybooks and sermon notes, they were unknown to me in 1970. In fact it was not until about 1986 that I first began to study them, and to trace my father's long struggle with evolutionary theory.

26

TORONTO AND SWITZERLAND

After studying Pearce, then rereading Ramm, my interest in creation was thoroughly aroused. Partly, I suspect, because both men quoted my father approvingly. I did not know of any other books on the subject; nor could I find anyone else to share my interest. To be honest, I don't think I looked very hard. At that time in Christian circles, English or Australian, even to admit that you believed in creation was to risk being labelled divisive, or a crank. And in scientific circles it was almost akin to admitting – as Thomas Huxley said of his early interest in Darwinism – that you had murdered your grandmother! Yet I had an increasing suspicion that the matter might be important. What should I do next?

I decided to follow a line I had used on a previous occasion. Since I knew so little about the topic, I would write a book on it. To some this may seem bizarre, even dishonest, but it had worked so well previously that I determined to try the same method again.

In an earlier chapter I explained how I decided to specialize in paediatrics during my student years. But this was during the War, and before I could start training I had to do service in the Royal Army Medical Corps, where I spent all my time looking after adults. However, on demobilisation, I determined to take the necessary paediatric examinations as soon as possible. But I had not seen a sick child since my student days. So in order to teach myself, I wrote a chapter of a book (an easy one!) and sent it to Messrs John Wright, the medical publisher. Many years previously they had published *A Synopsis of Physiology* for my father. Now I was asking them to publish *A Synopsis of Children's Diseases*[1] for me. This they agreed to do, and the book came out a few years later. Incidentally I learnt enough paediatrics to pass my specialist examinations.

The Miracles Book

My new book was to be entitled *Five Essential Miracles: A struggle for faith*. The five miracles were Creation, The Virgin Birth, The Resurrection, Personal Creation and Ecological Recreation.

I began to write in 1972, but progress was very slow as I was fully occupied with administering a university department, research, clinical work, teaching etc.; then there were family responsibilities and speaking at various Christian organizations. But progress was also slow because all the time my views were changing. Gradually I was moving away from a strictly evolutionist to a more creationist viewpoint.

The 'Diagnostica' Connection

Then a chain of events commenced which was to be of great significance in my life. I had returned to work following a holiday. As usual my secretary had opened and sorted my fairly voluminous mail, dealing with all the items she could. But a pile of circulars remained. These were put aside to be looked at later. I did not get around to sorting them for several days, and even then in a perfunctory and disinterested fashion. In fact, to save time on this occasion, I pitched those which seemed to be from drug houses into the wastepaper basket unopened. One letter landed in the basket along with the rest, but something about the envelope must have attracted me, and I later retrieved it. It contained an invitation to attend a committee in Rome, all expenses paid!

---

[1]John Rendle-Short, *A Synopsis of Children's Diseases* (Bristol: John Wright and Sons, 1st ed. 1954; 6th ed. with O. P. Gray and J. A. Dodge, 1985). My father continued to have books permanently in print with Messrs John Wright from 1911 until after his death in 1953. As I also have written some books on paediatrics which were published by the same firm, it so happened that either he or I were on their book lists for over eighty years until the firm ceased to exist.

At that time the multinational pharmaceutical firm Ames published a journal called *Diagnostica*. In order to improve the quality, they were establishing a panel of professional advisors. They chose people from different specialties – surgery, medicine, endocrinology, gynaecology, general practice, paediatrics – about ten in all. In addition to the mix of specialties, there were different nationalities. Most came from the United States, but also one each from Japan, Singapore, England, France, Columbia, and Australia. The group was to meet once a year.

God so ordained that I was invited as the paediatrician. I say 'God so ordained . . .' purposefully and with conviction. I am wary of well-intentioned people who say, 'God told me to . . .' do so and so. Sometimes what they purpose is manifestly ridiculous, and results in disaster. But Scripture, Christian biography and my own personal experience over a number of years, compel me to believe that sometimes God *does* guide us in unmistakable and beautiful ways. He has given us minds to reason with, and as long we obey the ground rules laid down in the Bible, we can safely exercise our common sense.

Quite apart from the value of the meetings to me (and I hope to the journal), the travel enabled me to visit places, and attend other conferences in a way which otherwise would never have been possible.

The first meeting, in six months' time, was to be in Rome. After that, as the delegates all had to travel considerable distances, it was decided that the venue should be varied, alternating between Europe and the Americas. So in July each year I travelled successively to Rome, Honolulu, Stockholm, Bogata, and Vienna. Then, to my regret, the journal ceased publication.

In 1974 the meeting was held in Stockholm. By what my father would have called one of 'the pretty ways of Providence', it happened that two other conferences were scheduled to take place on the days immediately preceding the Stockholm meeting. These slotted in very well, and I was able to attend them *en route*. The first was the International Convention of Christian Physicians held in Toronto; the second, the Billy Graham-sponsored World Congress on Evangelization, *'Let the Earth Hear His Voice'*, in Lausanne, Switzerland.

Toronto

Although I have been a member of the Christian Medical Fellowship for most of my medical life, this has been my only opportunity to attend the International Convention. The topics on this occasion included lectures on 'Drugs of Addiction' – very appropriate for a doctor working with youth.

One of the scheduled speakers was a well-qualified Professor of Pharmacology, Dr A. E. Wilder-Smith. At that time I had not heard of him. Although British, he lived in Switzerland and had been adviser in drugs of addiction to the American army in Germany. His lecture was fascinating and I bought an audio-tape.

On the Sunday of the conference, the delegates were taken to the People's Church in Toronto. Waiting in the coach to go back after the service, I found myself sitting in the same seat as Professor Wilder-Smith. Somehow, I do not know how, the topic of creation and evolution came up. Professor Wilder-Smith voiced his opinion that the world was created in six literal days, just as stated in Genesis. I was flabbergasted, overwhelmed. No-one of scientific integrity had ever said such a thing in my hearing before. I had never seriously entertained the possibility. Whether from astonishment, or because the coach started with a sudden jerk, I do not know, but I found myself suddenly precipitated onto the floor. The importance of six-day creation was firmly impressed upon me!

I had no further opportunity to talk to Professor Wilder- Smith in Toronto, or indeed for the next ten years. But on the convention bookstall I found a book he had written, *Man's Origin, Man's Destiny*.[1] This was the first publication I had ever seen by a man who openly stated his belief that the 'days' in the first chapter of Genesis are literal days and should be accepted as such.

A Search for Evidence

When I was in Toronto I was of, course, taken to see the Niagara Falls. As I peered over the rail into the impressive

[1]Arthur Wilder-Smith, *Man's Origin, Man's Destiny* (Wheaton, Ill: Shaw, 1968). I did not know it at the time, but Dr Wilder-Smith had three earned doctorates in various branches of science. He continued writing books and lecturing until his death in Switzerland in 1995.

gorge below the falls, I told myself that surely it must have taken millions of years for the river to erode that channel. I did not know then that Sir Charles Lyell had looked down into the same tumble of water about 130 years previously (see p. 14), and that the data he had collected formed an important part of his evidence for uniformitarianism.[1]

As I gazed at Niagara, I remembered other gorges I had seen; the Avon Gorge in Clifton, Bristol, and, far more impressive, the gorge of the Blue Nile in Ethiopia – so deep and inaccessible that to this day the floor has rarely been explored. Surely, I reasoned, it must have taken millions of years for a trickle of water to cut that deep ravine. Only years later did I discover that the gorge is part of the Great African Rift Valley, formed, not by the river, but by a geological fault. The river just happens to like flowing that way.

There is a lesson here for those who believe in evolution, or those who believe in creation: the danger of inaccurate evidence believed with dogged tenacity.

The Lausanne Congress

The second International Congress on World Evangelization was held in Lausanne, Switzerland. I do not remember evolution or creation being discussed as such, but then I was not particularly listening for the topic. More importantly, the official record of the congress, entitled *Let The Earth Hear His Voice*[2] published in 1975 makes no formal reference to the evolution/creation debate nor, incidentally, to so-called pre-evangelism.

However, the subject was not completely ignored. A paper by Kenneth Hamilton entitled *Apologetics and Evangelization* touched on creation. He considered how people have viewed the topic of apologetics down the centuries, pointing out that the writings of apologists rapidly become out of date. He instanced William Paley's *View of the Evidences of Christianity*[3] and asked, 'Who reads it now? No one.' I agree,

---

[1]See Taylor, *In the Minds of Men*. Taylor has worked in Toronto for many years.

[2]*Let the Earth Hear His Voice*, International Conference on World Evangelization, Lausanne, Switzerland (Minneapolis: World Wide Publications, 1975).

[3]William Paley (1748–1805), *View of the Evidences of Christianity*, 1794.

although Paley's 'watchmaker' argument[1] is still frequently quoted.

In Lausanne I had my only face-to-face meeting with Dr Francis Schaeffer, whose writings have had a profound effect on my Christian life.

Francis Schaeffer and L'Abri

I had discovered L'Abri late in 1971, when I purchased Schaeffer's *Escape From Reason* from another conference bookstall. This was soon followed by *The God Who is There*.[2] The teaching of the L'Abri Fellowship opened my eyes to a new world of Art, Literature, Philosophy and the relevance of these 'Arts-type' subjects to Christianity.

I come from a medical, scientific background, and when on the Professorial Board of the Queensland University I rubbed shoulders with members of other departments, I regret to say I often regarded the faculty of Arts as in some way inferior to other faculties which were more professionally based. Certainly, I felt, they did not deserve any big slice of the meagre university research funds!

You must understand that most medical doctors are woefully ignorant of the world of culture. They are so immersed in their clinical work that they have little time for wide reading. From L'Abri I soon found that, not only could 'cultural topics' be intensely interesting, but also of great assistance as I talked to young people about Christianity.

Swiss L'Abri, Huemoz

I visited L'Abri headquarters in Huemoz, Switzerland, while on the way to another *Diagnostica* committee, this time in Vienna. I had broken the journey in Zurich in order to visit a

---

[1]Paley develops this argument in his book *Natural Theology*. He describes a man walking across a lonely heath and coming on a watch which 'on inspection discloses design'. This could only have been produced by an intelligent being. Similarly as we consider the universe – especially the earth abounding with life – 'the works of design are too strong to be gotten over.' Design, Paley concludes, must have a designer, and that designer must be a person. That person is God.

[2]Francis A. Schaeffer, *Escape From Reason* (London: Inter-Varsity Press, 1968); *The God Who Is There* (London: Hodder and Stoughton, 1968).

child with autism. From there I hired a car to drive to Huemoz for the weekend. Unfortunately neither Dr Schaeffer nor his wife Edith were present at the time.

At L'Abri I attended the daily sessions. The form was that we were notified in which chalet to assemble. In due time (nothing started punctually), a staff member would appear and play one of Schaeffer's tapes to the small group present; questions would be asked, and a vigorous discussion developed. In fact so many were the questions, and so warm the argumentation, that no tape was completed. That did not seem to matter.

The group was drawn from various nationalities and occupations. My attention was particularly attracted to a young American couple, Peter and Petronella.[1] They had come to L'Abri 'because it sounded interesting. Something new. Another trip.' Both wore the obligatory uniform of the time: long hair with a head band, scruffy shirts, jeans and sandals. They were 'doing' Europe from a beat-up old VW. Unfortunately, it had insufficient power to climb the mountains. It seemed a pity to be in Switzerland yet stay all the time in the valleys, so I offered them a ride up a mountain in my hired car.

We sat in a meadow among the beautiful summer flowers, ate cherry pie and talked. I learned a lot. I remember Peter saying, 'Salvation, what do you mean by salvation? I've never done anything wrong, and if I have, who cares?' And according to his deterministic world-view, he was speaking the simple truth. If science has *proved* there is no God, then man cannot be made in his image. He is just an evolved animal, nothing special; so who minds what happens to you? Love is only sex. There are no moral absolutes. Everything you think or do is determined by your heredity and environment,[2] or if you prefer a more basic level, by your physics and chemistry.

Let C. S. Lewis explain what I mean. In his novel *That Hideous Strength*[3] he introduces a particularly unpleasant character by the name of Frost who is being chased by his enemies:

[1]Names altered.

[2]This word has changed its meaning over the years. By the middle of the last century it had come to mean, 'the conditions or influences under which a person lives'. Particularly in contrast to heredity, as the way, or circumstances, in which a child is reared (*OED*). This is the sense in which I use it here.

[3]C. S. Lewis, *That Hideous Strength* (London: Pan Books, 1945), p. 210.

In a dim way the possibility of destruction was never out of his thoughts. Now it seemed to be descending on him. He reminded himself that *fear was only a chemical phenomenon* [that is, mere physics and chemistry]. For the moment, clearly, he must step out of the struggle, come to himself and make a new start later in the evening.

As we parted, Peter wanted my address. I gave it to him, and asked in return, 'Would you mind if I prayed for you?' He replied, 'I can't very well stop you, can I?' I agreed.

Two months later, back in Australia, I got a letter from Berlin. It began, 'Dear Doc, Praise the Lord. I have been chosen and I have answered. To refresh your memory, I am Peter, one of two – Peter and Petronella. We met at L'Abri.' At the time he wrote, Petronella was not yet a Christian, and they had separated. Nine months later I received an invitation to their wedding in California. Unfortunately I was not able to attend.

Schaeffer at Lausanne

When I spoke to Dr Schaeffer at the Lausanne Congress, he told me how he had tussled over the section in the Lausanne Covenant on *The Authority and Power of the Bible*. He had insisted it should contain an unequivocal reference to the infallibility of Scripture. Probably this paragraph owes much to his authorship: 'We affirm the divine inspiration, truthfulness and authority of both the Old and New Testament Scriptures in their entirety as the only written Word of God, without error in all that it affirms, and the only infallible rule of faith and practice'. He signed it. But, then, so also did a number of others, including some who certainly do not subscribe to a literal interpretation of Genesis 1–11. Regretfully, for many, even in Christian circles, 'words mean what I mean them to mean'.

I invited Dr Schaeffer to visit Australia. 'Not yet', he replied, 'the situation there is not bad enough. I have other more needy places to visit.' He never managed to come. However, when I returned home I optimistically opened a file and marked it, 'Australian L'Abri'.

At the Congress Schaeffer contributed a paper entitled, 'Form and Freedom in the Church'.[1] In his inimitable phraseology he reiterated his favourite theme:

We must say with sadness that in some places, seminaries and institutions, individuals who are known as evangelical no longer hold to a full view of Scripture. The issue is clear: is the Bible true truth and infallible wherever it speaks, including where it touches history and the cosmos, or is it only in some sense revelational where it touches religious subjects? This is the issue and I would like to repeat it.

He then said it again with great emphasis and continued: 'The heart of neo-existential theology is that the Bible is a quarry out of which to hew religious experiences, but that the Bible contains mistakes where it touches that which is verifiable – namely history and science.'

According to Schaeffer, this type of reasoning has, unhappily, even invaded some who call themselves evangelicals. They hold the view that not *all* the Bible is revelational and in particular it teaches little or nothing when it speaks of the cosmos. That is, on the subject of natural history in its widest sense. By way of reply, Schaeffer quoted Martin Luther: 'If I profess with the loudest and clearest exposition every portion of the truth of God except precisely that little point where the world and the devil are at the moment attacking, I am not confessing Christ.'

But the opposite end of the spectrum, as Schaeffer pointed out, is dead orthodoxy. To counteract this we need 'a love of community':

We say man is different because he is made in the image of God. But we must not say man is made in the image of God unless we look to God and by God's grace treat every man with dignity. We stand against B.F. Skinner in his book, *Beyond Freedom and Dignity*, but I do not dare argue against Skinner's determinism if I then treat the man I meet day by day as less than really made in the image of God.

Schaeffer on Creation

What were Schaeffer's views on Creation? It is difficult to be quite certain. Constantly he stresses the infallibility of Scripture.

[1]Francis A. Schaeffer, 'Form and Freedom in the Church', in *Let the Earth Hear His Voice: A comprehensive reference volume on World Evangelization* (Minneapolis: World Wide Publications, 1975), pp. 361–79.

In the preface of his book, *Genesis in Space and Time*,[1] Schaeffer looks at the way in which various people regard the first chapters of Genesis. Some see it as 'a Jewish myth, having no more historical validity for modern man than the Epic of Gilgamesh or the stories of Zeus. For others it forms a pre-scientific vision that no-one who respects the results of modern scholarship can accept'. Some, on the other hand, view the early chapters of Genesis as revelational, *containing* religious truth, but lose 'any sense of truth in regard to history and the cosmos (science)'.

'Well then', asks Schaeffer, 'How should these early chapters of Genesis be read? Are they historical and if so what value does their historicity have?' He is vehement in underlining,

The tremendous value of Genesis 1–11 for modern man. In some ways these chapters are the most important in the Bible, for they put man in his cosmic setting and show him his peculiar uniqueness. They explain man's wonder and yet his flaw. Without a proper understanding of these chapters we have no answer to the problems of metaphysics, morals or epistemology [the science of the grounds of knowledge]. Furthermore, the work of Christ becomes one more upper-story 'religious' answer.[2]

Surprisingly, evolutionism also purports to give answers to the same deep questions concerning man and his place in the universe. According to the *Fontana Dictionary*,[3] 'Evolutionary humanism is a sort of secular religion or religion surrogate founded on the deeply held conviction that evolution is the fundamental modality of all change in the universe, so that all agencies that provoke change and all that retard it can be described as "good" and "bad" respectively.'

Schaeffer makes an important differentiation between what he calls 'true communication and exhaustive communication'. 'The Bible', he says, 'gives us true knowledge, although not exhaustive knowledge.' Indeed, since man is a finite creature, he is not capable of comprehending exhaustive knowledge.

---

[1]Francis A. Schaeffer, *Genesis in Space and Time* (Illinois: Inter-Varsity Press, 1972).

[2]Ibid. p. 9. By 'upper story "religious" . . .' Schaeffer is referring to events considered in the realm of philosophy, remote from the 'real' world.

[3]'Evolutionary Humanism', in *The Fontana Dictionary of Modern Thought* (London: Fontana/Collins, 1983).

Further, Schaeffer maintains that Scripture contains information concerning cosmic creation:

Because we need to know these things which were before the Fall. What the Bible tells us is propositional, factual and true truth, [but] it is given in relation to men. It *is* a scientific textbook in the sense that where it touches the cosmos it is true, propositionally true . . . [But] it is not a scientific textbook if by that one means that its purpose is to give us exhaustive truth or that scientific fact is its central theme and purpose.[1]

In a relevant footnote on p. 173, Schaeffer elaborates on the relationship of science to the Bible. There may be, so he tells us, a difference between the methodology by which we gain knowledge from the Bible or from scientific study, 'But that does not lead to a dichotomy of facts.' He illustrates this by considering the Tower of Babel. We can look at the story from a biblical or scientific point of view. The important fact is that whichever way we choose, 'either the Tower of Babel was there or it was not there'. The same can be said of Adam. 'Either he was a true first man, or he was not'. And, I would add, the same can be said of Eve, either she was a real woman created miraculously from Adam's side, or she was not.

In another important paragraph, Schaeffer maintains that 'there indeed must be a place for the study of general revelation'.[2] He continues:

There is no automatic need to accommodate the Bible to the statements of science. There is a tendency for some who are Christians and scientists to always place special revelation under the control of general revelation and science, and never or rarely to place general revelation and what science teaches under the control of the Bible's teaching. That is, though they think of that which the Bible teaches as true and that which science teaches as true, *in reality they tend to end with the truth of science as more true than the truth of the Bible.*[3]

---

[1]Schaeffer, *Genesis in Space and Time*, p. 37.

[2]God's general revelation is that which he has revealed of himself and his works in nature. (See, for example, among many Psalms 104, 107. See also Romans 1:18–21; 10:17–18, quoting from Psalm 19:1–4). General revelation is to be contrasted with special revelation, which is God's written word, the Scriptures. (See Galatians 1:11–12; Ephesians 3:3–5; 2 Timothy 3:15–16; 2 Peter 1:16–21).

[3]Schaeffer, *Genesis in Space and Time*, p. 173.

Schaeffer does not enter into the vexed question of the 'days' of Genesis 1. All he will say is that: 'The answer must be held with some openness'. And, 'From the study of the word in Hebrew, it is not clear which way it is to be taken'. He also maintained that there is 'a lack of finality in science concerning the problem of dating'.

What did Schaeffer think about Noah's flood? He writes, 'Christians who love the Scripture have discussed at length whether the flood was universal or not. I believe it was, but we should not make it a 'test of orthodoxy'. He rests his case on biblical passages elsewhere which refer to the flood,[1] pointing out that some of these parallel Christ's second coming.

Summary

When I first read Schaeffer's thoughts on the 'days' of Genesis 1, the problem of dating, and Noah's flood I found them less than satisfying. However, I now take into account the fact that Schaeffer spoke as a theologian and philosopher and not as a scientist. Apparently he did not feel free to pontificate on a topic which he would probably have regarded as outside his terms of reference. Furthermore, he was writing two or three decades ago. He never lived to see the recent explosion of scientific evidence against evolution and in favour of creation.

It was as an apologist to thinking men and women that Schaeffer excelled. Christians, he said, are often in need of 'honest answers to honest questions'. Atheists and sceptics, on the other hand, need to be brought face to face with 'the logic of their own presuppositions'. To such people he would ask such questions as, 'Have you an adequate explanation for the origin of that which you should know best, Yourself?'; 'Where did personality come from?'; 'Where did the appreciation of beauty and the ability to say "it is right", "it is wrong", come from?'; 'Where did morality come from?'; 'What is beyond the biological attraction that makes it meaningful for a man to say "I love you" to a woman?'.

With emphasis Schaeffer asserted, 'Evolutionary theory knows nothing of these things'.

[1]See, for example, Isaiah 54:9; Matthew 24:37–39; Hebrews 11:7; 1 Peter 3:20; 2 Peter 2:5. Also appendix 2.

Faced with questions like these, the humanist has no answers. Such a person is 'Without hope and without God in the world' (*Eph.* 2:12).

27

MAN'S ORIGIN, MAN'S DESTINY AND OTHER BOOKS

Until the episode in Toronto, I had never met any trained scientist who believed in a literal interpretation of the first eleven chapters of Genesis. (I talk about the 'first *eleven* chapters', because chapter twelve introduces us to Abram, thus chapter eleven is the end of what is called, in secular terminology, pre-history.) Of course, even before Toronto I would have said I believed the Bible was inspired, but what that meant for history and the cosmos, I had not really considered.

It was several years before I met another 'Creationist'; indeed, I had never heard the term. This ensured that my early research material was limited to the Bible, aided for the next few years by three helpful books.

The first of these was by Professor Wilder-Smith: *Man's Origin, Man's Destiny*,[1] to which I have already referred. I took this book with me on my journey to Stockholm, and read it in my hotel room during the long jet-lag nights. I had not considered the scientific aspects of evolution since my student days. I found Wilder-Smith's book far more scientifically plausible than anything I had read on the subject before. Early in the book Wilder-Smith considers the very practical question of why the creation narrative should be so unpalatable to most scientists. He suggests several reasons.[2]

---

[1]A. E. Wilder-Smith, *Man's Origin, Man's Destiny* (Wheaton, Ill.: Harold Shaw, 1968).

[2]For some further reasons see Richard Milton, *The Facts of Life: Shattering the Myth of Darwinism* (London: Fourth Estate Pub., 1992), pp. 163, 168, 234.

Firstly, because they believe that many phenomena once thought to be supernatural can now be explained on a natural basis. As someone remarked to me recently, 'The more science discovers, the less we need God'. But Wilder-Smith issues a warning: 'Surely', he comments, 'we should not extrapolate too far and assume that *every* phenomenon can be explained on a purely material basis'.[1]

Another suggestion by Wilder-Smith is that scientists dislike 'having to reckon with the entirely unpredictable, with a God who might do anything, and whom we cannot investigate.'

I can add another reason: many professional evolutionists would face severe disruption to their work, and probably finances too, if evolution was proved to be a myth.

Lastly, in the oft-quoted words of Sir Arthur Keith, 'Evolution is unproved and unprovable. We believe it because the only alternative is an act of creation, by a God, and this is unthinkable'. 'And', Keith might have continued, 'He might make unacceptable demands'.

At the end of the last century, there was a wave of optimism, spurred on by evolutionism. According to the *Fontana Dictionary of Modern Thought*, 'Evolutionism is normally associated with a belief in the inevitability of progress.'

But is this optimism justified? On the contrary, since the commencement of World War I, an incipient pessimism has crept in. True, there has been wave after wave of incredible inventions in many diverse fields: diseases have been controlled or cured, man has walked on the moon . . . and so on, and so on. But on the down side, new diseases have appeared, and weapons of mass destruction multiplied; there has been gross degradation of the environment, the suicide rate is increasing each year, the family is disintegrating. While people are living longer it is at great physical and mental cost. The result has been a rise in euthanasia. Young and old are in despair.

It is surely obvious that evolutionary humanism with its creed of optimism has failed mankind. Why? Because the theory is founded on the wrong premise. The present calamitous

---

[1]Wilder-Smith, *Man's Origin, Man's Destiny*, p. 23.

state of the world is the result of the Fall of mankind (*Gen.* 3:17–19). According to St Paul, 'the creation was subjected to futility [disorder], not willingly, but because of him who subjected it in hope.... The whole creation groans and labours with birth pangs together until now' (*Rom.* 8: 20–22).

Dr Wilder-Smith, quoting the Second Law of Thermodynamics, states that: 'Although the total energy in the cosmos remains constant, the amount of energy available to do useful work is always getting smaller.' Or, more briefly, 'Available Energy Constantly Decreases'.[1]

I found this section particularly useful, because for me, the law was just another long forgotten residue from my schooldays.

Since Dr Wilder-Smith lived in Switzerland, it is appropriate that he should illustrate this law by reference to the kinetic energy produced from hydro-electricity. But let me give an example from nearer home, based on my personal experience.

Recently I visited the hydro-electric power station at Wivenhoe dam, west of Brisbane. In the hills above the main reservoir is the smaller Split-Yard Creek dam. Here water is stored which can be delivered at will via four large tunnels to operate turbines in the power station far below at Wivenhoe. This enables the production of extra electricity at any time to meet sudden demand. The advantage of the system is its flexibility. Sixty kilometres away in Brisbane, the requirements of the Queensland electricity grid are monitored, and controlled. When extra power is needed, the Wivenhoe power station is switched on. But when not required to produce electricity, the turbines can be used to pump water back up the pipes to be stored again in Split-Yard Creek dam for future use. However, and here is the important point, because of the loss of useful energy accounted for by the Second Law, the system will only generate electricity for *five* hours, using water it has taken *seven* hours to pump back into the high dam.

What is the significance of the Second Law? Wilder-Smith writes, 'The Law seems to describe the situation of our present material world perfectly, and the Bible very clearly confirms this' (*Rom.* 8:22–23). There is this tendency for everything to go downhill to randomness, chaos and destruction.

[1]Ibid. p. 56.

It is obvious that the Second Law (sometimes known as the Law of Entropy) presents an enormous hurdle for believers in evolution. All nature is demonstrated to be in a state of decay, the opposite of evolution (*Rom.* 8:20–22).

Randomness

Linked with the Second Law is the principle of randomness. In his book Wilder-Smith illustrates this in such a personal and dramatic fashion, that I still remembered the passage when I re-read it more than twenty years later.[1] Briefly, he describes throwing 100,000 cards from a light aircraft. He asks: Would they sail to earth and land so as to form exactly the letters of his initials A-E-W-S? Obviously not. They would land in a random fashion. That is the universal state of things in any system, open or closed, unless there is intelligence acting, or some form of pre-existing programmed mechanism.[2]

*   *   *

The Origin of Life

Prior to the middle of the nineteenth century people believed in 'spontaneous generation'. They observed that if rotten meat is left lying about, it soon breeds maggots. Seemingly, new life has been formed. The Second Law has been broken.

[1] Dr Wilder-Smith's description is lengthy, but because it impressed me so much at the time I include it here: 'I take a small aircraft and fly at 6,000 feet over my home in Einigen/Thun in Switzerland. I have with me in the aircraft one hundred thousand unprinted white cards stacked in orderly little piles. When I am over my home, I open an escape hatch in the aircraft, and push out all these heaps of card with one almighty heave. The cards flutter down slowly and spread out in the breeze over the shores of the Lake of Thun and Einigen. Some come down over Interlaken and some over Beaten Berg. "What would be our reaction, however, if someone were to announce after our landing that all three hundred thousand cards had landed on the roof of my house in Einegen precisely in the form of my initials A-E-W-S? Impossible!"' He continues, 'Everyone knows that the cards would become more and more disorganized (random) as they fall, until they reach a more or less completely random distribution all over the area. And this is precisely what the second law of thermodynamics predicts and requires: order degenerates with passage of time into increasing randomness and chaos.' Wilder-Smith, *Man's Origin, Man's Destiny*, p. 57.

[2] A suggested exception is the growth of a crystal, but this not analogous to the origin of life, and in any case, the resultant order is 'encoded' on the molecules in the original solution.

Then Pasteur performed his famous experiments. He showed that, in a 'closed' system, this never happens. For new life to appear, 'life' in some form has to be injected into the system from outside. Only prior life can beget life.

Here we come to the central point in Wilder-Smith's thesis: 'Life can appear in an apparently closed system only when we open it to an outside *intelligence* or living influence.' So for the origin of life on earth, some intelligence (or evidence of it in the form of a programme) must have been 'injected' into the waiting inorganic chemicals. (See also a more modern book on the same subject by Werner Gitt, *Did God Use Evolution?*, Appendix 1).

But where does this prior life, this intelligence, come from? 'From outer space, probably in the form of DNA carried by meteorites', say Sir Fred Hoyle and Dr Wickramasinghe.[1] I listened to Sir Fred lecture on his theory before the Royal Society of Medicine in London. The audience, consisting mainly of Harley Street specialists, applauded mildly at the end. No one asked any questions. I doubt if most of them knew what to make of it.

Another theory, that of 'Directed Panspermia', was suggested by Nobel Prize winner Dr Francis Crick.[2] He postulates that 'the roots of our form of life go back to another place in the universe, almost certainly another planet; that it had reached a very advanced form there before anything much had started here; and that life here was seeded by micro-organisms sent on some form of spaceship by an advanced civilization'.

Despite these suggestions the majority of scientists still believe that life somehow evolved here on earth by a strange combination of chance circumstances. But if they do, why the intense interest in space exploration, costing billions of dollars? Probably because scientists also believe that if life did evolve on earth it must surely have evolved elsewhere as well, for example on Mars, and they are out to find it.

[1]Sir Fred Hoyle and Chandra Wickramasinghe, *Evolution from Space* (St Albans: Granada Publishing, 1983).

[2]Directed Panspermia is the brainchild of Francis Crick. Instead of solving the problem of life's origin, it merely transports the problem to another part of the universe. He won the Nobel Prize for Physiology in 1962 for his part in the discovery of the molecular structure of DNA. See *Life Itself, Its Origin and Nature* (London & Sydney: Macdonald and Co., 1981), p. 141.

Unfortunately most people reject the only reasonable alternative – that the living God provided the necessary 'intelligence' at the dawn of time.

Man's Origin, Man's Destiny thrilled me when I first read it. By its timing and content it was one of the most influential books I have read. Although written twenty-five years ago, and therefore somewhat dated, it remains fresh today.

More Books

In 1976 the Queensland University Senate granted me a year's study leave. My family and I spent most of the time in Cambridge. The excellent library facilities there enabled me to pursue my research into Autism, with a commencing interest in Minimal Brain Dysfunction.

One day I attended a research seminar on the latter subject at Guy's Hospital in London. I went by train, and changed at Waterloo Station. I don't think I had ever been there before. With time on my hands I wandered around and found in the centre of the vast concourse, an enclosed area. If it had been in the open air it would have been a tent or small marquee, but this was open to the roof. Inside, to my surprise, was a book-stall. Furthermore, it was a Christian book-stall. More remarkable still it contained a number of books on creation. What a bonanza! I bought one, and, lacking ready cash, resolved to return to Waterloo as soon as possible to purchase more. This I did. But the tent was gone. I have been to the station since but the tent and its hoard has vanished.

The book I obtained was *The Great Brain Robbery: Studies in Evolution* by David C.C. Watson.[1] Being written for high-school children I found it understandable. From Watson I learnt, among other matters, the inadequacy of uniformitarianism, the significance of the universal flood in the creation narrative, and in particular, the importance of the verse in Genesis, 'All the fountains of the great deep were broken up' (7:11). So here at last, was a logical reason for the vast number of fossils buried in sedimentary rock all over the earth.

[1] David C. C. Watson, *The Great Brain Robbery: Studies in Evolution* (Worthing, Sussex: Henry E. Walter, 1975).

*   *   *

On that same visit to Cambridge I found in the Municipal Library another intriguing book, *Darwin Retried: An Appeal to Reason*,[1] by Norman Macbeth. Arthur Koestler in a review wrote: 'This brilliant treatise highlights the shortcomings and inconsistencies of the neo-Darwinian theory . . .' And Sir Karl R. Popper called it, 'An excellent and fair, though unsympathetic retrial of Darwin. I regard the book as most meritorious and as a really important contribution to the debate . . .' Neither, of course, agreed with it in full.

Macbeth's intensely interesting, well-researched, and in places humorous book shows evidence of being written by a lawyer. In the first chapter he makes a very important point, which in some ways reminded me of *Omphalos:*

Courtroom experience during my career at the bar taught me to attach great weight to something that may seem trivial to persons not skilled in argumentation – the burden of proof. The proponents of a theory in science or elsewhere, are obligated to support every link in the train of reasoning, whereas the critic or sceptic may peck at any aspect of the theory, testing it for flaws. He is not obligated to set up any theory of his own, or to offer any alternative explanation.

This summarizes Macbeth's stance. He appears to hold no strong religious convictions. Indeed, his final verdict is, 'We say, "Not Proven" to Darwin's suggestion as to how and why, but we do not return to fundamentalism.' Here is an example of his style. He quotes Mark Twain, 'There is something fascinating about science. One gets such wholesale returns of conjecture out of such a trifling investment of fact.'

From Macbeth I learned that any intelligent layman, even if he makes no particular Christian profession, can readily find flaws in the theory of evolution. Indeed, Macbeth calls evolution, 'Religion in Reverse'. He writes: 'The determination

---

[1]Norman Macbeth, *Darwin Retried: An Appeal to Reason* (Ipswich: Gambit Press, 1971). Macbeth was writing before the popularization of the New Age Movement. Today evolutionary-based mysticism is more and more rejecting materialism and returning to the promise of future bliss after death, although in a different form more reminiscent of neo-paganism. Its practitioners have gleaned some comfort, no matter how inappropriate, from some of the more counter-intuitive conclusions of the so-called 'new physics'.

to exclude Christianity . . . is only a reflection of a far more significant fact: *"Darwinism itself has become a religion".*' He asserts this religion of Darwinism is demonstrated by the following dogmas:

(a) The 'All Who Are Not with Me Are Against Me' dogma.
(b) The 'Reproof of the Fainthearted' dogma. That is the belief that if a colleague becomes disillusioned with evolution he is no longer wholly reasonable.
(c) The 'Missionary Zeal' dogma. The conviction that, for example, evolution must be taught in every high school.
(d) The 'Perfect Faith' in any newly propounded idea dogma.
(e) The 'Millenarianism' dogma. He points out 'The distinctly religious idea of heaven on earth . . . [although] this has become a little threadbare in the course of the century'.

Finally, Macbeth makes the dogmatic pronouncement:

It is my conviction, after examining the literature, that intelligence and integrity are still very much alive among biologists. In their own circles they speak candidly and express their misgivings freely. Only when they popularize do they become pompous and pontifical. Perhaps they are reluctant to confess error. Perhaps they fear that the fundamentalists will gloat over their discomfiture . . . I urge the Darwinists to take the public into their confidence by a full disclosure.[1]

*   *   *

Five Essential Miracles. A Struggle for Faith

Meanwhile I continued work on my proposed book. It had a long gestation. I first contacted ANZEA Publishers of Sydney in 1972, and told them of my intention to write the book and received an encouraging reply. In 1973 I wrote again to say the book was almost finished, and explained in greater detail the proposed format.

After a general introduction, the first Miracle would be *Creation*. I proposed to discuss the problem of creation and evolution from the Christian perspective. However, as time went by this section had grown longer and longer, in fact,

---

[1]Ibid., p. 157.

ultimately it comprised over a third of the book. The next longest section was on the *Resurrection* which incorporated many of the arguments I had considered in my student years. I intended that there should be two appendices, one on Modern Miracles and a second on Pre-Adamic Man, but in the final version the second appendix was omitted, as was the sub-heading *A Struggle for Faith.* I suppose by that time I must have believed I had arrived. This underlines the problem I had with the book – the more I studied, the more my views changed, particularly after the Toronto episode.

In April 1975 I contacted ANZEA and again received a very cordial reply. They pointed out that they were a specialist publisher for Youth and Christian workers. They hoped the book would not be over-technical and academic in style. They received the completed manuscript in June of that year.

Then came the anxious wait, well known by all aspiring authors of books and articles – would it be accepted? In August a courteous reply came from the manager. The book had much of value, and could be of use to a thinking young person, etc., *but* it had come in for criticism from the reviewers. This was almost entirely concerned with the treatment given to miracles in general and the Creation v. Evolution debate in particular. The manager told me the reviewers criticized the range of data offered, and the actual accuracy of the evidence cited at certain points. They felt the manuscript was unacceptable in its present form, and a rewrite was required. The manager offered to send me a copy of the reviewers' criticisms. These turned out to be biting. Some examples are: 'Appeals to *design* argument. Needs to recognize difficulties in this.' 'Can actually build a stronger case than the author presents on evolution.' Another reviewer wrote, 'Creation from "dust" hypothesis – Author too much of a scientist and not enough of a Hebrew thinker. Dust was not literal but to emphasize the fragile, earthy nature of man . . . Re built-in illusion of age: Is the Wilder-Smith quote [from *Man's Origin, Man's Destiny*] just a fundamentalist sophistry? Is it not pushing the biblical text too far to worry about "growth rings" on trees?' Then a comment which will only be understood by Australians. 'This book might do in some parts of Queensland but not in Sydney.'

The whole tenor of the reviewers' comments surprised and distressed me. I have had acceptances and rejections of books and articles from many editors over the years, but nothing as unpleasant as this. However, I came to the conclusion that many of the criticisms, particularly those about science, could be justified. I decided to alter the book considerably, and try another publisher.

Living in Cambridge in 1976 had given me the opportunity to research in good libraries, and buy relevant books, so I was able to revise the text further. By July I was ready to try again. This time I sent a much altered manuscript to the Inter-Varsity Press. The chairman of the publications committee warned me that, owing to the summer vacation, it would be some time before I received an answer. It was. But one Thursday in mid-October I had the conviction that IVP had now considered the matter, and furthermore, whatever their decision, it would fulfil the Lord's will. The following week, I received a kindly reply which stated *inter alia,* that the subject of creation and evolution is one on which IVP has to be particularly careful, 'as the views expressed are so easily assumed to be the position adopted by UCCF in some way . . . On this particular subject we would need to be readier, I think, than you are yourself to acknowledge that there are several views which can be held by Bible-believing Christians, and to give them a fairly even treatment.'

I was very surprised, and phoned the chairman of IVP for confirmation. He felt I was too dogmatically creationist, and that I too strongly questioned theistic evolution, which, he said, was the standpoint of the Research Scientists Fellowship which dictates IVP policy in this area.

I asked his advice about other publishers. He thought both 'Lion, and Scripture Union would probably reject the manuscript for the same reasons as IVP; Paternoster might take it but probably not, as most of the younger Brethren with scientific training are members of the Research Scientists Fellowship'. He suggested either Evangelical Press or even 'Hodder and Stoughton because they would be neutral'. I asked Hodder but they refused as it did not fit in with the type of book they were currently publishing.

By now I was starting to appreciate something of the

spiritual warfare in which I had unwittingly become embroiled. I am no fighter. I have always shunned confrontation. I felt almost as though I had been conned into becoming a creationist. If I had known what I was letting myself in for, I would have been more careful. I felt like Jeremiah when he wrote, 'O Lord you have persuaded me against my will. You are stronger than I, and have prevailed' (Jer. 20:7, Alternative version).

At the time I was uncertain whether the block was a satanic ruse to stop me publishing a book which glorified God, or the hand of providence frustrating a publication which would dishonour him.

There is no doubt that when I started to write I had been a confirmed evolutionist. By the time I sent the manuscript to ANZEA Press I was wavering, so they had rightly rejected it. Now I was fast moving towards creation. I think best on paper, so I wrote a long memo to myself to help sort out why my beliefs had changed so radically. Here are some of the points I made at that time (1976).

It appears that classical Darwinian theory is being abandoned by modern scientists, and multiple new theories are being suggested, often antagonistic to each other. Since there is no proof, faith is required by scientists who hold these views.

Some areas of controversy for Christians who are evolutionists appear to be: Would a God of peace and love have used bloody struggle as his chief agent in creation? How did love, altruism and philanthropy enter the world?

What about man? Is he fundamentally lowly, descended from slime and apes, yet rising to better things? This gives the impression that, given time, man can make it on his own; or is he a fallen king who yet can be redeemed? Was there struggle, disease and death in the world before Adam sinned? In brief, what is the significance of the Fall for Christian evolutionists?

I also considered the various possibilities with regard to the 'days' of Genesis 1, e.g., the 'Gap' theory; maybe the 'days' were long periods of time. I favoured the idea that perhaps time commenced with the Fall, therefore anything before that is in God's timescale, and thus timeless as far as man is concerned.

The most important question I asked myself was, does what I think about evolution/creation matter anyway? Here is a summary of my reply:

Not if I am only trying to satisfy my own scientific curiosity. But yes, if my beliefs separate me from non-christian scientists by making Christianity look 'old hat', or if they cut me off from many fellow Christians.

Also, evolution is important if it makes people, especially young people, doubt God's Word by compartmentalizing their faith. That is believing in Genesis on Sunday, but in evolution for the rest of the week.

Lastly, anything which is contrary to the fundamentals of the gospel, as displayed throughout both Old and New Testaments, must be wrong.

Adding up these answers, I felt I had to pursue the matter to the bitter end. But there was still a lot I did not understand.

During my time in England, I wrote to a Christian academic and asked how he thought the creation-evolution debate affected the student world. He wrote back: 'The subject isn't much debated among students. In general, evangelicals tend to hold the view that God is the Creator, but that he used evolution in the development of various forms of life as they are at present. Only if a university lecturer oversteps the mark and tries to dismiss God altogether, do the Christian students rebel.' He added that the conservative books on the subject mostly came from the USA.

I confess when I received this letter in 1976, so indoctrinated had I become, that I accepted it unemotionally as an accurate assessment of fact. For the purpose of this present book, I reread the letter and showed it to a friend in Australia. He wrote, 'How awesome has been the decline in Christian belief not only among students, but among the English public in general with each passing year since evolution was first popularized.'

Back to the Miracles *Book*

I sent the despised manuscript to the Evangelical Press and received a prompt reply: 'The section on evolution requires different treatment', they wrote, 'we feel that on this particular issue it is better to take a position clearly.'

To Sum Up

The first publishers had refused the manuscript because they queried my science and Hebrew; the second because it was too creationist; the third because it was too evolutionary; and Hodder because clearly they were not interested. What should I do now? I took the manuscript back to Australia, put it under my bed, and slept on it.

How gracious the Lord is. Today, as I thumb through the weird hotchpotch of ideas it contained, I realise how soon I would have been ashamed of it, and what is worse, it could have done real harm to the cause of Christ.

28

WHATEVER HAPPENED TO THE 'GOOD' EARTH?

For many years after the Toronto episode, I was still trying to discover the relevance of science, history and philosophy to the Genesis story. I had moved a long way from my beliefs of 1972, but I still could not accept that the days of Genesis 1 were six literal days except by some sleight of hand to make them long periods of time. Creation ran counter to everything I had been educated to believe all my life through. The barriers were apparently insurmountable. What should I do? For a while I ignored the whole issue, but it would not go away. I felt I was jammed into a corner.

After my 1976 study leave, it was some time before I got around to considering the creation issue again. It was obvious I no longer saw eye to eye with my friends in the Research Scientists Fellowship camp, although I hoped I would retain good relationships with them. But neither would I be accepted by conservative creationists, if the reaction of Evangelical Press to my *Miracles* manuscript was anything to go by.

Good or 'Good'

Then in the summer of 1982, when returning alone from London to Australia, as I was waiting at Paddington Station for the airport bus, I suddenly remembered I had no book to read on the journey. The thought of thirty hours in a plane armed only with stale *Women's Weeklys* and unattractive airline videos appalled me. I looked at Smith's news-stand, but found nothing, so I went for a cup of coffee. But I must have *something* to read, so back to the bookstall again. The only book which caught my eye was *Zen and the Art of Motor Cycle Maintenance* by Robert M. Pirsig.[1] I am not into Zen, and motor cycles are not my scene. But someone had told me it was not as bad as it sounds, and I was desperate. One last look for an alternative was in vain. I bought the paperback.

On the plane, I took up the book with some reluctance but found it interesting enough. Pirsig's hero is a university lecturer in philosophy as well as a motor cycle enthusiast. One day he tells his students to write a 350-word essay answering the question, 'What is *quality* in thought and statement?'. Pirsig describes the students' embarrassment and frustration as they find it is impossible to define quality unless you have some point of reference, some absolute standard to refer to. After musing on the topic for about fifty pages, Pirsig writes, 'In the area of religion, the rational relationship of Quality to the Godhead needs to be more thoroughly established . . . For the time being one can meditate on the fact that '*the old English word for God and good appear to be identical.*'

Of course! At last I was beginning to understand. The repeated word 'good' in Genesis 1 does not refer merely to anatomical and physiological perfection, as my geologist friend had once explained. He was wrong, and for twenty years I had been misled by him. The word good encapsulates the whole character of God. *God* is good.

When Moses pleaded with the Lord to reveal his glory, God told him he would show his back and 'make all my *goodness* to pass before you, and I will proclaim the name of the Lord . . .' But Moses was not permitted to see the Lord's face, for 'no man may see me and live.' Later God proclaimed to him, 'The Lord, the Lord God, merciful and gracious, long-suffering and abounding in *goodness* and truth . . .' Such is the awful 'goodness' of God (*Exod.* 33:18–23; 34:6).

Years later the shepherd king tells us, '*Goodness* and mercy shall follow me all the days of my life' (*Psa.* 23:6). And in the New Testament we read that Jesus Christ went about doing 'good'.

The relevance of this to the subject of creation was to become

[1]Robert M. Pirsig, *ZEN and the Art of Motor Cycle Maintenance* (London: Corgi Books, 1974).

critical to my new thinking. Evolution theory majors on suffering and death. The theory demands it: During the millions of years which are said to have elapsed before man came on the scene, myriads of animals were born and died. Likewise for 'progressive creation'. How can Darwinian natural selection take place except by the elimination of the less fit by death?

Many godless evolutionists have appreciated that more is involved here than a mere debate about origins. They argue that a world created by any method which employed (or allowed for) cruelty can scarcely be called 'good' in the God-given sense of the word. That being so, how can the Christian belief in a God of love ever be retained? I had been reminded of this argument only two months before the plane trip when I had purchased a potted edition of Darwin's autobiography. In it I found that he had written, 'A Being so powerful, and so full of knowledge, as a God who could create the universe, is to our finite minds omnipotent and omniscient, and it revolts our understanding to suppose that his benevolence is not un-bounded, *for what advantage can there be in the suffering of millions of the lower animals throughout almost endless time?*'[1]

Had not Darwin subtitled *The Origin of Species* with the words, *The Preservation of Favoured Races in the Struggle for Life*?

I remember hearing Sir Fred Hoyle remark on a television interview that an 'Intelligence' was required to guide the universe. 'No, not the Christian God', he protested rapidly. 'An all-powerful intelligence would have to be rather peculiar to create a world with such horrible aspects as we find in this world.'

And Jacques Monod, Nobel Prize winner in molecular biology, made the same point in a radio interview. 'The struggle for life and the elimination of the weakest is a horrible process . . . I am surprised that a Christian would defend the idea that this is the process which God more or less set up in order to have evolution.'

Some Christian evolutionists counter this argument by saying, 'But animals don't feel pain'. I asked a Professor of neuro-psychology about this. I remember the occasion. We

---

[1] *The Voyage of Charles Darwin: His autobiographical writings selected and arranged by Christopher Rawling* (BBC, 1978), p. 164.

were in a departure lounge again. This time it was he who was travelling, I was only seeing him off. Just before the plane was due to leave, I asked him: 'Do animals feel pain?' He paused for a long while. At last, with a touch of reluctance in his voice, he replied, 'Yes, I think they must'. Then he went to catch his plane. It was an important admission. He fully understood the significance of what he was saying. He is a prominent Christian evolutionist.

We surely cannot accept Darwinism and deny the inevitable consequence to which Darwin himself drew attention merely by degrading the status of animals. God's care for animals is a constant theme in the Old and New Testaments. Even his covenant of the rainbow was made with both man and animals (*Gen.* 9:8–17). Many Psalms refer to animals, for example, Psalm 104. Look especially at verses 14, 18, 24, 25. When we come to the New Testament, we learn from no less an authority than Jesus himself that his Father feeds the birds of the air; not one lowly sparrow, we are told, 'falls to the ground apart from your Father's will' (see Matthew 10:29; 6:26; Luke 12:6 and other passages). We do not read the Bible aright if we suppose that it reveals a God who has no interest in the earth nor the welfare of animals.

My unexpected reading of Pirsig's book brought me to the fundamental point that the earth (indeed the whole universe) was originally created 'good', but in all theology and philosophy only Genesis provides a convincing account of why and how it has ceased to be good.

Genesis tells us that both man and woman were made 'good' – in God's image. The first man, Adam, was formed instantly from the dust, not from a countless line of ape-like creatures who had lived and died before him. Death entered the perfect world and began to reign only when Adam rebelled against his creator:

'Through one man sin entered the world, and death through sin' (*Rom.* 5:12).
'By one man's offence death reigned through the one' (*Rom.* 5:17).
'The wages of sin is death' (*Rom.* 6:23).
'As in Adam all die . . .' (*1 Cor.* 15:22).

Moreover Scripture shows us that it was not man alone who

had to bear the consequences of the fall: *the whole creation* was involved (*Gen.* 3:17–18; *Rom.* 8:22), including the animal kingdom and even the environment. If that were not so the promise that 'the whole creation' is to participate in the final restoration and glorification of the earth would be meaningless. But the promise is clear. Creation, now in 'the bondage of corruption', is promised a glorious future with the advent of Christ. For 'the earnest expectation of the creation eagerly waits for the revealing of the sons of God' (*Rom.* 8:19).

This 'creation' is clearly distinct from redeemed humanity and cannot merely refer to angels, either good or bad. As Martyn Lloyd-Jones says:

We are left with the material creation, animate and inanimate, organic and inorganic. What does this mean? It means animals. It means vegetation, flowers and grass; it means rivers and streams, mountains and hills; it means the earth itself; it means the visible heavens. In other words the Apostle is personalizing this irrational part of creation.[1]

Just as the second advent of Christ will bring the resurrection of the dead – 'Those who have done good to the resurrection of life, and those who have done evil to the resurrection of condemnation' (*John* 5:29) – so will it also bring the 'restoration of all things, of which God has spoken . . . since the world began' (*Acts* 3:21). Restoration (to restore) can only refer to a return of something to its original (good) state.

As the tedious plane journey continued, however, I found I was not so much concerned with the future as with the past: the proposition that the 'death' which entered by the fall was wider in the extent of its reign than the human race alone. Faced with the word 'good' in Genesis 1, I was forced to conclude that there could have been no animal death before Adam sinned – no bloodshed, no violence, no disease. Tennyson was wrong when he pronounced that from the beginning of time nature was 'red in tooth and claw' (*In Memoriam*). This is emphasized by Genesis 1:29–30, where we read that God gave man and the animals *plants* to eat. There is no suggestion of killing for food. Animals were herbivores at

[1]D. M. Lloyd-Jones, *Romans. An Exposition of Chapters 8:17–19, The Final Perseverance of the Saints* (Banner of Truth, Edinburgh, 1975).

first, and we may assume that it was only after he was excluded from the garden that man became a hunter. Furthermore, we read that God, in renewing the prescription of Genesis 1:29–30 *after* the flood, then added the liberty to eat meat: 'Every moving thing that lives shall be food for you. I have given you all things, even as the green herb' (*Gen.* 9:3).

But with this passage from Genesis 9 comes a specific prohibition which is relevant to our present discussion: 'you shall not eat flesh with its life, that is its blood' (verse 4). In biblical usage, 'blood' is synonymous with 'life' for both animals and man, 'The life of the flesh is in the blood' (*Lev.* 17:11, 14; *Deut.* 12:23). Thus the shedding of blood is equated with death, and always a violent death. Adam and Eve were forewarned that the penalty for sin is death (*Gen.* 2:17). After their fall the only deliverance from the immediate, visible consequence of sin – the shame of their nakedness – was that God covered them with the skin of a slain animal (*Gen.* 3:21).

Blood is the God-appointed symbol of the atonement which alone can cover sin. The blood of the sacrifice saved Israel's firstborn in Egypt: 'When I see the blood, I will pass over you' (*Exod.* 12:13).

In the whole Scripture, the shedding of blood is of prime importance because it is related to the forfeiture of life; and life has such significance that even the eating of blood was forbidden as a constant reminder of that fact (*Gen.* 9:4; *Deut.* 12:15–16, 23–24. See also *1 Chron.* 11:17–19).

The logical culmination of all this imagery is found in the New Testament when the spotless Lamb of God 'came to take away the sin of the world' (*John* 1:29). And Peter tells us that we are redeemed 'with the precious blood of Christ' (*1 Pet.* 1:19).

The inevitable question arises: Is God's appointment of such imagery consistent with an evolution process by which he allowed gallons of blood to be squandered by random violence for millions of years before ever man came on the scene?

The answer surely must be an emphatic, no! It is apparent that the record of Genesis *cannot* be accommodated to evolutionary belief. Darwin, Monod, Sir Fred Hoyle and many others are right. It is, to my mind, unthinkable that a God of love would use so cruel a process as evolution to fashion his beautiful world. Do we have to conclude, therefore, that there is no God of love? Perish the thought! Thus the only reasonable alternative is that there *is* a God of love but he did not use any method involving bloody evolution in the creation of the world.[1]

Unfortunately the word 'love' has become debased during the last decades. Commonly today it means erotic, sexual love not altruistic love of the type referred to in the New Testament by the Greek word *agape*. I remember a professor of animal psychology telling me he had no difficulty with the theory of evolution except for the origin of altruism. At the time I did not understand what he meant. He explained that Darwinian natural selection is essentially selfish ('Nature red in tooth and claw') and so is contrary to altruism, which means selflessness.

Richard Dawkins, a noted English evolutionist, in his book *The Selfish Gene* wrote, 'I shall argue that a prominent quality to be expected in a successful gene is ruthless selfishness . . . Much as we might wish to believe otherwise, universal love and the welfare of the species as a whole are concepts which do not make evolutionary sense.'[2]

Whatever the method of creation proposed by some evangelicals, be it 'Old Age Creation', 'Progressive Creation', 'Theistic Evolution' or any other — if it attempts to harmonize the Bible with the idea of a billion-year-old earth — if it contains the concept in any form, that God superintended an earth history in which disease, suffering, cruelty, violence and death occurred on a grand scale, then it necessarily clashes with the whole flow of events crucial to the gospel.   However, if the fossils were formed *after* Adam's disobedience brought death and bloodshed for a season, there is no conflict. The creation is 'groaning in pain' as it awaits its future restoration – not back to millions of years of death and bloodshed, but back to the sinless, deathless state in which it once was.

Let me end the chapter with a summary of the gospel:

We commence with Eden: the perfect, sinless, deathless world – 'good' in every sense –

---

[1]A. M. Stibbs, *The Meaning of the Word 'Blood' in Scripture* (London: Tyndale Press, 1948; 3rd ed. 1962). This is an excellent monograph on the subject.
[2]Richard Dawkins, *The Selfish Gene* (London: Granada, 1976), pp. 2–3.

To the time when, following the example of Adam and Eve, men and women universally turned their back on their Maker, and despite all his goodness and love had provided, preferred to say with Ernest Henley,

I am the master of my fate,
I am the captain of my soul.

Until God, in his mercy, provided *the* way of escape. His ultimatum was clear: 'If you sin you die'. The death penalty was required for sin. But in the Old Testament God revealed that atonement ('covering') could be by the substitutionary blood sacrifice of an acceptable animal.

Finally, to the incarnation of the perfect, vicarious sacrifice – the Lamb of God, the Maker of the universe himself, who came into his world in order to shed his own blood to atone for the sin of all those who believe in him.

29

BIAS, FAITH, EVIDENCE AND
PRE-EVANGELISM

Bowls is a game played with a ball which has a 'bias', that is a built-in tendency to veer to one side or the other. Sometimes we describe a person as 'biased', by which we mean he leans towards a certain viewpoint. When we consider the topic of creation and evolution, *everyone* is biased. The well-known evolutionist Stephen J. Gould agrees with this when he rejects the claim, so frequently made, that personal preference plays no key role in science. He continues, 'Our ways of learning about the world are strongly influenced by the social preconceptions and biased modes of thinking that each scientist must apply to any problem. The stereotype of a fully rational and objective 'scientific method', with individual scientists as logical robots . . . is self-serving mythology.'

Another writer on the subject, Richard Milton, makes the same point when he asserts that the determining factor for both the evolutionist and the creationist is something other than actual scientific knowledge. He writes:

I am not a creationist and do not hold any religious convictions . . . I think those who believe in a creator, and those who believe in Darwinism do so as an act of faith or belief, because they find it intellectually and emotionally repugnant to acknowledge and live with open-minded ignorance.

So according to Milton,[1] a possible solution to the creation/

---

[1]Milton, *The Facts of Life: Shattering the Myth of Darwinism* (Forth Estate Publishers, Cambridge University Press, 1992).

evolution controversy might be to reject bias and live with open-minded ignorance. But according to the Bible, open-mindedness is something man cannot attain, for the simple reason that since the Fall all humans assert *themselves* and their own wisdom over against God. Far from being 'open' to the truth, our fallen mind is 'at enmity against God' (*Rom.* 8:7).

We learn from Scripture, that when nature speaks about creation – together with all that true science can learn from creation – this *ought* to be enough to establish all men in the knowledge of God. (See for example Psalm 19:1–4 [NIV], 'The heavens proclaim the glory of God, the skies proclaim the work of his hands', and *Rom.* 1:20, 'For since the creation of the world his invisible attributes are clearly seen, being understood by the things that are made, even his eternal power and Godhead; so that they are without excuse'.) However, in reality since the Fall, sin has so blinded and prejudiced our reason that it always favours our pride and resists the truth.

Furthermore, since the Enlightenment (otherwise known as the Age of Reason) in the eighteenth century – and increasingly since Darwin – the world has provided more and more of what it would call scientific evidence, to enable us to dismiss the knowledge of God innate in the human heart. Thus for the last one hundred and more years, *everyone* has been indoctrinated from childhood on, in schools and universities, by books and magazines, and increasingly by television, to accept evolution (and the associated millions of years) not just as a theory, but as an assured fact.

So thorough has this indoctrination been, that people who hold the evolutionary view regard themselves as straight, mainstream – even unbiased. A few years ago, I attended an evangelical church in an English university town. One day I asked whether I might speak for a few minutes at their weekly Bible Study on the subject of creation. After deliberation, the pastor replied slowly, 'I'm sorry, we can't allow it. You see, we don't want to appear biased in this church.' I ask you, was he really unbiased on that occasion?

As Sedgewick predicted over a hundred years ago in his grim prognostication of the future, the consequences of Darwinism have been catastrophic. Traditional belief that man was made in God's image has been swept aside. It is true that this

[250]

belief alone falls far short of the full Christian message, but it is fundamental and at least supports some respect for a high moral code. People, even until the mid-twentieth century, generally believed it was wrong to murder, to steal, to commit adultery and so on. Instead of this, evolution has taught people to think of themselves as mere animals: no God, no after-life, no absolute rules. Truth is relative: no absolute difference between good and evil, and increasingly the God-given distinctions between the roles of male and female are blurred into non-existence.

*   *   *

What is Faith?

My father often preached on the subject of faith. First, he would dismiss the small boy's suggestion: 'Faith is believing what ain't true'. Then he might recount the story of the Reformers who were prepared to be martyred for their faith so that the English Bible could be brought to the common people. Or he would illustrate from the story of Christopher Columbus who ventured out into the Atlantic to look for the New World. No one had ever seen it, but he was certain it must be there from the evidence of an unknown civilization – strange animals or trees; occasionally a curiously carved artefact – washed up on the shores of Europe.

'The Faith' is an early New Testament name for Christianity. Paul calls Timothy, 'My true son in *the faith*'; deacons were required to have 'boldness in *the faith*'; and in his valedictory address Paul declared, 'I have kept *the faith*' (*1 Tim.* 1:2; 3:13; *2 Tim.* 4:7).

Secondly, there is saving faith: we are saved only '*by faith*', which is given as the gracious gift of God (*Eph.* 2:8).

But not only do we start the Christian life with faith, we have, thirdly, to walk by faith, exercising faith in our daily life. I take this to mean constantly referring to God and asking his help. Not infrequently I am comforted to remember that he has told us that if we lack wisdom, we can ask him, and he will give it, 'liberally and without reproach', provided we ask 'in faith, without doubting' (*Jas.* 1:5–6).

[251]

The writer to the Hebrews tells us that it is 'by faith we understand that the worlds were framed by the word of God'. And, 'without faith it is impossible to please him, for he who comes to God, must believe that he is, and that he is a rewarder of those who diligently seek him' (*Heb.* 11:3, 6). Similar passages occur constantly throughout the Bible.

An aphorism my father often quoted ran: 'Faith steps out on the seeming void, and finds the rock beneath'. His message was plain: faith is not just a philosophical or theological concept: faith should lead to action.

The 'Conversion' Experience

My personal journey from a tenacious belief in the evolution of the universe over billions of years to a child-like acceptance by faith of a six-day fiat creation, was a process which took many years. I don't remember specifically praying for help; I certainly did not do so with any enthusiasm. The simple fact is that I still didn't really want to believe.

Then one day (I don't recall the place or time) I suddenly said to myself, 'I'm getting nowhere. There is no alternative. I *must* believe that God created the world in six days. Scientific evidence won't get me any further.'

So then and there, rather grudgingly, I told the Lord that, by faith, I accepted he *had* created the world in six literal days, and that the creation story as recounted in Genesis 1 and 2 was true after all.

And, unexpectedly, but of great practical importance, I found that for me, the earth, from being billions of years old, suddenly shrank to become physically quite young, with all that flowed from that momentous discovery: historically, scientifically, theologically and philosophically.

It was a conversion experience as dramatic as my turning to Christ for forgiveness when I was eight years old; or the Swanwick episode during the dark days of World War II. I felt intensely relieved and rejuvenated. The battle was over. The whole Bible was trustworthy after all. All that miracle business fell into place. I had learned the truth of Augustine's dictum: 'We are not required to understand in order to believe; but to believe in order to understand.'

[252]

Sudden 'conversion' experiences such as this are in no way uncommon. Numbers of people have told me about their change-about from belief in evolution to faith in creation. A girl wrote that when she heard a sermon on the relevance of creation, 'It shocked my socks off'. She immediately accepted that biblical creation was true, and a week later became a Christian. Very soon she had brought her young brother to the Lord.

A striking instance of this 'conversion' experience is recorded by Whittaker Chambers in his book, *Witness*. He is considering the question, 'Why do men break with the Communist party?' Chambers tells how this came about in his own life:

I date my break from Communism to a very casual happening . . . My daughter was in her high chair. I was watching her eat. She was the most miraculous thing that ever happened in my life. I liked to watch her even when she smeared porridge on her face or dropped it meditatively on the floor. My eye came to rest on the delicate convolutions of her ear – those intricate, perfect ears. The thought passed through my mind, 'No, those ears were not created by the chance coming together of atoms in nature (the Communist view). They could have been created only by immense design.' The thought was involuntary and unwanted. I crowded it out of my mind. But I never wholly forgot it or the occasion. I had to crowd it out of my mind. If I had completed it, I should have had to say: Design presupposes God. I did not then know that, at that moment, the finger of God was first laid on my forehead.[1]

Some years later Chambers became a Christian and left the Communist party.

How does Sudden 'Conversion' Occur?

I am using the word 'conversion' in its basic dictionary sense, as the 'act of rotating one's ideas' (*OED*), not with any particular theological meaning.Something of the conversion experience of 'Evolution-to-Creation' can be seen in the behaviour of the disciples when they first saw the risen Lord after his resurrection.

[1]Whittaker Chambers, *Witness* (Chicago: Henry Regenery Co., 1969).

In Luke 24 we read that two disciples (one was named Cleopas) met the risen Christ on that memorable Sunday evening as they returned from Jerusalem to their home in Emmaus. As they were walking along, Jesus joined himself to them, and the three started to discuss the Jerusalem events of the weekend. Despite the fact that they knew him so well, and he explained to them in detail the reasons for his death, we read: 'But their eyes were restrained, so that they did not know him' (verse 16).

How was it that for so long 'they were kept from recognizing him' (verse 16, NIV)? I suggest it was because the very idea was something which their minds blotted out as totally unreasonable. They had watched with amazed shock as before their very eyes the Saviour had died in agony. It was inconceivable that he could now be walking and talking with them.

I remember a friend telling me how on one occasion his father saw him off on an express train from Manchester to London. His father said he was on the way to York. However, unknown to him, the father intended to go to London first, but wanted to keep the fact a secret from his son. So just as the train left, he jumped into the last coach.

Some hours later, walking through the crowds in Oxford Street, it so happened that my friend passed within a few yards of his father. They did not greet each other. The son told me, 'I remember I observed a likeness, but I had seen him in Manchester that very morning going in the opposite direction. It was quite impossible for him to be in Oxford Street. So, to me, the man I saw in London had to be someone else.'

To return to St Luke: 'When they reached Emmaus, Cleopas and the other disciple [was this Mrs Cleopas?] begged Jesus to rest in their home and have a meal with them. Not until they had finished did the unknown stranger take 'bread and blessed it and brake, and gave it to them'. Then 'their eyes were opened' and they knew him (verse 31).

St Thomas had not been present when the Master first appeared to the disciples after his resurrection (*John* 20:24). He refused to believe that Jesus had risen from the dead until he, personally, had put his finger into the print of the nails and thrust his hand into the Saviour's side.

One week later Jesus appeared again, this time to all the disciples. He offered Thomas his hands and his side for inspection, and said, 'Thomas, because you have seen me you have believed. Blessed are those who have not seen me and yet have believed' (*John* 20:29).

Notice two things:

First: God often provides evidence (also called signs, miracles, means, or his works, John 20:30–31) to aid his unbelieving followers. On this occasion we are told the means he used: breaking the bread in the house of Cleopas, and showing the print of the nails to Thomas.

Second: We are told by Luke, 'And their eyes were opened and they knew him; and he vanished from their sight.' So another unrecognized dimension was involved: the action of the Holy Spirit who alone can open blind eyes.

To repeat the words of Chambers: 'The finger of God was laid on my forehead.'

God's purpose in giving us evidence is that people may believe his Word (the Bible) totally. Essentially, he desires men and women, Christians or non-christians, to exercise faith and believe in him. But this is not 'blind faith', or faith against reason. Often he does not give us as much evidence as we would like, but always adequate. I believe the key verse is *Hebrews* 11:1, 'Now faith is the substance of things hoped for, the evidence of things not seen'. (Other translations give variations of this verse, but the word 'evidence' is essentially the same.)

I have asked myself many times why it took me so long to abandon Darwinism and especially the idea of a six-day creation and a young earth. I believe the main reason was that I just did not think God could have done it. In fact this was the substance of my answer to Prof. Wilder-Smith on the bus in Toronto. 'It's impossible.'

As I look back on this episode today I remember the story of Abraham and his wife Sarah before the birth of Isaac (*Gen.* 18: 1–15). For twenty-five years God had repeatedly promised Abraham that he would have a son who would be the ancestor of a great nation. Furthermore, the child would be by Sarah. But years had gone by, and Abraham was now one hundred years of age, and his wife was ninety. It was too late!

Impossible! So when the Lord told Abraham yet again, confidently (verses 10–12), it is not surprising that Sarah laughed (she had been hiding by the door of the tent).

And 'The Lord said to Abraham, "Why did Sarah laugh, saying, 'Shall I surely bear a child, since I am old?' *Is anything too hard for the Lord?* [1] At the appointed time . . . Sarah shall have a son." But Sarah denied it, saying, "I did not laugh", for she was afraid. And he said, "No, but you did laugh!"'

In his commentary on Genesis, Calvin is very gentle with Sarah. He writes, 'Sarah foolishly set her age and that of her husband in opposition to the word of God. Yet she does not charge God with falsehood. But having her mind fixed on the contemplation of the thing proposed, she only weighs what might be accomplished by natural means, without raising her thoughts to the consideration of the power of God . . . As often as we measure the promises and work of God by our own reason, and by the laws of nature, we act reproachfully toward him, though we may intend nothing of the sort, for we do not pay him His due honour . . . Sarah did not intend to make God a liar. Her sin consisted in this alone, that having fixed her thoughts too much on the accustomed order of nature, she did not give glory to God by expecting from Him a miracle which she was unable to conceive in her mind.'

Blaise Pascal wrote, 'It is the supreme achievement of reason to know that there is a limit to reason. Using his reason alone, man finds his reason is not sufficient.'

Pre-evangelism

I believe that today the acceptance of evolution theory is probably one of *the* major stumbling blocks preventing people from becoming Christians, and stunting the spiritual growth of many who call themselves Christian.

Over the years people have been indoctrinated to believe there is no God, the Bible is not reliable, Jesus was just a man who never rose physically from the dead. There may be a

---

[1]This truth is repeated in a number of contexts in Scripture, see Job 42:2; Jeremiah 32:17, 27; Luke 1:37; Matthew 19:26; Romans 4:20–22.

heaven, but there certainly is not a hell. In brief, all this spiritual stuff is just a myth. So what is the use of saying 'Jesus loves you' to such people?

For many Christians, Genesis is a closed book. A new convert told me recently: 'I don't read the Old Testament, it's such a waste of time. I concentrate on the gospels.'

Even some pastors are nervous about the first chapters of Genesis, and avoid them. Instead they present what they call the 'simple' gospel. One such pastor told me, 'I rarely preach from the O.T. I preach only about the Lord Jesus Christ and his love.' He added that he did not really believe the Genesis account of creation or the flood. I asked whether he believed any of the supernatural elements of Scripture. 'What about Jonah and the big fish, for example, and the feeding of the 5,000, and the virgin birth of Jesus; then what about Christ's resurrection?' There was a long pause. 'You mean,' he asked, 'if I start saying about Genesis, but that I can't believe, and that, and that . . . there comes a time when there isn't much of the Bible left. – It's like being on a slippery slide?' 'Yes', I replied. 'I think,' he said, in a slow whisper, 'I think I'm on that slippery slide.'

Because modern men and women do not know about God, the starting point for evangelism should be Hebrews 11: 6: 'He who comes to God must believe *that he is*'. This is the essential message of the first chapters of Genesis. We must sweep away the myth of evolution and substitute the biblical doctrine of creation before we can expect today's men and women to accept salvation in Jesus Christ by faith alone. Before we can successfully plant the seed of the Word, the ground must be prepared. And this is the task of pre-evangelism.

When I say that in evangelism we must not start by proclaiming the love of God, some people will disagree. They will instance many who have come to salvation primarily through the message of God's love (see for example the story of Nicky Cruz in *The Cross and the Switchblade* by David Wilkerson). But most of these were men and woman of the past who had not had all knowledge of God completely knocked out of them by evolution theory. Some, for example, may have been brought up in a Roman Catholic home. If you do meet such a person, of course, you should start with the New Testament message of the love of Jesus, not with Genesis 1. To quote Francis Schaeffer, 'To do otherwise is just plain stupid.'

The Relevance of Genesis (see also Appendix 3)

Over the years I have talked to a large number of people (particularly young people) who agree that the evolution story is ludicrous. They rightly say:

The universe could not possibly have started with a Big Bang. Where did the matter come from? What about the space the Big Bang banged into? It's mathematically impossible for life to start from non-life just by chance. Did a whale really evolve from a cow? (Or was it the other way round?) There must be some better explanation. Perhaps there is a Creator God after all.

But unfortunately the next step, how all this is linked with the gospel, continues to elude them. So what is the *relevance* of the first chapters of Genesis to the whole Bible plan of salvation? I stumbled across this *relevance* almost accidentally.

Ten years ago a group of scientists were invited to speak at a neighbouring university. I was asked to go with them. But I do not class myself as a scientist in the test-tube sense of the word. I am a medical doctor. I felt quite incompetent as I stood up in the lecture theatre. I am not normally daunted by a tiered theatre with a bench and sink and taps. But this was different. I feared I was expected to speak on a scientific topic outside my field of expertise.

At the end my fears seemed to be confirmed when a student came up and confronted me with: 'That wasn't a lecture, that was a sermon.' I had been caught out and felt distinctly uncomfortable. After a pause I answered, 'Was it any the worse for that?' I was somewhat relieved by his grudging reply: 'I suppose not.'

On the way home I pondered over the incident. So far from being 'no worse', maybe it was better. Perhaps that was what was urgently needed. My message as a non-scientist should not be to show scientifically *how* the earth came into being (frankly I don't know apart from what the Bible tells us), but *why* in God's providence, it did so.

As the late Professor Wilder-Smith said, 'Creation man has two legs: the biblical and the scientific.' Scientific learning alone cannot bring an individual to a true saving faith in God, but that does not mean science should therefore be ignored as we confront people with the Christian faith. On the contrary, as we have seen, God provides necessary evidence so that people can come to believe in him. And at the present time he is providing more and more hard scientific evidence of the truth of the Bible.

30

'THEN YOU WEREN'T A CHRISTIAN!'

Towards the end of a lecture on creation, I mentioned that for over forty years I had been a Christian who believed in evolution. A man leapt to his feet and shouted, 'Then you weren't a Christian!' The implication was clear: it is impossible for a 'real Christian' to believe in evolution.

Before I tell you how I personally replied to the man, let me ask my companions on this difficult road, whether they were Christians. 'Mr Philip Gosse, you are the eldest, and are obviously well acquainted with courts of law, what is your answer?' I think Gosse would have replied something like this:

I can certainly affirm that I am a Christian. Ever since that time in Newfoundland when I heard Charles Wesley's hymn, 'And can it be that I should gain an interest in the Saviour's blood?', I have been able to continue, 'He died for me, who caused His pain, for me, who Him to death pursued'.

In the early years of the nineteenth century, I observed a slow steady increase in 'evolutionary-type' thinking. But you must realize we didn't use the word evolution in those days. The word only slowly came into vogue in the general sense, to include the embryological development of animals, the origin of species from earlier forms and the formation of heavenly bodies, in about the year 1850. Lyell had pioneered the way with his *Principles of Geology*, which rubbished the idea that Noah's flood covered the whole earth. This allowed the hypothesis that the universe was millions of years old to gain ground rapidly. Then came Darwin. And I wrote *Omphalos* . . .

Philip pauses for some minutes. At last he goes on, 'I certainly considered what is now called Darwinian evolution very carefully, but I don't know that I ever really believed it.'

*   *   *

We will have to question George Romanes on one of the last days before his death, for at that time his views were changing so rapidly. 'Yes,' he replies with real difficulty:

> Yes, I was converted years ago, back in my student days. At that time I was certain of it. I loved the Lord and wished above all to follow him. But then as you know, I met Mr Darwin and he was so kind to me, and so persuasive about evolution, that I began to have doubts. I studied a lot, did a lot of biological research, and mixed with the men at the Royal Society. As I did so, gradually my love for Darwin and science increased, and my love for God and the Bible decreased. I became a disciple of evolution and a materialist, despite what it cost me in affection and happiness. Yet even as I embraced evolution, I saw it as a horrendous storm which was already engulfing the land. I even wrote that the effects would be disastrous for all civilization.
>
> About a year ago, I noticed that verse in the Gospel of Saint John (7:17) – you know it, of course: 'If any man wants to do God's will, he shall know concerning the doctrine'. I found I really did want to do God's will; I longed that Christianity should be true after all. And because of that, I found I was more and more knowing the doctrine – and doing it.

I cannot say for certain whether Romanes would go on to say that this, for him, included discarding the theory of evolution, though the evidence seems to favour that likelihood. Was Romanes really a Christian at the same time that he was a rabid evolutionist? That question you must answer for yourself. It is true his original conversion is not recorded in the modern, 'born again' sense of the term. But then Ethel was not an evangelical herself, and did not use that sort of terminology. Personally I would answer, 'Yes'. I believe he was undoubtedly a Christian although he had backslidden grievously. But it is for the Lord to determine. He alone knows those who are his.

Let me review Romanes' life. What do we find? A man rich in worldly goods, with a loving family, high intelligence, academic knowledge and insight, and an excellent knowledge of the Scriptures; a man with no evidence of a wicked life in the sense of profligacy, alcoholism or sexual sin. However, we find also a man who turned his back on God and enthroned the goddess of Nature. By so doing he walked straight into the trap set by Satan for the academically minded: a trap carefully designed to snare the scientist, the psychologist, the philosopher and the theologian.

Overwhelmingly, his story demonstrates the amazing love of God to those who are lost. It illustrates that the repentant sinner with a glimmer of faith, God will not despise. George cried out, 'Lord I believe, help thou mine unbelief.' And the Lord did so. More than this, to the best of his increasingly limited physical ability, he was starting to show the fruit of repentance on his deathbed.

What brought Romanes back to Faith?

Even in his hour of deepest gloom, Romanes was aware of the danger of the road he was treading and, in the midst of despair, his poems began to show a flicker of hope.

And God in his mercy disciplined George with suffering, but softened by the love of many Christian friends. Specifically, he directed his eyes to the scriptures; in particular Psalms 137 and 138; and the verse in John 7:17. Above all he revealed to his seeking child Christ's crucifixion love.

How can all this be? It is because God is merciful, and regards the forgiven Christian as righteous, as part of his family, everlastingly his child. So if I sin now, I am not sinning against God's Law, but against his love. My sin is no longer the action of a criminal, but it *is* the act of a rebellious and unworthy child.

Romanes is an illustration of the verse, 'How hard it is for those who trust in riches to enter the kingdom of God'; and another verse: 'Not many wise according to the flesh . . . are called. But God has chosen the foolish things of the world to put to shame the wise' (*Mark* 10:24; *1 Cor.* 1:26–27). The 'riches' in which George trusted were particularly his academic ability. In my experience it is often the brightest and keenest university students who as graduates forsake their Christian profession.

I wonder what Romanes' final understanding of creation was. I don't know for certain. After his death, his wife Ethel became convinced that a reconciliation between Christianity and Darwinism, 'as proposed by Professor Dana', was possible.

She wished her husband 'had come to the same place of certainty'. By which she was referring to Dana's compromise position between evolution and Christianity. Clearly this meant that such a compromise was unacceptable for him.

*   *   *

With regard to ARS? Let me briefly review his life. By 1900 the fierceness of the Darwinian storm had somewhat abated, but every year the after-effects were becoming more apparent and disturbing. There is no doubt of my father's Christian faith, yet he was a convinced and active evolutionist. In his younger days he was in spiritual turmoil and determined to find the truth for himself both scientifically and theologically. To this end, in addition to medicine and surgery, he studied physiology and geology in depth, and also textual and higher criticism of the Bible. Later he became interested in archaeology as it related to biblical apologetics. Always he was searching to confirm the utter reliability of the Scripture: that it was God's revelation to man, 'true truth' throughout, including especially the first chapters of Genesis. He would quote the words of Archbishop Cranmer, 'Explain the obscure passages by those which are simple. Scripture by Scripture. Seek, pray and he who has the key of David will open to you.'

In the later years of his life as his sermon notes seem to indicate, he appeared to come ever closer to a straightforward understanding of Genesis. Though he remained uncertain at some points he rested in a conclusion of which he had no doubt at all:

If, as we believe, the Eternal God of infinite Truth and Wisdom is at once the Creator and Controller of all material things, and the Author both of Holy Scripture and natural law, then it stands to reason that conflict between science and revelation is an impossibility. God cannot deny Himself.

With this statement I would wholeheartedly agree, as long as it is realized that 'science' here means *the raw data; the experimental facts of science*; not the man-made theories built upon that data. Thus to look at the rocks and observe that they are stratified and contain fossils is one thing. To say that therefore they were laid down over long periods of time is quite another.

I have every sympathy for Gosse, Romanes and ARS. All three earnestly hoped that biblical creation was true, but they lacked the evidence and insights to confute the near universal claim of their day that overwhelming scientific proof existed to the contrary.

What was my father's particular contribution? For the first half of the twentieth century he, almost alone in Britain, held the fort. By his writing and speaking in the defence of the Bible he saved the faith of countless Christians.

*   *   *

And for myself? As I told my interrogator at the lecture, I have no doubt of my conversion at the age of eight years. I could have added that as a student this was confirmed by the event at Swanwick. I was certainly a Christian. But for many years I was so ignorant of the importance of the creation/evolution issue that it did not much worry me whether creation was true or not. By default I sided with evolution.

When I did start to consider it, perhaps my greatest deficiency was my inability to accept the *absolute* sovereignty and power of God. This is illustrated by my pathetic efforts to 'help' God by thinking up improbable ways in which he could have performed some of the miracles recorded in Scripture.

I believed it was physically impossible for God to have created the world in six literal days. (Not to mention performing many of the subsequent miracles recorded in the Bible, such as the floating iron axe-head, 2 Kings 6: 6). So God did not create in six days because he did not have the *power* to do so. Therefore, he must have used some method involving evolution, and thus he could not be the *fiat* Creator who made the world in six days.

This vicious circle could only be severed by the sword of the Spirit, the Word of God (*Eph.* 6:17; *Heb.* 4:12) which God in his mercy gave to me. By all this I learned the lesson that the key to God's character is in the word *absolute*: his *absolute* sovereignty, *absolute* power, *absolute* goodness, *absolute* justice, *absolute* love, *absolute* mercy. I would have been saved a lot of trouble if I had heeded Esther Lloyd's words: 'But Master John, dear, God can do anything. What's the problem?'

[264]

You may exclaim, 'But you had God's revelation in nature and the Scriptures, so you are without excuse' (see Romans 1:18–20). With great sorrow I have to agree. Even real Christians have many sins and failures and I see now that my lack of faith in the Genesis account was dishonouring God. I deserved the same rebuke that the Lord directed to Peter after his ill-fated attempt to walk to Jesus on the water: 'O you of little faith, why did you doubt?' (*Matt.* 14:31).

When I did finally trust in the narrative of Genesis as literal history there were still spiritual truths about which I was unclear. In particular, I believed it had been my own decision to abandon evolution theory. I had to be corrected on this point also. It happened years later. I remember the occasion vividly. It was a holiday morning; I was sitting up in bed reading a Scripture portion, when I came to the words of St Paul recorded in 2 Timothy 2:24–26:

A servant of the Lord must not quarrel but be gentle to all, able to teach, patient, in humility correcting those who are in opposition, if God will perhaps grant them repentance, so that they may know the truth, and that they may come to their senses, and escape the snare of the devil, having been held captive by him to do his will.

Here, I thought, is a message to me and to all who proclaim the creation message: we must be gentle, patient, humble, and careful to teach only what is undoubtedly true. Regretfully, in the past some creationists – including sometimes myself – have been arrogant and polemic in their opposition to those who do not agree with them, especially perhaps to fellow Christians.

I read the passage again. As I did so, by an unexpected twist, my mind was concentrated on the words repeated below in italics:

. . . if God perhaps will grant *them* [those who are in opposition] *repentance*, so that they may know the truth and *that they may come to their senses, and escape the snare of the devil*, having been held captive by him to do his will.

All of a sudden I saw that my appreciation of creation through the eyes of faith was God's doing. It was not I who by scientific skill had suddenly discovered the superiority of the creation account over evolutionary theory. On the contrary, it was the Lord who had delivered me from a powerful snare from which I could not deliver myself. Forgetful of the influence of the god of this world I had not heeded the warning of Scripture: 'Let no one deceive himself . . . For the wisdom of this world is foolishness with God. For it is written 'He catches the wise in their own craftiness'; and again, 'The Lord knows the thoughts of the wise that they are futile' (*1 Cor.* 3:18–20). Had I heeded these and similar Scriptures, I might have realized earlier that it was not any superior scientific training which had enabled me to grasp the historical truth of the Genesis narrative and the utter foolishness of Darwinism. On the contrary, to a large extent it was because of my supposedly 'superior modern education' that I had found Genesis so difficult. This meant therefore that I had now to ask God to forgive me for my years of blindness.

Finally, how did I reply to my interrogator? I told him that if a person does not accept the Genesis account of the universe created in six days; the creation of Eve from a bone of Adam; the worldwide flood of Noah, and other evidences of creation; following the plain and obvious words of Scripture, he or she is wrong, illogical, and in a situation highly dangerous to their eternal soul. But this does not therefore mean they are not Christians.

Whoever you are, you will know where you personally stand before the Lord on this issue.

I conclude with words spoken by Moses towards the end of his life: 'See I have set before you today life and good, or death and evil . . . all the words of this law [the Pentateuch]. For it is no vain thing for you, because it is your life . . . Therefore choose life' (selected from Deuteronomy 30:15; 32:46, 47 and 30:19).

31

EVOLUTION: HOW SERIOUS AN ISSUE FOR CHRISTIANS?

Creation/evolution is still often a 'bone of contention' for Christians. I have in front of me an article by a Christian academic entitled, *'Why not Creation by Evolution?'* He points out that many true Christians believe in the theory of evolution, which is certainly true. Some were evolutionists when they were converted and have never seen the need to change their view. Others believed in creation when they first became Christians, but later decided this was not necessary as an article of faith, and reverted to evolution. There is a mix of reasons.

Most people, whether Christians or not, regard evolution as a purely scientific matter. They are taught it at school or college and are easily influenced by peer pressure, even in church, to ignore the whole issue. They have never had the biblical or philosophical/sociological importance of creation explained to them. When the subject is raised, they may make enquiries of evolutionist friends who convince them that scientific evolutionism is totally compatible with the first chapters of the Bible.

Christians often maintain that to urge a literal understanding of Genesis is divisive and should be rejected for that reason. They argue that Christians are already separated by varying doctrinal beliefs – mode of baptism, speaking in tongues, differing methods of church government – so why add another? With sorrow I have to agree, 'Yes, it is divisive'. After my new-found beliefs on creation, I personally experienced a coldness, or even a loss of fellowship, with several Christians whose friendship I had greatly valued in the past. But then, Jesus himself warned his disciples that his message would be divisive (*Luke* 12:51–53).

Still other Christians go further and suggest that young people seeking Christ may be put off by what they regard as an old-fashioned, conservative, fundamentalist viewpoint (select which term you prefer). And this again may be true, but even so it should not deter us from being faithful to Scripture.

Mark you, I fully accept that we should do all that we can to lessen a spirit of divisiveness and obscurantism among Christians. Belligerence should have no place amongst us. Quarrels among Christians are a bad witness to the watching world, especially if accompanied by a loveless spirit. *The Great Evangelical Disaster* cites the late Francis Schaeffer on 'The Mark of a Christian'.[1] He quotes Christ's words, 'A new commandment I give to you, that you love one another; as I have loved you, that you also love one another. *By this will all men know that you are my disciples*, if you have love for one another' (*John* 13:34–35).

Schaeffer maintains that if I fail in my love towards a fellow Christian, that does not thereby prove that I am not a Christian. However, Jesus is telling me that, if I do not show the love I should, then *the world has the right to judge* that I am not a Christian. He adds that unless we, as Christians, show love to one another, we cannot expect the world to listen to us, even if we give them all the right Christian answers.

Schaeffer goes on to emphasize that if we are called to love our *neighbour* as ourselves, how much more should we love all Bible-believing Christians, even those with whom (perhaps justifiably) we contend. If we do not, 'then in the eyes of the world, and in the eyes of our own children, we are destroying the very truth we proclaim.' Thankfully there have been, and are, Christians who take this lesson seriously.[2]

---

[1]Francis Schaeffer, *The Mark of a Christian* (Inter-Varsity Press). Quoted in *The Great Evangelical Disaster* (Crossway Books, 5th Ed., 1984).

[2]George Whitefield and John Wesley, the great eighteenth-century evangelists, differed profoundly on an important matter of doctrine, Whitefield taking a Calvinist stance, and Wesley an Arminian. But Whitefield could write: 'I truly love all that love the glorious Emmanuel, and though I cannot depart from the principles which I believe are clearly revealed in the book of God, yet I can cheerfully associate with those that differ from me, if I have reason to think they are united to our common Head.'

Granting these very real pitfalls, would it not be better to put the whole matter into the 'too hard' basket? To say, with a friend of mine, 'I'm agnostic. I just don't know.' If it were just a matter of science, as I earlier thought, I might agree. But faith in creation is not a faith which can be discussed in separation from faith as a whole. All Scripture constantly goes back to Genesis as the starting point for the understanding of the most fundamental truths of redemption: the original holiness of Adam, the devil's lie, the entrance of sin, the place of woman –these things, and more, are related to whether or not we read the Genesis account as real, space-time history, or we see it as just another myth akin to the Australian Aboriginal 'Dream-time' legends.

In the Bible the whole plan of salvation is presented in terms of 'the first man', Adam, and the 'second man', the Lord from heaven (*1 Cor.* 15:45–47). I do not deny that evangelicals may hold a non-literal view of Genesis and yet believe in Christ; but belief in the one cannot be rejected without weakening the other also. It is a short step between doubting the power of God to create all things in six days to doubting the mystery of the Trinity, the divine nature of Christ, and the resurrection of the dead.

It is not uncharitable to observe that professed evangelicals who are concerned to advocate some allegorical interpretation of the Genesis creation account are commonly indefinite on other great issues of Scripture. Too many preachers endeavour to take no clear position on Genesis. Dr George Carey, the Archbishop of Canterbury, for example, speaks of what he calls this 'primal tragedy' and goes on:

Humanity has fallen from its destiny and calling. Adam and Eve . . . were made for fellowship with God and for sharing in his love and generosity. Their fate, through rejection of his love was to be separate from his life. They 'fell' from grace, and it became our fall. As with the account of our creation, so with our fall, there are different ways to take the story. Some hold that unless we believe in a literal, historical fall, that actually affected the whole human race, we undermine the central Christian facts of sin and salvation. Others see the Genesis story as plainly figurative describing poetically the deep alienation between God and humanity. The story is saying that we are sinners and need God. Every person is 'Adam', and every person has fallen from the righteousness God intends for us.[1]

Dr Carey clearly intends to take no side on the issue. But if the figurative view is an error it belongs to that category which 'eats like a cancer' (2 Tim. 2:17, AV). Once seeded, we cannot set limits to it. If Christ was wrong in basing his teaching about marriage on two actual persons, Adam and Eve (Matt. 19:3–6), how do we know he was not wrong on much else? If he was mistaken in depending upon Genesis for his words, 'Have you not read, that he who made them at the beginning made them male and female?' (Matt. 19:4), how can his assertion concerning the Old Testament, 'the scripture cannot be broken', ever be trusted? The testimony of Genesis to the creation of Eve is crucial to the whole case of literal versus 'figurative' interpretation of Genesis. Obviously nothing is left of Darwin's origin of species argument if Eve was supernaturally created, as categorically maintained in Genesis 2:18, 21–25, and confirmed by Christ in Matthew. Eve was presented to Adam as a full-grown woman, with no history, created by the act of God. Womanhood did not evolve from a pre-existing line of ape-like creatures.

It is interesting to note that my father, despite his desire to make Scripture amenable to apparent scientific evidence, yet wrote in 1924:

The greatest difficulty in the earlier chapters of Genesis, as it seems to us, is to be found in the origin of woman. We do not pretend to be able to say anything in explanation of this; except to remark that even those who reject the Genesis account still have great problems to face.

The historicity of Adam and Eve belongs to the unity of Scripture. As Martyn Lloyd-Jones has written:

There is no such thing as isolated truth . . . all aspects of truth are interrelated. Very often people who are scientifically inclined get into difficulties over their faith because they forget this principle. They are confronted by what purports to be scientific evidence. Something is offered to them by scientists as fact, and the danger is that they will accept that particular statement as it stands, without realizing the consequence of that acceptance in another department of truth. For

[1]George Carey, The New Archbishop Speaks (Lion Paperback, 1991), pp. 20–21.

instance, I always say that one very good reason for rejecting the theory of evolution is that the moment I accept it I am in trouble and difficulty with the doctrine of sin and the doctrine of faith, and the doctrine of the atonement. Truth is interrelated; one thing affects another.[1]

Lloyd-Jones returned to the same subject in his series of sermons on the Epistle to the Romans.[2] For example, when discussing the words, 'Wherefore, as by one man sin entered the world, and death by sin, and so death passed upon all men, for that all have sinned' (*Rom.* 5:12 AV), he ponders such questions as: How can you account for the universality of sin and death? Why this conduct, this misbehaviour of which we are all guilty? He looks first at supposed non-biblical answers, based on man's materialistic philosophies. Essentially, he writes, their claim amounts to this:

Man had never been perfect, but is a creature who had evolved and is evolving out of the animal. The animal lives in response to its own lusts and passions and desires. But man has evolved somewhat beyond that; the convolutions of the brain have developed more; the cerebrum, the highest part of this brain, has developed over against the rest . . . Yet there is conflict in man. The conflict between the higher and lower parts.

According to this view there is really no such thing as sin, because man has always been like this. it is not that he was once created perfect, fell into sin, and thereby became guilty of sin. The proponents of the evolutionary view heartily dislike the term *sin*. What the Bible calls sin they regard as something negative in man's constitution . . . The trouble is not that man is positively bad or evil, but that he has not yet sufficiently developed his good and better qualities.

With the above Lloyd-Jones contrasts the biblical answer, as follows: 'It is the teaching of the whole Bible that both sin and death "entered into" the life of man and into the story of the human race as a direct result of the one man Adam's act of disobedience'. He continues emphatically:

It is not a matter of indifference as to what view you hold of Genesis 1, 2 and 3. If you do not believe there was a literal Adam, and that what

[1]D. M. Lloyd-Jones, *Faith on Trial: Studies in Psalm 73* (London: Inter-Varsity Fellowship, 1965), p. 28.
[2]D. M. Lloyd-Jones, *Romans: Exposition of Chapter 5, Assurance* (Banner of Truth, 1971), pp. 190–91, 196–97.

Paul says about him in this Epistle is true, why is there any need for forgiveness? Why is there any need for the Atonement? Why did Christ have to take human nature upon him?

Reject a literal Adam and the whole Christian case and the Christian message . . . collapses . . . The one great theme of the Bible from beginning to end is man and his relationship to God. It tells us how he went wrong and the consequences of that; but thank God it also tells us how he can be put right. Adam! Christ! 'As in Adam, so in Christ'.

In summary, as Lloyd-Jones stated elsewhere, the theory of evolution is 'the biggest hoax in the world in the past 150 years'.

An individual with weak faith may sit on the fence for a while, but this is a most uncomfortable position in which to remain permanently. No Christian should be satisfied to believe in Christ and yet to remain in doubt on creation. The fact that there are differing measures of faith among different Christians is no excuse for unbelief. As I have watched the unfolding careers of some Christians, it would appear to me that it is often unbelief on this topic which robs them of much usefulness and fruitfulness in serving Christ. My personal appreciation of this truth was one reason which impelled me to write this book.

A friend has told me that in 1959 he was working as a young engineer on the banks of the Euphrates river. There, cut off from Christian companionship, his faith began to waver. As he re-read Genesis chapter 1, it came home very forcibly to him that if he could not trust the first chapter of the Bible, how could he safely trust his whole life to the rest of it?

While in this situation he met the noted Christian archaeologist, Dr Donald Wiseman, who gave him a copy of a book by his father, Air Commodore P. J Wiseman, entitled *Creation Revealed in Six Days*.[1] In 1946, Wiseman had reached the conclusion that the six days of Genesis 1 were not successive days in which God had made the universe, but days occupied by God in revealing the creation story to Adam in what we could call six 'seminars'.

At the time, the book seemed to have helped him, as apparently it has many others. Yet my friend did not find it established him further in the faith. Some years later he

---

[1] Reprinted as *Clues to Creation in Genesis*, ed. Donald Wiseman (London: Marshall, Morgan & Scott, 1977).

abandoned the idea when he realised there is no biblical or scientific evidence to support Wiseman's proposal. He wrote, 'My faith has since been greatly strengthened as I have seen so much evidence which overwhelmingly supports a literal reading of Genesis and condemns evolution as a lie and a myth.'[1] I can personally witness to the popularity of Wiseman's theory. I purchased the book myself, and have since been given three copies by others!

Not only does disbelief in the biblical account of creation impair the effectiveness of our own Christian lives, it can also, through us, harm others. This is particularly relevant to those who are called to teach.

In the 1960s and 1970s I greatly enjoyed speaking at young people's and church family camps. Although I didn't make a speciality of speaking on evolution, the subject inevitably surfaced from time to time. Quite recently the pastor of a large Baptist church told me that at some camp in 1967 he heard me mention the topic of creation and evolution. I have no recollection of the occasion. At that time the pastor was a Christian of about three years' standing and believed in a literal interpretation of the first chapters of Genesis. However, as a result of my talk he became a convinced theistic evolutionist, which belief, so he told me, nearly wrecked his faith. Twenty years later he was surprised to learn I had changed my beliefs on the subject. By then he had read a book on creation and was convinced that I had misled him. When he recounted this to me he was visibly upset. I apologised for leading him astray.

This episode reminds me again of my encounter with my friend the geologist back in the sixties. His explanation of the meaning of the word 'good' greatly (and I now realize, adversely) influenced me at the time, and probably did many others too. I have often thought about that man. What a difficult position the establishment geologist (or biologist) is in if later he comes to abandon evolution theory for biblical creation. By rights he should write to all his thousands of ex-students to say that much of what he had taught them was wrong!

Among my father's papers, I found notes of a sermon he gave

[1]Personal communication from Arthur Tuck, BSc.

at a graduate student conference in about 1938. It was addressed primarily to scientists who were Christians. In it he referred particularly to their awesome responsibility to expound the Scriptures without error!

Jesus warned the Jews of the danger of the blind leading the blind. How much worse if a blind teacher leads a sighted pupil into a ditch. One of the curses in those terrible chapters near the end of Deuteronomy reads, 'Cursed is the one who makes the blind to wander off the road. And all the people shall say "Amen"' (*Deut.* 27:18).

What lessons can we learn from the life of ARS? Primarily that he was a great man of faith, who brought 'many to righteousness'. In his youth he was arrested by what at that time seemed to be a virtually insoluble problem – how to reconcile Scripture and science. He achieved a form of compromise, but as we can gather from his frequent cry for more light, he obviously never regarded this as completely satisfactory. I say the problem was virtually insoluble. Why? Because at that time Darwinian evolution was seemingly as rock solid as the Berlin wall. The first crack in the 'wall' did not occur until December 1953 when it was shown that Piltdown man was a hoax. Since then the wall has crumbled more and more due to the research efforts of many scientists, both Christian and non-christian, in many different disciplines. So many new and exciting discoveries! But *my father never knew of all this*. I often think of the sermon of St Paul to the Athenians, in the expressive words of the Authorised version, 'The times of this ignorance God winked at; but now commandeth all men every where to repent' (*Acts* 17:30, AV).

And here is the essential reason I have written this book.

The same problem as faced ARS faces all thinking Christians today, yet many still rely on some compromise solution. But for them there is far less excuse. Today, relevant information is freely available.

SOME MAJOR SCIENTIFIC AND HISTORICAL EVIDENCE FOR SPECIAL CREATION

In this section I give scientific and historical data which to the best of my knowledge is not in dispute. Any difference of opinion should, therefore, be concerned only with the interpretation placed on this data, not on the facts themselves. The object of the Appendix is to indicate some of the recently highlighted major evidences for special creation, as opposed to general evolution.

I have concentrated on recent material which was not available prior to the middle of the twentieth century. Since that time there has been a spate of new and important research. A theme I have stressed throughout this book is that before about 1950 was a 'time of ignorance' (*Acts* 17:30). However, in view of the evidence I shall present (which is only a tithe of that available), I believe that Christians today, with a mass of well-accredited facts available, are indeed without excuse if they ignore special creation.

Natural Law

All systems of matter or energy have a relentless tendency to move towards the most probable arrangement of that system. In the absence of either a specific programmed mechanism or action by an intelligence (*Information*, see below), even open systems tend to flow from *order to disorder*, and from higher to lesser degrees of energy availability. This was a lesson I learnt from Wilder-Smith's illustrations of the

Second Law of Thermodynamics. It is the ultimate reason why heat flows from hot to cold.

Information

Gitt writes:

Next to matter and energy, information is the third fundamental entity on which both technical and biological processes are based . . . Information is established (formulated, transmitted, stored) by means of a unique code. An agreed-on set of symbols is used (e.g., the alphabet to form words). The words have conventional meanings, they are combined into sentences according to established grammatical rules for the purpose of conveying (meaningful) information.[1]

Any piece of coded information must have originated in a person (the sender) and is meant for somebody (the recipient).

Thus: The sender   uses his voice
       Speech   is the code
       The recipient uses his ear.

The above thesis, when applied to the origin of first life, denies that biological order can possibly arise *except* if information from outside is somehow impressed onto the matter. It explains why the sun's energy will make the leaf of an African violet stuck in a pot of potting-mix sprout and grow, whereas a knitting needle in the same pot will not. The difference, of course, is that only the leaf contains information (specific, pre-programmed machinery).

Thus regardless of the length of time available – even millions of years – 'micro' changes in living things will always be heading in the 'wrong direction', and therefore 'micro' can not be extrapolated to support the idea of 'macro' evolution, the amoeba-to-man scenario.

Selection, whether artificial or natural, from information already present in a population (e.g., DDT resistance in mosquitoes) is not a gain, but causes a net *loss* of variety of

[1]Werner Gitt, *Did God Use Evolution?* pp. 138–44, 151. In this excellent book Gitt answers both scientifically and biblically the question he poses in his title. Gitt is a well-qualified scientist, having written numerous scientific papers in the developing field of information science. Many of these have been translated from German into other European languages.

genetic information in that population. Thus mutations (copying mistakes), on both information-theoretical and experimental grounds, are incapable of causing any functional, or teleonomic,[1] increase in information or complexity. Instead they result in a downhill flow of information. This observation is consistent with the concept that gene-pools in plants or animals originally contained a much larger degree of variability than – following years of breeding – they do today. This fact is becoming increasingly recognized by environmentalists who are anxious to find and preserve 'primitive' plant seeds uncontaminated by man-introduced mutations.

Fossils

Throughout his life Darwin was able to point to only very few, if any, transitional fossil forms. This was a great disappointment, and he recognized it as a fatal flaw in his theory of natural selection which was largely dependent on the fact that they must occur. Darwin rationalized that the lack was because in his lifetime comparatively few fossils had been discovered worldwide. But the situation is not substantially better today after 150 years of diligent search by hundreds of scientists all over the globe.

Luther Sunderland[2] quotes Dr Colin Patterson (a palaeontologist on the staff of the British Museum of Natural History, London) as writing,

I fully agree with your comments on the lack of evolutionary

---

[1]Teleonomy (Greek *telos* = purpose, intelligent design; *logos* = word, doctrine) is the doctrine that everything has a final purpose, especially living beings. Biological 'machinery' also has teleonomy; so do man-made buildings and machines. Teleology states that the purposefulness observed in all living beings, and in the structure of the world, point to a purpose-giving creator. This doctrine contradicts evolutionary thought which claims that development occurs without any purpose. Purposeful processes are still recognized by evolutionists, but an originator of purposes is excluded beforehand.

[2]Luther D. Sunderland, *Darwin's Enigma: Fossils and Other Problems* (California: Master Books, 4th ed. 1988), p. 89. During 1978 the New York State Education Department invited Dr Sunderland to conduct taped interviews with leading fossil experts from five natural history museums containing some of the largest fossil collections in the world. All of them were in the USA except for Dr Colin Patterson from the British Museum of Natural History, London. The records were edited by the speakers, and the full texts are available for scrutiny in any public library in the United States. (For reference see Sunderland, p. 11.)

transitions in my book.[1] If I knew of any, fossil or living, I would certainly have included them . . . I wrote the text of my book four years ago. If I were to write it now I think it would be rather different. Gradualism [evolution in slow small steps, rather than big 'jumps'] is a concept I believe in, not just because of Darwin's authority, but because my understanding of genetics seems to demand it. Yet Gould and the American Museum people are hard to contradict when they say there are no transitional fossils. As a palaeontologist myself, I am much occupied with the philosophical problems of identifying ancestral forms in the fossil record. You say I should at least 'show a photo of the fossil from which each type of organism was derived'. I will lay it on the line – there is no such fossil for which one could make a watertight argument.

All the other leading palaeontologists interviewed by Sunderland admitted there were huge gaps in the fossil record. Even the oft-cited *Archaeopteryx* shows no sign of the crucial scale-to-feather or limb-to-wing transition.

The Age of Things

We cannot directly measure the length of time which has elapsed before our own lifetime, so all chronometric arguments for either a long or a short age of the earth are necessarily indirect and have to depend on the assumptions on which they must be based.

Evidence for a young earth/universe is, inescapably, evidence for creation, as naturalistic evolution (if it were possible) would require aeons of time.

Recently many items of evidence have been discovered which are opposed to the billions-of-years scenario. These include, among many others: DNA and other fragile organic molecules found in fossils supposedly millions of years old; not enough helium in the atmosphere; not nearly enough salt in the sea; C-14 found in objects and strata supposedly millions of years old, and so on. A particularly cogent argument much in

[1]Colin Patterson, *Evolution* (British Museum, 1978). He has come under fire for making this and similar admissions which have delighted creationists, and has sought to soften the meaning retrospectively. Overall, however, the statement is not only unambiguous, but is in line with a host of similar comments by equally authoritative experts.

favour of the young-earth, catastrophist position is the realization that billions of the fossils in earth rocks – for example fish – show well preserved soft parts which must have required rapid deposition and rapid hardening of the sediment for their very existence.

Catastrophe versus Uniformitarianism

As we have seen, since the early nineteenth century, the central unifying theme in geology has been uniformitarianism – that fossil-bearing deposits have been laid down slowly and gradually by uniform processes similar to those going on today. The well-known slogan is 'The present is the key to the past'. The contrary idea is catastrophism, the occurrence of volcanic eruptions, meteor strikes and other massive natural disasters. These two theories have been bitter rivals for the last two hundred years with uniformitarianism apparently the clear winner, thus wiping out any suggestion of a universal flood. The first serious attack on uniformitarianism was a book by Immanuel Velikovsky published in 1950 called *Worlds in Collision*, followed shortly by *Earth in Upheaval*. These two books were universally vilified by scientists. However, the situation has recently changed. In April 1984 *Nature* magazine devoted five articles and two editorials to the topic. Writes Sunderland, 'We have experienced a complete revolution in evolutionary-uniformitarian thinking over the last 30 years.' The current view is that there has been a major fossil-depositing catastrophe about every twenty-six million years, with possibly others besides.

Mount St Helens

On 18 May 1980, Mount St Helens, a volcano in Washington State, USA, exploded with an energy output reckoned as equal to 20,000 atomic bombs. Even so this was small compared with some of the great volcanic catastrophes of the past: Krakatoa in 1883 was fifteen times greater than Mount St Helens, and Mount Tambora in 1815 was so large (computed as eighty times bigger) that the resulting accumulation of airborne ash caused 1816 to be known worldwide, as 'the year without a summer' (*National Geographic*, January 1981, p. 55).

The 1980 Mount St Helens eruptions caused landslides, and ash-falls. It emptied a large lake and the wave action from this uprooted millions of trees and caused massive erosion. Then on 19 March 1982 the volcano erupted again, this time when there was snow in the crater. A vast mud flow resulted which in one or two days breached through the rockslide-and-pumice deposits from the previous 1980 eruptions to form a canyon system over one hundred feet (thirty metres) deep, some of it cut through solid crystalline rock. Later the Toutle River, which had been dammed back by the landslide, burst its banks and started to make its path down the new canyon. This system is now known as 'The Little Grand Canyon of the Toutle River'.

Of great interest is the stratified appearance of the walls of the Little Canyon. Just like the Grand Canyon[1] in Arizona, and sedimentary rocks all over the world, it shows layering. In the Little Canyon this layer formation is known to have occurred within a matter of only a few hours.

All the above scientific data, and much more, are consistent with the view that the earth/universe is far younger than is believed by evolutionists.

Design and Complexity

It is scarcely necessary to show, nor would space permit, how complicated and beautiful is the world in which we live. It has been my pleasure over the years to attend countless lectures on research subjects, particularly on medical topics. As I have listened to the enthusiasm of the lecturer, and have been led to understand something more of the intricate wonders of the human body, I have often worshipped God more fully in a physiology lecture theatre than in many churches.

The glories of the world around us have been opened up particularly in the last two decades. [2] Surely the superb design

---

[1]Steven A. Austin, *Grand Canyon: Monument to Catastrophe* (Santee, California: ICR, 1994). Geologist Dr Austin has spent many years researching into the Grand Canyon; the catastrophe of Mt St Helens; the rapid formation of coal; the origin of fossil tree stumps going upright from one coal seam through sediment into another coal seam; the origin of petrified forests, etc.

[2]See for example, David Attenborough, *The Trials of Life* (BBC, Collins, 1990), and many similar books and films.

and beauty of the earth reveal that a Supreme Intelligence must be in control. As any honest mathematician will agree, even to contemplate that the whole world could have come about by material plus time plus chance alone is outside the realm of mathematical computation. We read in Romans 1.20, 'Since the creation of the world, God's invisible attributes are clearly seen, being understood by the things that are made, even His eternal power and Godhead, so they [those who reject Him] are without excuse'.

Cultural-Anthropological Evidence

Worldwide there are traditional stories of a global flood, even including the rescue of a special group of people (named as eight) in a boat. Many such stories, for example, exist among the Australian Aborigines. [1]

Linguistic and biological evidence has recently revealed hitherto unrecognized genetic closeness among the 'races' of man. Mitochondrial DNA studies suggest that all people alive today can trace their maternal inheritance to one woman.

Further Reading

Bohlin, M. and Lester, L. *The Natural Limits to Biological Change* (detailed arguments from biology for the creation model).

Denton, M. *Evolution: A Theory in Crisis*, 1986 (Powerful arguments, especially from the author's own field of molecular biology).

Humphreys, D. R. *Starlight and Time* (solving the puzzle of distant starlight in a young universe).

Lubenow, M. *Bones of Contention* (the human fossil record falsifies the notion of human evolution).

Morris, J. *The Young Earth* (easily comprehended material from a Ph.D. geologist).

Wilder-Smith, A. E. *The Natural Sciences Know Nothing of Evolution* (Information theory; organic chemistry; thermodynamics.)

[1] See also, C. H. Kang and Ethel R. Nelson, *The Discovery of Genesis: How the Truths of Genesis Were Found Hidden in the Chinese Language* (St Louis: Concordia Publishing, 1979).

APPENDIX 2

THE SIGNIFICANCE OF A GLOBAL FLOOD

The testimony of Scripture has long been weakened by the commonly accepted view that the Flood was not worldwide in its extent. My father argued for this view, as mentioned already.

Since the middle of the nineteenth century it has been the established belief of secular geologists that there never was a worldwide flood; vast inland seas (or what is sometimes known as a 'tranquil flood') that came and went over the land masses (for example Australia), depositing sediment and sometimes fossils – this is allowed, but a Noah-type flood? Impossible. And theologians have followed the lead of the scientists.

My father, among many others, frequently referred to the Flood as 'the deluge'. This commonly means only a severe downpour of rain, whereas the text of Scripture makes clear that far more was involved: 'in the second month, the seventeenth day of the month, the same day were all the fountains of the great deep broken up' (*Gen.* 7:11). So the huge quantity of water necessary to flood the earth did not have to come from rain alone; the flood was almost certainly accompanied by massive, volcanic action and the outpouring of subterranean water.

More than that, in Genesis 6:5–7 we are told that the Lord saw the wickedness of man was so great, that he said, 'I will destroy man whom I have created from the face of the earth, both man and beast, creeping things and birds of the air, for I am sorry that I have made them.'

The express purpose of the flood, therefore, was to destroy *all* human, animal and bird life on earth because of the evil of mankind. (Also, Genesis 6:12, 13, 17; 7:4, 21–23; 9:11; 2 Peter 3:5–6). How could a local flood have achieved this? It could not even have destroyed the bird life in any local area, as these could fly for safety to the nearest mountain range. Human beings had been on earth at least 2,000 years, many of them living to a great age. The population of both humans and animals must have been very great and geographically widespread. Only a global flood could have achieved God's purpose.

Divine intervention in such a worldwide catastrophe refutes uniformitarianism. As Scripture asserts (*2 Peter* 3:3–4), 'all things' have *not* continued as they were from the beginning.

Quite apart from the categorical statements of Scripture concerning the extent of the Flood, there is increasing scientific evidence. For example, the 'slow and gradual' uniformitarian theory cannot explain how animals could be buried so quickly that their soft parts remain in well-preserved fossilised form, nor how, in vast graveyards, the bones of different species are jumbled together in improbable confusion – whale remains mixed with the bones of a possum in one place![1]

Moreover, since the fossils obviously show evidence of death, and often of struggle and even disease, the 'slow and gradual, over long ages' view undermines the biblical concept that such evils only came into the world after Adam sinned.

While it is not necessary for us to assert that *all* fossil remains come from the era of the Flood, the fact of that gigantic judgement helps us to see that the theory so generally accepted by evolutionists may not be the correct interpretation of the fossil evidence. A global Flood judgement is the only viable explanation of how billions of dead things could have been laid down by water all over the earth *after* Adam sinned.

[1]M. R. Banks, 1957, 'The stratigraphy of Tasmanian limestones' in T. D. Hughes, *Limestones in Tasmania* (Miner. Resour. Tasman.), 10:39–85; R. Tate and J. Dennant, 1896, 'Correlation of the marine Tertiaries of Australia', Part III, *South Australia and Tasmania* (Trans. Roy. Soc. S. Aust.) 20(1):118–48; R. D. Gee, 1971, 'Table Cape' Tasm. Dept. of Mines, Geol. Survey Explan. Rept. Geol. Atlas, 1 mile Series, Zone 7, Sheet no. 22.

APPENDIX 3

WHY IS THE BOOK OF GENESIS SO IMPORTANT?

For five principal reasons which I summarize here.

1. Because the Bible from Genesis 1 to Revelation 22 reveals the whole plan of God for the world. It is his story. Genesis is the chronological foundation of the *Total Bible*. Genesis is historically continuous with the rest of the Pentateuch, and so on through Joshua and to the rest of Scripture (see, e.g., *Josh.* 1:7–8; *1 Kings* 2:1–3; *Neh.* 10:28–29; *Luke* 24:27).

The Bible is a unity because, although written by about forty men over a period of more than 1,500 years, God is the author. The first chapter of Genesis must have been given by direct revelation to Adam as no human was present to witness the events it records.

The historicity of Genesis 1 makes it obligatory that the earth was created in six literal days as the plain and obvious words of Scripture make clear. Jesus Christ himself trusted Genesis and frequently quoted from it. If any part of his word is found to be inaccurate, Christianity is compromised. If you reject any part, you undermine the whole. You can't safely pick and choose.

The history of redemption does not commence with Abraham. It starts with Genesis 1:1 (confirmed by John 1:1–5).

2. In particular Genesis 1–3 tell us about *the character of God*. God is revealed as the Almighty, Sovereign, Infinite Creator. He said: and it happened. Just like that. Every time. No potentially harmful mutations were required. He is *all*-powerful and has *all*-knowledge. The world as he originally made it was *good*, perfect, beautiful in every respect, with no bloodshed or death.

God is the supreme communicator – with other members of the Trinity (God said, 'Let *us* make . . . one of *us* . . .'. Genesis 1: 26; 3:22), and also with Adam and Eve. We read of his care for the human race; of his awful justice, yet tempered with mercy.

3. *Man* is made in the image of God. He is not just an animal, alone in a hostile universe. He (or she), whoever they are, is a person of infinite worth in the sight of Almighty God.

4. God has established *Creation Ordinances.* These are divine decrees to show man how he should conduct himself. These ordinances antedate Christianity and even Judaism, and so are binding on all men and women everywhere and in all ages.

For example: man was given one day in seven as a day of rest in which to worship God. He was given dominion over the earth and all its creatures. He was commanded to work, to till the ground. This is the origin of the Protestant work ethic.

Historical information is given about the creation of woman (Eve), and particular instructions were given concerning the relationship between men and women; husband and wife. In these chapters we find the foundation for the biblical view of sexuality and feminism.

5. *The Gospel.* Genesis chapters 1 and 2 contrasts the *good* earth, before there was sin and death, with chapter 3 in which we read of the temptation of Eve and Adam. Without the Fall leading to death, spiritual and eventually physical, there would have been no need for the Creator God, in the person of Jesus Christ, to come to earth and die on the cross for you and me.

INDEX

Index

Index